SOVIET STRATEGY AT THE CROSSROADS

SOVIET STRATEGY AT THE CROSSROADS

Thomas W. Wolfe
The RAND Corporation

HARVARD UNIVERSITY PRESS · CAMBRIDGE, MASSACHUSETTS

1964

CARL A. RUDISILL LIBRARY
LENOIR RHYNE COLLEGE

355.0947
W 83s

50634
Sept. 1965

© Copyright, 1964, by The RAND Corporation · All rights reserved · Distributed in Great Britain by Oxford University Press, London · Library of Congress Catalog Card Number 64–25056 · Printed in the United States of America

ACKNOWLEDGMENTS

This book is an outgrowth of the author's long interest in Soviet military affairs, and in the role of military power as an instrument of Soviet policy in particular. Like most books, however, it could hardly have been written without the encouragement and suggestions of many colleagues and friends. Few of those who have given generously of their time and ideas in the course of the book's preparation would agree with everything the author has had to say; some would certainly differ strongly with particular findings. Among the persons to whom the author is indebted in one measure or another are the following: Bernard Brodie, Robert D. Crane, Herbert S. Dinerstein, Raymond L. Garthoff, Matthew P. Gallagher, Joseph M. Goldsen, Leon Gouré, Ian C. C. Graham, Irwin Halpern, Donald Harris, Robert A. Kilmarx, Jane Moody, Philip E. Mosely, Melvin J. Nielsen, John S. Patton, Sol Polansky, Thomas C. Schelling, Ellen R. Seacat, Helmut Sonnenfeldt, William S. Stewart, and William W. Taylor. An especially grateful word is reserved for those who suffered most in seeing the manuscript through to completion: my research assistant, Anita Magnus, together with Bette Logsdon, Rosalie Fonoroff, and Bonnie Lieb.

This study was prepared as part of a continuing program of research undertaken by The RAND Corporation for the U.S. Air Force. Portions of the work, in somewhat modified form, have previously appeared in *Foreign Affairs, Problems of Communism,* and *Europa Archiv,* whose consent to use of the material is appreciated.

Thomas W. Wolfe

Washington, D. C.
June 4, 1964

CONTENTS

Contents

Contents

Contents

SOVIET STRATEGY AT THE CROSSROADS

INTRODUCTION

In much of the extensive Western literature on Soviet affairs it has come to be recognized increasingly in recent years that a process of change is at work within the Soviet system. In politics, diplomacy, economics, education, culture, science, and military affairs, to mention a few relevant fields, there have been signs of change and adjustment to new conditions as the Soviet system has emerged from the Stalinist era into that under Khrushchev's leadership. To be sure, Western students of the Soviet scene are by no means agreed on the nature of this process of change or the direction in which it is moving. One may find quite disparate views on certain fundamental questions.

There is the view, for example, that the Soviet Union is gradually evolving into a society similar in many basic respects to the modern societies produced in the Western world by the phenomena accompanying industrialization and urbanization. Offsetting this theory of convergence, another view holds that the Soviet system is developing in its own way, *sui generis*, along lines that are unlikely to shape it to a common political and socioeconomic mold with the rest of the Western world.

On a second salient question, some observers feel that the process of change has brought substantial modification in the hostile aims and attitudes of the Soviet Union toward the West. Others find no convincing evidence that underlying sources of conflict between the Soviet system and its adversaries have been significantly allayed. Still others profess to believe that Soviet relationships with the West are in transition along a spectrum from conflict and competition at one end to increasing cooperation at the other.

On a third major question, the view is advanced that the process of change in the Soviet system has been greatly influenced by Western policy and power, and that the future course of Soviet development will be substantially affected by interaction between the two systems. An offsetting opinion, on the other hand, holds that change and evolution in the Soviet Union stem mainly from forces over which the West has little control or influence.

It is not to be expected that such questions as these will yield readily to studies of Soviet affairs in the future, any more than they have done in the past. However, the very recognition that the Soviet outlook is susceptible to change, rather than fixed and monolithic as was once so generally assumed, seems to represent a step toward fuller insight and understanding. In this connection, it is worth noting that students of Soviet military affairs and strategic thinking were among the first to suggest that the old image of the monolithic Soviet mind was no longer apt.

Perhaps this can be explained by the fact that the post-Stalin period happened to begin at about the same time that the scientific-technological revolution of the nuclear age was also beginning to make itself strongly felt in the Soviet Union. Thus, it is not surprising that among the first fields in which Soviet thinking tended to break away from the static conceptions and tight conformity of the Stalinist era was that of military policy and strategy. One may recall that even before the "de-Stalinization" drive brought revision and innovation into many areas of Soviet life following the 20th Party Congress in 1956, some Soviet military men had already begun to question the sanctity and permanence of "Stalinist" military theory. And in Khrushchev's own case, his initial venture in the role of "creative developer" of Marxist-Leninist theory was directed toward nuclear-age strategic problems, when he amended the Leninist thesis of "inevitable war" at the same 20th Party Congress. In any event, whatever the sources of ferment and change in post-Stalin Russia may be, it seems fair to say that one of the most important new elements in the outlook of the Soviet leadership has been a growing awareness of the implications of nuclear-age weaponry. Certainly, the revolution in military affairs has been a prime factor in shaping the general political and strategic climate in which Soviet policy has unfolded in the decade since Stalin.

In this study I have been concerned mainly with developments in the field of Soviet military policy and strategy during the period since the Cuban crisis of October 1962—a period in which the Soviet leadership has sought some form of limited détente with the United States. It is not possible to predict how long this policy of détente will endure. To some extent, the durability of détente will doubtless be conditioned by the success of the Soviet leadership in dealing with the various problems of strategy and military policy which were brought into sharp focus by the Cuban crisis. This is not to say that there is necessarily an exclusive correlation between Soviet interest in cultivating a détente atmosphere and inadequacies in the Soviet military posture. Many other factors enter the picture. Neither does détente necessarily connote that Khrushchev's position of leadership is shaky in general, making a breathing spell imperative while he mends his fences at home and abroad. On the contrary, the argument might be advanced that it takes an extraordinarily firm grip on the levers of leadership to negotiate moves toward détente, to back away from crises, and to survive reverses, especially under criticism from rival leaders within the Communist camp in Peking.

Nevertheless, while recognizing that a détente policy need not be interpreted as solely the product of unresolved problems and circumscribed opportunities, there is a tendency to give these factors predominant weight in accounting for Moscow's pursuit of such a policy during the past couple of years. Indeed, it is a central thesis of this study that the Soviet leadership has been

3

seeking both time and freedom of action to deal with an accumulation of difficulties, among which some of the most stubborn are various issues of strategy and defense policy. The author's aim in the present work is to provide an analysis of Soviet thinking and debate on these issues, against the background of numerous problems arising out of the new technological and political environment of the modern world. The remainder of these introductory remarks will be given over to summarizing in a general way the more detailed examination to be found in the body of this work.

A central problem confronting the Soviet leadership relates to the allocation of resources. The need for greater investment to sustain a high rate of industrial growth and to shore up a faltering agricultural sector, a rising level of consumer expectations, growing labor requirements in the face of a man-power pinch, the costs of keeping up the space race—these are some of the competing demands upon the Soviet economy which evidently have made it more difficult than usual during the past year or two for the Soviet leaders to decide what share of their resources should be devoted to military purposes. To a considerable extent, economic difficulties may lie at the bottom of Soviet efforts to promote an atmosphere of détente in East-West relations. At the same time, the Soviet leadership has asserted that remedial economic measures must not impair Soviet defenses.

Another fundamental problem, growing out of the military-technological revolution of modern times, centers upon Soviet awareness of the destructiveness of nuclear war. A nuclear environment not only has made war look extremely dangerous; it also has helped to undermine traditional Marxist-Leninist doctrine on the link between war and politics, and has given rise to disturbing questions on the political utility of the use of military power, or the threat of its use, in the nuclear-missile age.

4

The continuing Sino-Soviet rift represents another problem of great magnitude. Its ramifications are widespread. Besides feeding the centrifugal forces at work within the communist camp and sharpening the competition between Moscow and Peking for the allegiance of "national liberation movements," the conflict may have called into question some of the basic strategic assumptions upon which Soviet planning has been based. Together with a stirring toward greater autonomy among the East European countries, the growing estrangement between Moscow and Peking has obliged the Soviet leadership to give more attention to internal military relations within the communist camp.

At the same time, two years after the abortive deployment of Soviet missiles to Cuba, the development of a military posture suitable to Soviet needs in the power contest with the United States apparently presents troublesome and unresolved problems. Both the internal military debate within the Soviet Union and the external strategic dialogue with the United States bear witness to the fact that there are still differing schools of thought in the Soviet Union on many matters that have been under discussion for some time.

The military debate that has been taking place in the Soviet Union during the past few years has furnished a good deal of insight into the kinds of military policy problems that preoccupy the Soviet leadership. It can be said, too, that there is now somewhat more latitude than formerly for the expression of divergent views. The amount of latitude fluctuates, and there is still a fairly elaborate ritual for conveying high-level criticism by indirection in order to preserve the myth of communist solidarity. Nevertheless the conditions of Soviet discourse today do allow more room for public airing of differences than formerly.

As for the military debate itself, the mainstream has been fairly well-defined since the late 1950's, when the consolidation of Khrushchev's political primacy coincided with the prospect that the Soviet Union might soon count on having advanced weapons in some numbers. From that time, the debate has centered essentially on the efforts of the political leadership, including particularly Khrushchev himself, to reorient Soviet military doctrine and forces in a direction considered more suitable for the needs of the nuclear-missile age. These efforts have met with varying degrees of resistance from some quarters of the military, perhaps with tacit backing among elements of the party-state bureaucracy whose interests were engaged in one way or another.

It would oversimplify the picture, however, to regard this as merely an institutionalized contest of views between political and military leadership groups. The debate probably has been shaped as much by the nature of the issues as by purely institutional differences. In fact, there has been a continuous tributary stream of discussion within the military itself, with "modernist" and "traditionalist" outlooks at each end of the spectrum and a body of "centrist" opinion in the middle.

The modernists have tended more or less to sympathize with the kinds of views advanced by Khrushchev, and to argue for a more radical adaptation of modern technology to military affairs. They have suggested that this approach might permit reducing the size of the armed forces—that quality, so to speak, would replace quantity. The traditionalists, on the other hand, while recognizing the impact of technology on military affairs, have nonetheless tended to argue against discarding tried and tested concepts merely for the sake of adopting something new.

Neither the modernist nor the traditionalist viewpoint can be said to dominate "official" Soviet military theory today, although the main trend of the past few years seems to have been in the direction of establishing modernist concepts as the type of thinking most favored by Khrushchev and the political leadership. At the same time, there are signs that a countertrend may also be setting in, representing as it were a reaction in some military quarters against the new "orthodoxy" embodying such Khrushchevian strategic notions as the absolute primacy of nuclear-missile weapons. If nothing else, the unsettled status of the modernist-traditionalist question testifies to the continuing vitality of the military debate in the Soviet Union.

Unresolved issues in the Soviet military policy debate include the following:

1. *The size of the armed forces that should be maintained in peacetime, and the prospects for mobilization of additional forces in wartime under nuclear conditions:* Khrushchev's proposal in December 1963 for further troop reduction, perhaps to complete his earlier 1960 troop-cut program which was suspended in 1961, met with notable lack of enthusiasm among high-ranking Soviet officers. In fact, Marshal Chuikov, commander of the Soviet ground forces, spearheaded a rather thinly disguised lobby against the proposal. In December 1963 he pointed out that the Western powers had recognized the pernicious effects of "one-sided" military theories and were building up their ground forces along with their strategic nuclear power. While it would appear that the lobby against the troop cut has lost its case, Khrushchev also seems to have yielded some ground by giving public assurance that the reduction would be "reasonable."

2. *The kind of war—short or protracted—for which Soviet forces should be prepared:* This issue involves two divergent viewpoints. One view, usually identified with the modernist school of thought, places major stress on the *decisive* character of the initial period of a nuclear war and on the need to prepare the Soviet armed forces and economy for bringing the war to a conclusion "in the shortest possible time, with minimum losses." The second view pays more heed to the possibility of a pro-

tracted war and the consequent need to make strenuous preparations economically, militarily, and psychologically for such a war.

3. *The question whether limited wars can be fought without danger of escalation into general nuclear war:* Contradictions still exist between Soviet avowals of support for "national liberation" wars and the Soviet doctrinal position that small wars pose a great danger of escalation if the nuclear powers become involved. Some signs of a shift in the Soviet view on the escalation potential of local wars have been evident, particularly in the strategic discourse with the United States.

4. *The respective weights of strategic nuclear operations and combined-arms theater operations in any future general war involving a powerful overseas adversary like the United States:* Although the primacy of the strategic missile forces has now become an established tenet of Soviet military doctrine, considerable debate continues over the ways in which theater campaigns on the Eurasian continent should be related in scope, character, and timing to global strategic operations. Such issues as the size of the armed forces and the duration of a war also are interwoven with this question.

5. *The prospects of survival under conditions of surprise nuclear attack:* This issue has many ramifications, including ultimately the question whether a nuclear war can be won—or lost—in any meaningful sense. In the immediate context of the military debate, one school of thought holds that seizure of the strategic initiative by the enemy at the outset of a nuclear war could bring irreparable losses and defeat. This view has led to great stress on high combat readiness of forces-in-being and also to veiled advocacy of a pre-emptive strategy, which tends to conflict with the political-propaganda position that the Soviet Union would not strike the first blow. Another school of military thought concedes the importance of moving swiftly to the strategic offensive in the initial period of a war, but argues that

there is a high likelihood that the war would stretch out after the initial nuclear exchanges. Some adherents of this view advocate preparation for a protracted war in which, it is argued, the superior political-morale qualities of the Soviet side, plus its residual economic and military capacities, would operate to ensure victory.

6. *The question whether the criteria for developing the Soviet armed forces should stress mainly their deterrent and intimidational functions, or their actual war performance value:* A substantial group in the military apparently feels that a military posture patterned strictly in accordance with Khrushchev's strategic ideas would leave the Soviet Union in an unsatisfactory position if deterrence should fail. Views on this issue probably reflect differing estimates of the likelihood of war. Although both political and military spokesmen customarily join in tendentious charges that the West is preparing for a "preventive" war against the Soviet Union, Khrushchev's private view for the past few years appears to have accorded rather low probability to the danger of a deliberate Western attack on the Soviet Union under conditions short of extreme provocation.

7. *The question of finding a military strategy for victory in a possible future war against the United States:* Soviet military thinkers appear to be increasingly aware of the inadequacies of traditional doctrine and forces for war against a formidable overseas opponent like the United States. However, there continues to be a good deal of uncertainty as to whether one could count on paralyzing the U.S. will to resist by quick nuclear blows against the American homeland or whether it would be necessary to defeat the U.S. armed forces in detail and occupy the United States to achieve victory. This uncertainty is compounded by the question whether nuclear war can any longer be regarded as a rational instrument of policy. In general, Soviet military theorists and ideologists continue publicly to spurn the concept of "no victor" in modern war, but real doubt appears

9

to be at work in the minds of many Soviet leaders whether in fact anything that could meaningfully be called victory could be salvaged after the damage the Soviet Union would suffer in a nuclear war.

In addition to such unresolved issues in the immediate area of military policy and strategy, there also has been continuing evidence of a certain amount of underlying strain in Soviet political-military relations. Symptomatic of this strain is the renewed emphasis placed since the fall of 1962 on the principle of political supremacy in military affairs. Various problems, some of long standing, are involved. One of these concerns the proper role of the military in the formulation of defense policy and strategy. The party-oriented view tends to hold that the military leadership should confine its attention to the professional aspects of preparing the Soviet armed forces for their assigned tasks. Among the military, on the other hand, there is a tendency to feel that the complex nature of modern warfare means the military profession should have greater weight in preparing the country as a whole for a possible war. This view implies a claim for more influence in the shaping of basic national policy.

While the internal military debate indicates that doctrine is still in flux on many points, it is important to bear in mind that a consensus on basic matters still binds the various elements of the Soviet leadership together and that the areas of agreement on purpose and policy are doubtless broader than the areas of contention. On a number of military questions, a large measure of agreement is apparent in Soviet thinking over the last couple of years. This is the case, for example, with regard to: the primacy of strategic nuclear weapons in modern warfare; the critical importance of the initial period of a war; the need for maintenance of a high state of combat readiness; adoption of a target philosophy emphasizing destruction of both military and civilian targets; rejection of the concepts of targeting restraint and controlled response; and recognition of the economic difficulty of maintaining large standing forces in peacetime.

On still other matters, a new degree of emphasis is to be found in recent Soviet military discussion. To mention a few examples, there has been: more attention to limited war; increased confidence in the ability of early warning to reduce the chances of successful surprise attack; greater stress on the hardening and mobility of strategic weapons and on the contribution such measures make to the credibility of the Soviet deterrent posture; upgrading of the strategic role of missile-launching submarines; some downgrading of long-range bomber prospects for the future but an upgrading of the bomber's role against targets at sea; more emphasis on antisubmarine operations and amphibious landing capabilities; and further stress on the importance of developing both antimissile and antisatellite defenses. There has also been growing Soviet interest in the military potential of space, centering around charges that U.S. intentions to exploit space militarily make it incumbent upon the Soviet Union to take corresponding steps for its defense.

The views of Soviet political and military leaders on problems of war and strategy are of great interest in the context of the external strategic dialogue with the West, principally the United States. As a form of communication between adversaries, much of the strategic dialogue has been and probably will continue to be concerned with advancement of the policy interests of the two great nuclear powers in a more or less narrow sense, with each side using public declarations to enhance its deterrent posture, to obtain political advantage from its military power or prevent the other from doing so, and to impress the authority of its position on allies and onlookers.

At the same time, however, both sides tend perceptibly, though in varying degrees, to look upon more precise strategic

communication as a means to clarify the complexities and mitigate the dangers of their strategic relationship in the nuclear-
missile age.

In the past year or so, the Soviet side has made several
contributions to the discussion of strategy which are of notable
interest in the context of the external dialogue, as well as
internally. One of these was a revised and expanded edition of
the Sokolovskii volume, *Military Strategy*, published in the fall
of 1963, a scant fifteen months after the widely-publicized first
edition. Another was a direct Soviet riposte in the newspaper
Red Star to American commentary on the first Sokolovskii edition. In these and certain other expressions of strategic thinking
by Soviet military and political figures there has been a tendency
to refine the arguments, partly in order to counter or modify
Western interpretations of Soviet military posture and policy.
Some Soviet writings have contained "corrective messages" on
such questions as escalation of local conflicts, Soviet second-
strike capability, pre-emption, military-political relations, and
so on.

The Soviet leadership's recent difficulties have left their
imprint on strategic discourse with the West, which reflects an
evident Soviet awareness of the need to adjust Soviet policy to
changes in the character of the strategic environment.

There has been, for example, an insistent effort to enhance
the credibility of the Soviet strategic deterrent in Western eyes.
This theme, argued with greater technical sophistication than
previously, has been coupled with an attempt to disabuse the
United States of any idea that it can count on a successful first
strike or draw political advantage from its strategic position
vis-à-vis the Soviet Union. Increasing emphasis has been placed
on the strategic missile forces as the main element of Soviet
military power and a major tool of Soviet foreign policy. While
asserting the qualitative superiority of Soviet missiles, and alluding to the Soviet Union as the sole possessor of weapons of "50–
100 megatons and more," the Soviet spokesmen have continued

to avoid numerical comparison of their long-range missile forces with those of the United States.

Another feature of Soviet discourse on warfare at the strategic level has been a consistent rejection of the idea of controlled use of strategic weapons and damage-limiting restraints in the event a major war should occur. Since Secretary McNamara's Ann Arbor speech of June 1962, in which he outlined a strategic philosophy stressing that military targets rather than cities and population should be the object of attack in case of nuclear war, Soviet commentators have devoted much criticism to what they call a U.S. attempt to popularize a "counterforce" or "city-sparing" strategy. At the same time, there have been some signs of Soviet sensitivity to implications that the Soviet strategic concept is rigid and less humane than the position of Western advocates of damage-limiting measures.

In contrast with the rigid Soviet image of war at the strategic level, there has been a new tendency to redefine the Soviet position on the link between small wars and global war. For some years this position was marked by a rather high degree of doctrinal rigidity, exemplified by stress on the great danger of escalation. Today, however, there are some efforts, particularly in military media, to make the point that Soviet doctrine does not preach the "inevitable" escalation of limited wars into general war. While not necessarily indicating that the Soviet Union has suddenly developed a fresh interest in waging local wars, the new trend of argument suggests that the Soviets are at least seeking to soften the old line on escalation. One reason might be to counter Chinese criticism of Soviet failure to give vigorous support to "national liberation" struggles. Another reason might be to correct any impression that the West enjoys greater freedom to act in local conflicts because Soviet doctrine indicates a hypersensitive concern over escalation.

The apparent desire in some Soviet quarters to convey an image of greater flexibility in the handling of potential local conflicts has tended to stop short of Central Europe, where the

possibility of keeping a local war within limited bounds is rejected by Soviet opinion. However, there has been some suggestion in Soviet discourse that, in case of certain third-power
conflicts involving possibly West Germany and Eastern Europe,
the Soviet Union might try to avoid expanding the conflict by
withholding attacks against the United States in return for U.S.
abstention. This suggestion seems to relate to a general Soviet
concern to reassure the United States against a Soviet first strike
under borderline conditions in which the question of pre-emption might arise.

At the same time, however, the Soviet position on pre-emption
remains somewhat ambiguous. There is still a veiled hint in the
statements of many Soviet leaders, perhaps intended to reinforce
the Soviet deterrent image, that under some circumstances the
Soviet Union may entertain what would be in fact, if not in
name, a pre-emptive strategy. Thus, for example, one finds
Marshal Malinovskii and others still asserting that the Soviet
armed forces must be prepared for the high-priority task of
"breaking up the enemy's aggressive plans by dealing him in
good time a crushing blow."

Much of the East-West strategic discussion to date has centered on the question whether the balance of military power
in the world favors one side or the other. The predominant note
in Soviet discourse has consistently been the need for military
superiority over the West. However, there are some obvious
liabilities in professing a policy of achieving and maintaining
military superiority, for if the Soviet military posture is made to
look excessively formidable the result may well be simply to
spur the West to greater efforts, and to leave the Soviet Union
relatively no better off in the military sphere, and perhaps a
good deal worse off economically. For a country whose resources
already seem strained by the high cost of arms competition, this
is a serious consideration. Soviet cultivation of a détente atmos-

phere indicates recognition of the problem, for it aims in part at slowing down the competition for military pre-eminence. Furthermore, in a tactical sense, untimely emphasis on military superiority could jeopardize other immediate goals that détente seems meant to serve.

Some tentative signs of wavering on the wisdom of proclaiming a policy of military superiority have appeared in recent Soviet discourse, but whether this connotes merely a temporary softening of the superiority doctrine or a deeper reassessment of its pros and cons remains to be seen. Certainly the Soviet leadership faces one of its more vexing problems in deciding whether to strive for strategic superiority over the West or to settle for a second-best position. Not only is the Soviet Union at a relative disadvantage in the resources available for the task of achieving significant superiority, but as experience shows it has managed to live for a considerable period in a position of strategic inferiority to its major adversary without being subjected to the "imperialist attack" so often predicted.

The prospects for further development of a useful strategic dialogue between the Soviet Union and the United States seem moderately encouraging in the light of some recent expressions of Soviet strategic thinking. Even though Soviet perception of U.S. motives and intentions is still not free of gross distortion, a slightly more objective image of the United States as a powerful but responsible adversary emerges from recent Soviet discourse. Improvement in the quality of communications on the strategic relationships between the super-powers has paralleled certain tentative steps in the arms control field, such as the nuclear test ban treaty, the Moscow-Washington "hot line" agreement, the U.N. resolution against orbiting of nuclear weapons in space, and the joint declarations of cutback in nuclear materials production. Although these measures do not directly involve disarmament, they can be said to reflect a mutual desire to slow the tempo of the arms race and reduce the danger of war by misunderstanding. Together with the strategic dialogue, such measures seem to represent what might be termed an exploratory effort to "manage" the U.S.-Soviet confrontation so as to keep it within certain bounds without damaging the political interests of the adversaries.

The U.S.-Soviet confrontation is likely to remain the dominant feature of the international scene during at least the next decade or so. At the same time, one must recognize that the conflict will be carried on within a system of world relations that is undergoing some fundamental changes. The bipolar structure of the past fifteen years, dominated by the two super-powers, is in the process of being superseded by a new and somewhat less rigid pattern. Within the two major blocs, each super-power finds itself increasingly obliged to cope with centrifugal political and economic forces. Each side has its heretics, and each is exposed in some degree to a process of fragmentation.

A major, though by no means the only cause of change from a rigid, bipolar confrontation to a looser pattern of international relations can be traced to the military-technological revolution of the nuclear-missile age. As it has become increasingly apparent that no one could expect to win a nuclear war in any meaningful sense, the likelihood of deliberate resort to arms on a general scale has declined. By reducing the danger of deliberate attack, mutual nuclear deterrence has also helped loosen the cohesion of the two great power blocs. Within the communist bloc, the Eastern European countries (and, in a measure, Red China) can afford the luxury of seeking greater autonomy precisely because Soviet nuclear power has made the danger of a direct attack by the West seem rather remote. A similar situation in reverse permits the European members of NATO to pursue more independent policies under the U.S. nuclear shield. The danger of irrational or accidental origin of nuclear war remains, but the obligation of avoiding irresponsible actions which could lead to "unwanted" nuclear war rests most heavily on those few powers which possess the means to wage nuclear warfare.

This in itself furnishes an incentive to improve strategic communication between the United States and the Soviet Union, and may to some extent contribute to a blurring of the sharp ideological lines of the bipolar confrontation of the past fifteen years. However, there is no assurance that an international system developing in the direction of multipolarity will necessarily prove more stable than hitherto. In fact, the potential sources of conflict may well increase as greater freedom of action is sought by a larger number of states. The process of fragmentation could subject the U.S.-Soviet relationship to accentuated pressures from two different directions. On the one hand, if new alignments and greater turbulence characterize the international scene, there might be an increased premium on formal or tacit U.S.-Soviet cooperation to stabilize the situation and dampen the risks of escalation to major military conflict. On the other hand, these same features of the fragmentation process might seem to offer opportunities for political exploitation which would be difficult to resist, particularly by a Soviet leadership under pressure from Peking to show results in the world revolutionary struggle. Should the Soviet leaders yield to such temptation, this would of course tend to sharpen rather than alleviate the U.S.-Soviet confrontation. No one can predict with confidence what the future will bring, but on the basis of past relationships, it might be expected that new crises will arise from time to time, and that they will be followed by remedial efforts to improve cooperation and communication, which hopefully will serve to keep the East-West conflict under control.

Chapter I

IMPACT OF THE NUCLEAR AGE
ON SOVIET MILITARY POLICY

Few people anywhere remain unaware today that the scientific-technological revolution of modern times has had an enormous impact on social and political institutions, and has helped to stimulate great ferment and change in the world. Military affairs and the relationship of military power to politics have felt the impact of the scientific revolution in a particularly immediate sense. This is no less true in the Soviet case than in our own. To understand the debate over military policy and strategy that has unfolded in the Soviet Union over the past decade, as well as the strategic dialogue with the West, it may be useful first to view the situation of the Soviet leadership in the light of several considerations arising out of the new technological and political environment of the modern world.

The first of these considerations is the Soviet appreciation of the destructiveness of a nuclear war and the desire of the Soviet leadership to reduce the risk that such a war will occur and perhaps undo the achievements of more than four and a half decades of socialist construction. This appreciation has served to undermine some of the fundamentals of prenuclear age communist doctrine, especially that concerning the link between war and revolution. It was Lenin's view that war had what may be described as the legitimate sociopolitical function of enhancing the conditions for, and triggering off, socialist revolutions. While prenuclear age communist doctrine neither took cognizance of the notion of violence for its own sake, nor stressed, except for brief intervals, the spread of revolution by virtue of red bayonets, it did certainly, in the Marxist idiom, regard war as "the midwife of revolution." The experience of two world wars seemed to confirm this notion, for it was after each of these wars that communism enjoyed its greatest success and expansion in the world.[1]

Today, the nuclear environment has made a world war look extremely dangerous and consequently has tended to put a brake on many forms of revolutionary conflicts that might escalate into large nuclear wars and jeopardize the Soviet system itself. This situation clearly has had a striking impact on Soviet doctrine and policy. It accounts in large measure for Khrushchev's revision of the dogma of inevitable war and his vigorous advocacy of the strategy of peaceful coexistence as the safest and most reliable form of class struggle in the international arena. One may recall the sentiment expressed in the CPSU's riposte to the Chinese Communists, contained in the former's open letter of July 14, 1963:

The atomic bomb does not adhere to the class principle: it destroys everybody within range of its devastating force.[2]

In relation to classical communist doctrine, this is a truly corrosive statement, for once it is admitted that there are powerful phenomena which do not obey the laws of Marxism-Leninism the door is open to increasing doubt about the validity of other features of the creed. This seems to be sensed by the Chinese Communists in their defense of ideological orthodoxy against what they regard as Soviet revisionism. The nuclear-age revolution in weaponry thus lies close to the heart of the dispute between Moscow and Peking over the choice of means toward attainment of communist objectives in the world. While the Soviet leadership still clings upon occasion to the doctrinaire assertion that a nuclear war between the West and the communist camp would end with victory for the latter, this assertion is advanced with lessening conviction. Khrushchev's own appraisal of the difficulty of erecting a communist order on the radioactive rubble of a war that might cost, as he has said, from

700 to 800 million casualties[3] seems to reflect a more candid Soviet view of the outcome of a general nuclear war than the doctrinaire formula of inevitable communist victory.

A second general consideration that may bear upon the basic policy decisions confronting the Soviet leaders is uncertainty as to the outcome of unlimited arms competition with the United States. An important facet of this question is whether the intensified build-up of military forces in an arms race against an opponent with superior resources would bring added or diminishing returns so far as Soviet security is concerned. Past experience, such as that relating to the closure by the United States of the so-called missile gap, would seem to suggest that, from the the Soviet viewpoint, challenging the United States to a numbers race in modern weapons might have the effect of leaving the Soviet Union relatively worse off than before the challenge was made. There are signs, to be discussed in detail later, that the Soviet leadership appreciates and is caught in this particular dilemma.

A third and closely related consideration is the question of economic pressure and constraints upon Soviet decisions in the field of military policy and strategy. The Soviet political leaders seem well aware of the rising costs and rapid turnover of modern nuclear weapon systems, piled atop the fixed costs of a large conventional military establishment, at a time when they face major problems of resource allocation to meet a rising level of consumer expectation and to fulfill very substantial investment requirements for a faltering agricultural sector.[4] Further, there are increased demands on Soviet resources to meet the economic growth goals set by current plans and implied by the Party Program. These demands come at a time when, according to informed Western estimates of Soviet economic performance, the Soviet rate of economic growth has declined considerably.[5] There is also a man-power pinch, which arises from expanding labor requirements, not to mention the resource claims of space

programs. All of these competing pressures upon Soviet resources undoubtedly pose for the Soviet leaders difficult problems of choice between defense needs and other requirements.
In the past, it is true, when the Soviet economy was smaller than
it is today, they managed to strike a workable, if not necessarily
happy, balance between meeting military and nonmilitary requirements.

Each of the broad considerations sketched above tends to
raise many questions concerning the policies and programs
applying to the Soviet armed forces, particularly as regards the
matter of devoting further large resources to their development.
Before the Soviet leadership can satisfy itself as to the wisdom
and feasibility of embarking on radical changes in the policies
that have hitherto governed the development of the Soviet
armed forces, there is a second class of general considerations
also to be taken seriously into account.

First among these, as the Soviet leadership seems abundantly
aware, is the fact that the power position and political standing
of the Soviet Union in the world today rest to a large extent
on Soviet military strength and the technology associated with
it. Indeed, one might say that the Soviet Union's status as a
"superpower" was not confirmed in the world's eyes until the
Soviet Union became a full-fledged member of the "nuclear
club." Modern arms, in short, have given the present Soviet
leadership a capability for influencing events on a global scale,
such as no previous generation of Soviet leaders has enjoyed.

Along with a heady sense of international power, which the
Soviet leadership derives from its armed forces, goes a strong
conviction that these forces are an indispensable safeguard of
Soviet security against the hostile designs of the capitalist world.
Further, Soviet military power also has a major role to play in
support of Soviet political strategy generally. In Soviet eyes,
military power backs up Soviet political strategy, both by discouraging Western initiatives in troubled areas and by discour-

aging dangerous Western responses to Soviet moves. The heart of the coexistence policy itself, as the Soviet leaders have been arguing in their polemics with the Chinese, is the proposition that Soviet nuclear-missile power deters the "imperialists" and keeps them from launching a war against the communist camp. This is a danger the Soviet leaders profess to believe inherent in the situation as long as imperialism exists.

The Soviet leaders are not likely to lose sight of the fact that their position within the communist bloc is also intimately affected by their military posture. Uncertainty as to the eventual course of Sino-Soviet relations and intrabloc unity could make this concern even more important in the future. Should an open split in the bloc occur, for example, Soviet military power of a significant order might be needed as a check upon Chinese pretensions. It might also prove indispensable for keeping Moscow's own satellites in line within a restive and fragmented communist camp. Apart from this intrabloc policing function of Soviet military power, the Soviet Union has taken on the self-appointed role of "nuclear shield" for the communist states within its orbit. This too places a drain on Soviet resources beyond what is required for direct self-defense.

The Soviet relationship with China involves the special problems arising from the possibility that the Chinese may acquire independent nuclear capabilities. The larger freedom of action that even limited Chinese nuclear capabilities would give Peking must be a cause of some concern to the Soviet leaders. This is particularly true in so far as Chinese actions might lead to a dangerous confrontation with the United States in which China might have to call upon the Soviet Union to honor tacit agreements or treaty obligations relating to the rescue of a fellow communist country in distress. The Soviet leaders for some time past have been trying to prepare a position under which they would not be obliged to back up China if the latter pursued parochial interests not coinciding with those of the

Soviet bloc as a whole. Nevertheless, the stubborn problem of what to do if a crisis should develop is still one with which the Soviet leadership must contend.

Even with regard to the dangers of nuclear war, the Soviet leaders find themselves in a somewhat ambivalent position. On the one hand, they understand that if a nuclear war should occur, it could put them out of business altogether. This furnishes a strong incentive to seek solutions of the Soviet security problem through avenues other than build-up of the Soviet armed forces, such as arms control and disarmament. On the other hand, the Soviet leaders obviously recognize that the world's fear of nuclear catastrophe provides a potent emotional issue around which the "peace struggle" and other forms of political warfare can be mobilized. Given the nature of their political aims, there is thus a built-in temptation for the Soviet leaders to capitalize on the threat of nuclear disaster. This means, among other things, that they have a large political stake in keeping the disarmament pot boiling without actually seeking to consummate genuine disarmament arrangements as a serious alternative to the possession of impressive military power. The Soviet leadership appears to be quite aware that, while the prospects of using war as an active instrument of policy have gone down in the nuclear age, the potential political returns from exploiting the possession of modern military power have gone up. In a sense, the Soviet leaders seem to have grasped what may be the salient strategic truth of our times: that men's minds are by far the most profitable and perhaps the only suitable target system for the new weapons of the nuclear age.

At the same time, this consideration, too, is tempered by the practical lessons of experience. At the most optimistic level of Soviet calculation, it may have seemed only a few years back that the combination of Soviet missiles and space technology plus "Bolshevik iron will" offered a good prospect of facing down the imperialists in a series of crisis situations, and that this process would in time hasten the decline and fall of Western power and influence in the world.[6] However, things turned out otherwise. Spurred by the *sputnik* challenge and revived threats against Berlin in the late 1950's, the Western powers shook off the suggestion that the balance of strategic power had turned irrevocably against them. They responded to Soviet initiatives with actions that dissolved the myth of the missile gap and strengthened the material and political bases for Western resistance around the world. Cuba capped the process in the fall of 1962, when the tool of missile diplomacy plus "Bolshevik iron will" came apart in Soviet hands and left Moscow with no reasonable alternative but to back off and salvage what they could of an unhappy situation. Looking back upon their experience, the Soviet leaders may well be facing the question whether the declining worth of a missile-blackmail diplomacy justifies further great effort and investment to restore its plausibility. These, then, are some of the broad considerations that confront the Soviet leadership in making decisions with regard to their armed forces and the role military power can be expected to play in the conduct of Soviet political policy.

Over the past decade, changing concepts and practical necessities have influenced the policies governing the development of the Soviet armed forces. These influences, often pulling in diverse directions, are still at work. The leaders of the Soviet Union are pursuing a variety of domestic and foreign policy goals, and these often come into conflict with the aims of military policy as well as with each other.

The immediate problems of Soviet defense policy arise in several identifiable areas and undoubtedly are perceived differently at various levels of the Soviet bureaucracy. A first difficulty stems from the nature of modern war itself, which gives rise to fundamental questions as to whether war or the threat of war can any longer be regarded as a rational instrument of policy. A second difficulty appears in the allocation of resources to the military establishment in the face of urgent competing claims upon the economy from other sectors of Soviet society. A third set of problems arises in the overlapping zone where military strategy and political purpose meet. It involves such questions as how best to maintain the credibility of Soviet deterrence, how to resolve the discrepancy between actual military posture and the foreign policy utilities claimed for it, and what to do about any gaps that exist between Soviet military capabilities and those of potential enemies. A fourth difficulty lies in the organization and training of the Soviet armed forces themselves. It reflects all the practical problems that are generated when policy must be meshed with service roles and responsibilities. And finally, cutting across each of these problem areas, is the question of dealing and communicating with the adversary, a process in which the strategic dialogue with the West plays its part.

Few of the problems in these several categories are unique to the Soviet Union. At the same time, they are not necessarily perceived and dealt with along the same lines as the corresponding problems facing Western policy-makers and strategists. In this book we shall be concerned with Soviet thinking in all of the areas mentioned above. And, as we shall see later when we examine the substance of Soviet strategic thinking and debate, the Soviet leaders seem to stand at a crossroads in making decisions concerning many issues of military policy and strategy. Perhaps this is the natural state of those who guide the destinies of great powers in the nuclear-missile age.

Chapter II

THE INTERNAL SOVIET
MILITARY DEBATE

The structure and what might be called the ground rules of the Soviet military debate deserve some comment. First, there is the question whether a genuine policy debate, in the customary Western sense of the term, has been going on at all in the Soviet Union. Open discussion of strategic problems and military doctrine certainly has taken place more or less continuously in the decade since Stalin's death. This reflects a process of adjustment in Soviet thinking to the revolution in military affairs brought about first by nuclear weapons and jet aircraft, and then by ballistic missiles and space technology. Policy discussion of such matters undoubtedly has gone on in private as well. But does such internal discourse and communication, whether public or private, necessarily constitute a debate?

Much of it doubtless is merely the product of normal processes of professional military inquiry, policy formulation, and indoctrination of appropriate audiences, with no particular polemical significance. In fact, the areas of consensus in Soviet military discourse are a good deal broader than the areas in which disagreement can be discerned. At the same time, however, it seems quite clear that Soviet discourse has spilled over onto controversial terrain, often with important practical implications for defense policy and strategy. In this sense, it can properly be said that a genuine debate involving divergent views on military issues has been taking place, a debate interwoven with foreign policy and internal political-economic considerations. The essential point, over which confusion sometimes arises, is that the airing of divergent opinions in the Soviet Union in the past few years does not necessarily imply, as it once did, that those who lose the argument must also lose their positions of authority. Policy differences, in short, are not inextricably bound up with a power struggle. There is now somewhat more latitude than formerly for both public and private expression of differences of view, not only on military but also on economic, literary, and even some political matters. The amount of latitude fluctuates, and there is still a fairly elaborate ritual for conveying criticism by indirection so that the myth of communist solidarity may be preserved. Nevertheless the conditions of Soviet discourse today do allow more room for the airing of differences than before.

A distinction must be made between officially encouraged expressions of variant viewpoints, such as one occasionally finds for example in Soviet military journals, and the unsolicited interplay of competing views, the special pleading, and the bureaucratic axe-grinding that find their way into print from time to time in the Soviet Union. In both kinds of discussion, it can be assumed that the discussants recognize limits beyond which it is not expedient to press departures from the accepted policy line of the moment. Nevertheless, the attentive outside observer benefits from the partial evidence available and makes what he can of the problems and issues that preoccupy the Soviet discussants. This brings up the question whether such "listening in" on Soviet internal discussions can yield reliable insights into Soviet military thinking.

It seems characteristic of modern government, even under a totalitarian system, that it needs to foster communication among its elites, and between these and other internal audiences, on all sorts of matters. Governments have learned that the most expeditious way to do so is not necessarily through restricted private channels. In the Soviet system much more undoubtedly goes on beneath the surface through private and confidential communications than in a democratic society. Even so, a great deal of communication is necessarily carried on publicly. Consequently, when Khrushchev delivers a long speech criticizing Soviet agricultural and industrial management, literature, or defense industry, as he has done publicly on various occasions, he faces the problem of outsiders listening in and obtaining insights they would not get if this message had been conveyed in closed sessions. Indeed, Khrushchev has recognized this problem explicitly, as when he spoke to a construction workers' conference in Moscow in April 1963:

After today's conference, my speech will be published. There is a great deal of criticism in it. Our enemies will again howl: look, there is a crisis in the Soviet Union. There is this and that in the Soviet Union. We should not be afraid of this, comrades. If we start to hide our shortcomings, we will impede the creation of conditions for swiftly eliminating them.[1]

It is not to be supposed, of course, that the exigencies of internal communication and argument in the Soviet Union are likely to reveal what is customarily regarded as "classified" military information. However, even with regard to the kinds of military information that should be kept out of public discussion, there has been some change in the Soviet Union. For example, a pamphlet by Marshal Malinovskii, published in late 1962, contained the following comment pertinent to a change in the ground rules for discussion of military matters: "We nowadays set forth the basic theses of Soviet military doctrine openly—both in its political and in its technical aspects—not hiding such details as even in the recent past were considered great state secrets."[2]

The comparatively greater openness of Soviet internal discourse does not mean, to be sure, that Soviet military writings can now be regarded as a mirror of "objectivity," divorced from the propaganda functions that even professional military expres-

28

sion is intended to serve in the Soviet Union. As made clear by the authors of the Sokolovskii work, *Military Strategy*, which was recently republished in a revised edition and to which we shall give detailed attention later, Soviet military writers are explicitly aware that it is not their job to take an "objective" and "neutral" attitude toward their material:

Soviet military theory . . . reflects the laws of war as an armed struggle in the name of the most progressive social class—the proletariat. Consequently, in this work the study of various aspects of war could not be in the nature of an objective investigation. Although war, as a two-sided process of struggle, has a number of objective features, the authors, as representatives of the Soviet Armed Forces naturally could not consider these features from the position of an outside observer, but always started with Marxist-Leninist concepts of the essential nature of war in the modern epoch, its causes, and how it starts. According to Marxist-Leninist dialectics, objective evaluation of the various phenomena of social development means that the investigator cannot be neutral, but is always the representative and proponent of the ideology of his class.[3]

Obviously, military literature produced within the framework of Marxist-Leninist ideology will be colored throughout by a doctrinaire "propaganda" that distorts the reality perceived by non-Marxist eyes. This kind of propaganda distortion, however, does not make Soviet work any less valid as an expression of what Soviet writers believe to be relevant to their subject. Nor does it run counter to the purposes of internal indoctrination and instruction which Soviet military writing also is meant to serve. A consciousness of their obligation as proponents of Marxist-Leninist ideology does not mean that Soviet discussants are never drawn into debate over the merits of alternative policies or propositions. Apart from serving a legitimate need for internal communication, Soviet military discourse has the function of helping the leadership to communicate with and influence external (non-Soviet) audiences. This aspect of Soviet discourse will be taken up separately when we come to the question of the external strategic dialogue with the United States. For the moment, however, the internal Soviet debate over military questions merits some further comment.

MAIN LINES OF THE DEBATE

The character and history of the Soviet military debate from the time of Stalin's death to the publication of the Sokolovskii work on military strategy in the late summer of 1962 have been treated elsewhere at some length by the author of this volume and by others.[4] Only the main lines of that debate need be recalled here, since the present purpose is merely to provide a background for the discussion of current issues in subsequent chapters.

The mainstream of the military debate has been fairly well defined since the late 1950's, when the consolidation of Khrushchev's political primacy coincided with the prospect that the Soviet Union might soon possess advanced weapons in some numbers. Since that time, the debate has centered essentially on efforts of the political leadership, Khrushchev himself being deeply involved, to reorient Soviet military doctrine and forces in a direction considered more suitable for the needs of the nuclear-missile age. These efforts have met with varying degrees of resistance and dissent from some quarters of the military, perhaps with tacit backing among other elements of the party-state bureaucracy whose interests were engaged in one way or another. It would oversimplify the picture, however, to describe this as merely a contest of views between the political and military leaders, for the debate probably has been dominated more by the nature of the issues than by purely institutional differences between the political and military leaderships.

In fact, there has been a continuous tributary stream of debate within the military itself, with "modernist" and "traditionalist" outlooks at each end of the spectrum and a body of "centrist" opinion in the middle. The modernists have tended to be more or less in sympathy with the kinds of views advanced by Khrushchev, arguing for more radical adaptation of the fruits of modern technology to military affairs, and suggesting that this approach might lighten the strain on resources—that quality, so to speak, could replace quantity. The traditionalists, on the other hand, while recognizing the impact of technology on military affairs, have nonetheless tended to argue against discarding tried and tested concepts merely for the sake of adopting something new.

Khrushchev's own strategic ideas were most fully and forcefully laid out in a January 1960 presentation to the Supreme Soviet.[5] This speech, which appeared to represent Khrushchev's definitive assessment of the requirements for Soviet defense policy and structure in the nuclear-missile age, is one of the major landmarks in the debate. In it, he described the changes wrought by modern weapons in the character of a future war. He noted the probable decisiveness of the initial phase and thus implied that the war would be of short duration. He stressed that nuclear weapons and missiles were the main element in modern war and said that many types of traditional armed forces were rapidly becoming obsolete. He advanced the view that a large country like the Soviet Union, even though it might be struck first by nuclear weapons, would always be able to survive and retaliate. Expressing confidence that the imperialist camp was deterred by Soviet military might, he held that the Soviet Union was therefore in a good position so far as its military posture was concerned. Finally, he capped this presentation of his basic strategic notions with the announcement that the Soviet armed forces would be cut roughly one-third, from around 3.6 million to 2.4 million men, and went on to say that this reduction meant no loss of combat capability, since the firepower provided by new weaponry would make up for the man-power cut.

Khrushchev's policy position of January 1960 and the programs through which it was to be implemented did not remain intact for long. By the summer of 1961, the troop reduction program had been halted. The confident assessment that Soviet defenses were in good shape seemed to be implicitly contradicted by other measures—an increase of one-third in the Soviet military budget and the resumption of nuclear testing, including weapons of supermegaton yield. A new formulation of military doctrine, differing in some notable respects from Khrushchev's January 1960 views, was advanced at the 22nd Party Congress in October 1961 by Marshal Malinovskii. This was followed in 1962 by the comprehensive Sokolovskii work on military strategy, which reflected Malinovskii's position on certain touchstone issues more closely than Khrushchev's. In the realm of practical moves on the international strategic scene, the Soviet Union took an unprecedented step in the fall of 1962 with the deployment of missiles to Cuba.

The factors that brought about these various modifications in the Khrushchev prospectus of January 1960 are not fully known, though some of them can be identified. Soon after the January 1960 policy was enunciated, a reluctance to accept it *in toto* became apparent in the Soviet military press, not in the form of open opposition, but often through statements stressing matters that Khrushchev had either glossed over or omitted altogether. Concurrently, signs appeared in the Soviet press that many officers being returned to civilian life were encountering difficulties of adjustment, which raised questions about the effect of the troop reduction program on military morale. External events also had their impact on the situation. In May 1960 the U-2 episode posed the possibility that Soviet military security had been compromised by loss of secrecy. It also left the international situation more tense after the break-down of the Paris Summit meeting.

In 1961 a new American administration took office and responded to the threats that had been raised against Berlin by increasing U.S. defense appropriations, strengthening conventional forces, and improving the posture of U.S. strategic forces. In the fall of the same year, the United States began to express new confidence in the margin of Western strategic superiority, on the basis of improved intelligence. A year later, the Soviet Union's attempt to redress the strategic imbalance through its Cuban adventure came to nought. In the aftermath of the Cuban missile crisis the Soviet leadership was faced with a painful reappraisal of its worldwide position.

While Khrushchev's policies had to face a certain amount of internal criticism as well as the challenge of events, the striking thing about his role in the military debate is the constancy with which he seems to have stuck to his basic strategic ideas.[6] His views, both publicly and privately expressed, have tended to run along much the same lines as those in his January 1960 presentation. Moreover, as we shall see later, these views took on renewed currency in the military debate of 1963 and 1964.

Throughout the entire debate, the role of Marshal Malinovskii, the Soviet Defense Minister, is of particular interest. Like other high command appointees, Malinovskii is beholden to Khrushchev for his job and is further constrained by party discipline and presumably by his own prudence not to be so bold in opposition as was, for example, his predecessor Marshal Zhukov. In a sense, Marshal Malinovskii has seemed to search for a mediating role in the military debate. He seems to have sought to reconcile the general thrust of Khrushchev's views with the reservations probably felt by a substantial body of conservative opinion within the military. The result has been that Malinovskii's public pronouncements have tended to reflect the centrist position in the military debate, although he has also displayed fluctuations that may reflect pressure from either side or perhaps merely the pull of his own convictions.

Malinovskii's military report to the 22nd Congress of the CPSU in October 1961 is another of the major landmarks in the military debate.[7] This presentation of a "new Soviet military doctrine" reflected many of the points Khrushchev had made in his January 1960 speech concerning the changed character of the war, the primacy of strategic missile forces, and so on, but it also included some notable amendments. Most significantly, Malinovskii reaffirmed the importance of the traditional forces. Unlike Khrushchev, who conspicuously omitted the point, Malinovskii stressed that mass, multimillion-man armies would be required for victory in any future war. While Malinovskii himself curiously avoided taking a clear position on the issue of a short versus a protracted war, the burden of his argument on the continued need for large armies implied that the Soviet Union must prepare itself for a long war as well as for a short, decisive one. This view had implications for Soviet military policy quite different from Khrushchev's notion of a war that would run a very brief course after the initial nuclear exchanges. On the whole, while Malinovskii shared Khrushchev's emphasis on a military posture that would deter the West, he also reflected a concern, evidently felt by the Soviet military, that the kind of peacetime forces envisaged by Khrushchev might prove inadequate for fighting a war successfully if deterrence should break down.

The much-discussed Sokolovskii work on military strategy, which appeared a little less than a year after Malinovskii's Party Congress report, can be regarded as another important landmark in the military debate. This jointly written work, while not an "official" exposition of views held at the highest level of the Soviet government, was the most ambitious treatment of doctrine and strategy attemped in the Soviet Union in many years. With its joint authorship, it could hardly avoid becoming a forum in which both divergences and areas of agreement were brought into view. On the whole, the work appears to have tried to strike a kind of balance in the debate, and to have used the formulations advanced by Marshal Malinovskii in October 1961 as "middle ground" between competing viewpoints. However, this effort at compromise clearly failed to end the debate. Some of the issues on which ambivalent and sometimes contradictory positions were taken in the first edition of the Sokolovskii book were, briefly:

1. *The Size of the Armed Forces.* Does modern technology and its effects on the nature of any future war reduce the need for massive multi-million-man armed forces? Is Soviet security jeopardized by attempts—like those sponsored by Khrushchev in January 1960—to cut down on military man-power levels by substituting missiles and nuclear firepower? When competing claims on Soviet resources are great, should today's priority investment go into technology for its potential payoff in the future, or into maintenance of very large armed forces for present security?

2. *The Nature of the Initial Period of a War.* How "decisive" is this phase of a war likely to be under conditions of nuclear-missile warfare? What implications should be drawn and what practical steps taken with regard to force posture, readiness, and pre-emptive capability?

3. *The Length of the War.* Will a future war be short and decisive as a result of nuclear-missile attacks in the initial period, or will it be protracted with major campaigns in widespread theaters of war? Must one expect that only combat-ready forces-in-being at the outset of the war will be able to contribute to the outcome, or can one count on extensive economic and military mobilization in the course of a nuclear war? If forces-in-being are the critical factor under modern conditions, can the economy support adequate forces on a constant, peacetime basis?

4. *The Best Military Strategy for Dealing with the United States.* What kind of military posture will provide the most convincing deterrent against the United States? In the event of war, what strategy holds the most promise for a victory against a formidable overseas power like the United States? Can one

35

count on paralyzing the U.S. will to resist by quick nuclear blows against the U.S. homeland, or will it be necessary to defeat the U.S. armed forces in detail and occupy the United States to achieve victory?

5. *The Escalation of Small Wars.* What is the likelihood that such wars will occur and that they can be kept limited, or is it "inevitable" that any limited war into which the nuclear powers are drawn will rapidly expand into global, nuclear war?

6. *The Proper Role of the Military in the Formulation of Defense Policy and Strategy.* Should the military confine its attention strictly to the narrow professional aspects of preparing the Soviet armed forces for their assigned tasks, or does the complex nature of modern warfare mean that the military should have greater weight in preparing the country as a whole for a possible war, with consequently more influence upon the shaping of basic national policy?

Critical discussion of the Sokolovskii work in the Soviet Union indicated not only that it had stepped on political toes, but also that neither the modernist nor the traditionalist schools of thought were altogether happy with the compromise formulations advanced by the book. As will become apparent later when we take up developments in Soviet military thinking since publication of the first Sokolovskii edition, and since the appearance of a revised edition in the fall of 1963, many of these issues in the internal Soviet military debate still remain unresolved.

There is, indeed, ample Soviet testimony to the fact that a military debate has gone on continuously over the past few years without attainment of a unity of views. For example, the editor of a Soviet military journal, Major General P. Zhilin, wrote in the spring of 1961 that in view of all the military and political changes taking place in the world, "now, as never before, it is necessary to have a unity of views on all the most important problems of military art and employment of troops." After observing that many discussions of these problems had been taking place "in the pages of the military press and within the walls of the General Staff Academy," General Zhilin found it necessary to add: "Unfortunately, in these discussions, no unity of views has been achieved."[8]

Three years later one finds another Soviet military writer voicing virtually the same conclusion. In an exceptionally forthright treatment of the various stages of internal debate over the development of Soviet military theory in the postwar period, Colonel I. Korotkov in April 1964 alluded to the inconclusive discussions of the 1960–1961 period which had been remarked upon by General Zhilin, and in which differing points of view had been advanced. "Unfortunately," Colonel Korotkov wrote, "these discussions have still not been brought to completion. As before, there is no unity of views on the subject matter, the content and component parts of military science."[9] Nevertheless, Korotkov found, the debate had not necessarily been fruitless, for "it had speeded up the process of working out the foundation of military science."

Chapter III

THE SOVIET VOICE IN THE
EAST-WEST STRATEGIC DISCOURSE

CHARACTER OF THE DISCOURSE

The views of Soviet political and military leaders on problems of war and strategy are of great interest not only in the context of internal Soviet discussion and debate over military issues, but also in the context of the external strategic dialogue with the West, principally with the United States. Widespread appreciation of the fact that the modern world cannot, as President Kennedy put it, "survive, in the form in which we know it, a nuclear war"[1] accounts in part for the growing significance of the strategic dialogue between the United States and the Soviet Union. This is especially true in so far as the dialogue represents a means by which the two great nuclear powers may seek to clarify the complexities and mitigate the dangers of their strategic relationship in the nuclear-missile age.

By and large, the strategic discourse to date has not been especially impressive in terms of balanced and mutually instructive discourse between the two sides. They are, after all, in an adversary relationship, which involves basic differences of purpose and policy. A broad conceptual gulf lies between them. They are not likely to find it easy to explore the interacting problems and ambiguities of their strategic positions in any dispassionate and nonpolemical fashion. Indeed, as a form of communication between adversaries, much of the strategic dialogue has been and will probably continue to be concerned with advancement of the policy interests of the two great nuclear powers in a more or less narrow sense. Each side will use the dialogue to enhance its deterrent posture, to obtain political advantage from its military power or to prevent the other from doing so, to impress the authority of its position upon allies and onlookers, and so on. In particular, the dialogue up to now has tended to center on the question whether the strategic power balance in the world favors the Soviet or the Western side.[2] So long as the world's everyday judgment concerning the balance of military power continues to be a weighty factor in international politics, one can expect that much of the dialogue will turn, as before, on this question.

At the same time there is a perceptible tendency for both sides, in varying degrees, to look upon more precise strategic communication as a means to clarify the complexities and mitigate the dangers of their strategic relationship in the nuclear-missile age. In these circumstances, it is understandable that any new expressions of strategic thinking from the Soviet side should be scrutinized in the West with great interest. Over the past year or so there have been occasional statements by prominent Soviet political and military leaders, as well as books and articles by lesser figures, which qualify as significant contributions to the strategic discourse, not for the unassailability of the arguments they present but because they seem intended to convey messages to audiences abroad, as well as at home. One of the more notable of these contributions is the revised and somewhat expanded second edition of *Military Strategy*, written by a collective team of Soviet military experts headed by Marshal V. D. Sokolovskii.[3]

The first edition of this work, which was published in the Soviet Union in the late summer of 1962, was, as mentioned earlier, an important document in the Soviet internal military debate. Described by the Soviets as the first comprehensive work on military strategy to appear in the Soviet Union since 1926, the book aroused so much interest abroad that it was soon brought out in different English translations by two American publishers, and almost by a third, not to mention versions in other languages. Whether its Soviet sponsors anticipated the extent of attention the Sokolovskii work was to receive in the West is problematical. At any rate, a wide audience abroad was introduced for the first time to a full-length specimen of contemporary Soviet writing on military doctrine and strategy—a subject hitherto known to the Western world mainly through the works of a relatively small group of professional students of Soviet military affairs.

The new edition, in the same format and by the same "collective" or team of authors as its predecessor,[4] did not come as a complete surprise to interested observers, though the interval between editions—fifteen months—was unusually short for such a work. In the spring of 1963 a Soviet listing of forthcoming publications carried a brief notice that a revised version of the Sokolovskii book could be expected in the fall of that year. The announcement appeared at a time when the original volume was meeting with mixed critical comment in the Soviet Union,[5] and this heightened the impression, already held abroad, that the book, while it gave evidence of a broad consensus on many matters of military policy and strategy, also reflected divergent Soviet views on various issues. Whether plans for a second edition so soon after publication of the first were prompted by a need to take account of developments since mid-1962 or simply by the need for larger distribution (the first edition of 20,000 copies was quickly exhausted, while the new edition was double this number), was not at all clear. In any event, the new version was awaited with more than routine interest as a possible barometer of important changes in Soviet thinking and emphasis on a broad range of military policy issues.

As if to give the new Sokolovskii volume a vigorous send-off, a prominently headlined article appeared in the newspaper *Red Star* on November 2, 1963, coincident with the appearance of the work in Moscow bookstores. There seemed to be an official awareness of the book's potential as a vehicle for external as well as internal communication on strategic problems of the nuclear age. The article, signed by four members of the Sokolovskii team,[6] was in the form of a riposte to the interpretive introductions that had accompanied the two U.S. translations of the original Sokolovskii work.[7] The main burden of complaint was that American commentators, "directed from a single center in the U.S.A.," had systematically distorted the "peace-loving policy of the Soviet Union."[8] The article, despite its peevish tone, contained a number of substantive observations that made it a noteworthy document in the strategic discourse between the United States and the Soviet Union. Like a number of other recent expressions of Soviet strategic thinking, it gave evidence of Soviet sensitivity to Western interpretations of Soviet military policy and posture. It contained "corrective messages" on such questions as escalation of local conflicts, Soviet second-strike capability, and pre-emption.

Another example of the kind of direct discourse with Western military analysts that has tended to bring Soviet views into sharper focus is afforded by an article by L. Glagolev and V. Larionov published in the November 1963 issue of *International Affairs*.[9] The authorship of this article represented a rather interesting combination. Glagolev is a Soviet specialist on international relations and disarmament affairs who has been active in promoting the informal discussion of disarmament questions with various American scientists and government officials.[10] Colonel Larionov, a Soviet military expert and a prolific writer on strategic topics, including the military uses of space, is one of the authors of the Sokolovskii work. The collaboration of these two men marked a departure from customary Soviet practice. It suggested that the particular competence of a military specialist like Larionov was deemed desirable to reinforce the policy arguments of the *International Affairs* article.

This supposition was borne out by the contents of the article itself. Besides reacting to the alleged inference abroad that there are "contradictions between the Soviet policy of peaceful coexistence and the propositions of Soviet military strategy,"[11] the article also contained a rather detailed elaboration of military factors designed to demonstrate the credibility of the Soviet retaliatory posture. The latter exposition, which we shall take up in detail presently, introduced into the strategic discourse a somewhat more informed style of argument than usually has been encountered in Soviet writing.

Not the least interesting example of this new genre in Soviet strategic discourse was an article that appeared in the March 1963 issue of the *World Marxist Review,* under the signature of "General A. Nevsky, Military Commentator."[12] A trail-blazer of sorts, this article laid out many of the arguments on limited war, counterforce strategy, and other matters that were subsequently found in the revised Sokolovskii edition and the Glagolev-Larionov piece. Indeed, the close correspondence of content and style suggested that "A. Nevsky"—by curious coincidence the name of a traditional Russian military hero—may have been a *nom de plume* for one or more of the writers who had a hand in the Sokolovskii work. This impression was strengthened by at least two other circumstances: no Soviet general by the name of Nevsky could be found in any list of Soviet periodical literature; the list of contributors to the March 1963 issue of *World Marxist Review* identified all contributors with the conspicuous exception of General Nevsky. Furthermore, it is the custom for flesh-and-blood Soviet general officers to be identified when signing articles by their full title of rank, such as Major General of Aviation, Colonel General of Artillery, etc. There does not happen to be a Soviet rank of just plain "General." Whoever General Nevsky may be, his article helped to introduce the more informed style of argument that has been noticeable in recent Soviet strategic writings.

REFLECTION OF SOVIET INTERNAL
ISSUES IN THE DISCOURSE

Woven into the strategic discourse with the West have been some of the issues under internal debate in the Soviet Union, especially those growing out of the critical relationship between economics and defense. A case in point has been the central question whether to increase the Soviet military budget and to adopt a correspondingly tough declaratory policy that might provoke more vigorous Western defense efforts, or to take a path toward détente, using among other things the tactics of "negotiation by example" to bring a downturn in the level of military preparations. Throughout the period of internal Soviet reappraisal to determine what should be done to retrieve the Soviet strategic position after the reversal in Cuba, there was obviously considerable pressure for an increase in the military budget. An early sign of such pressure appeared in a pamphlet by Marshal Malinovskii in November 1962. One of the lessons he drew from the Cuban experience was that "real reasons exist which force the government and the Communist Party to strengthen the Soviet armed forces."[13] Khrushchev himself recognized this pressure in a major speech of February 27, 1963, when he made the painful admission that satisfaction of consumer needs would again have to be postponed so that the "enormous resources" required to keep Soviet military capacity from falling behind that of the West might be made available.[14] Shortly thereafter, the creation of a new Supreme Economic Council was announced, with D. F. Ustinov, a defense production expert, at its head.[15] This move suggested that a decision might have been made, or was pending, to increase allocations for military purposes. No hint was forthcoming, however, as to how any increased defense expenditure might be apportioned within the military establishment. Should it go to satisfy the prevailing military demand for continued support of large, combined-arms, theater forces, or to strengthen the strategic missile forces, by which Khrushchev himself seemed to set greater store? The possibility that the strategic forces might receive the greater attention was suggested by the elevation at about this time of Marshal Biriuzov, a Khrushchev supporter and commander of the strategic missile forces, to the position of Chief of the General Staff.

At this point in the spring of 1963, however, the internal policy debate evidently took a new turn that was to culminate before long in a Soviet decision to seek at least a limited détente with the United States. In a long speech on April 24, 1963, Khrushchev shifted his sights to the need for giving priority to economic development and for the more efficient use of available resources by defense industry. At the same time, he indicated that the Soviet armed forces were now already "equipped with the most advanced weapons for repulsing aggressive forces."[16] This statement and his remarks in early June to Harold Wilson, the British Labour Party leader, about the Soviet Union's ceasing production of strategic bombers and surface warships[17] suggested that Khrushchev was again prepared to take the line that Soviet defenses were in good enough shape not to require a large increase in military expenditures. Moreover, the view expressed by Khrushchev in January 1960 that firepower rather than massive man power should govern the scale and composition of Soviet military forces began to come back into vogue in some Soviet publications before the middle of 1963.[18] This implied a policy of "holding the line" on defense spending. These signs of an impending shift toward détente culminated in the test ban treaty of August 1963 and the October UN resolution banning nuclear weapons in space. By that time, despite such aberrant notes as the Berlin autobahn incidents, an atmosphere of détente had been unmistakably established.

In December 1963 Khrushchev's remarks at the Central Committee plenum on "chemicalization" of Soviet industry and the publication of the new Soviet budget immediately thereafter disclosed that the Soviet Union intended to reduce its military budget for 1964 by 600 million rubles, or about four per cent.[19] This action was immediately reflected in the strategic discourse with the West, as various Soviet spokesmen including Khrushchev himself pointed to the budget reduction as a token of Soviet good intentions and an example the United States should emulate.[20] The announcement of the military budget cut appeared to make a virtue of necessity. As in his earlier military policy speech of January 1960, when he combined an announcement of Soviet troop reduction with disarmament proposals aimed at the then forthcoming 10-Nation Disarmament Conference in Geneva, Khrushchev seemed to be seeking political advantage from military policy moves that he was bent on making for other reasons anyway.

Soviet moves in the process of "negotiation by example" are not always as prompt as in the case of the budget reduction announcement of December 1963. For example, no immediate response was heard from the Soviet side when, in early January 1964, the United States announced its intention of cutting back production of nuclear materials and invited the Soviet Union to do likewise.[21] Two and a half months later the Soviet Union joined the United States and Great Britain in a simultaneous announcement of plans to reduce nuclear production.[22] During the interval, as Khrushchev's April 20 statement indicated, the Soviet government evidently had been weighing the situation to determine whether a production cutback would be compatible with Soviet military requirements.

It is hard to say whether any differing views between Soviet political and military leaders on the assessment of military requirements made it difficult for the Soviet government to make up its mind on this occasion. However, a potential source of discord seems to exist in such cases. It is interesting, for example, that while Soviet military leaders in general gave public approval of the Soviet military budget reduction announced in December 1963, no military leader came forward immediately in the Soviet press with specific comment on Khrushchev's remarks in his December 13 plenum speech that the Soviet government was considering "the possibility of some further reduction in the numerical strength of our armed forces."[23] In fact, the most conspicuous public military utterance in the wake of Khrushchev's statement carried the unmistakable inference that it was unwise for the Soviet Union to contemplate further reduction of its ground forces at a time when the West was building up its own ground strength. Marshal Chuikov, commander of the Soviet ground forces, whose special interest in countering the NATO build-up of ground forces was probably great, implied this conclusion in an *Izvestiia* article in December 1963.[24] We shall return to Chuikov's views later in connection with the internal controversy over what the size of the Soviet armed forces should be.

Soviet reaction to the program of conventional force build-up urged on NATO by the United States has tended to vary in a way that has shown up on the Soviet end of the strategic discourse. Marshal Chuikov's evident worry about the changing relationship of Western and Soviet ground strength typifies one kind of response, expressed also by others who have asserted that the West is building up massive ground forces along with its nuclear forces.[25] Another response has been the standard political propaganda line that the NATO build-up demonstrates the aggressive aims of the Western bloc, particularly the Bonn "revanchists."[26] At the same time, there has been a discernible tendency, especially since the onset of Khrushchev's détente overtures, to accept some increase in NATO's ground forces as a fact of life, and to turn it to Soviet political account instead of challenging it head on.

Khrushchev himself, for example, has taken note of Western conventional strength increases in Europe, but has suggested that if these forces are as strong as American spokesmen say then there is no reason why the West should hesitate to enter into arms reduction agreements.[27] There also has been some Soviet commentary on the question of U.S. policy concerning the employment of nuclear weapons in the event of a Soviet attack on Europe that could not be contained by conventional means. The Glagolev-Larionov article stated that a U.S. nuclear initiative was justified by some people in the United States as a response to "the possibility of an attack by conventional Soviet forces on Western Europe, which allegedly does not have enough conventional forces to defend itself." The article then went on to assert that this argument "does not hold any water," since Western forces are deployed in greater strength in Europe today than formerly.[28] This statement seems to constitute an interesting admission that the Western build-up of conventional strength in Europe makes for greater stability of the military situation there. Although the article did not offer such an interpretation, the general effect of this treatment of the NATO situation was to moderate internal Soviet arguments for further strengthening of the Soviet ground forces.

"MESSAGES" TO THE WEST

The foregoing examples of ways in which internal issues have tended to become interwoven with the external strategic discourse suggest the difficulty of interpreting the "messages" that Soviet spokesmen and writers may intend to convey to the West. The Soviet voice may sometimes contradict what appears to be the main line of Soviet policy at a given moment. On the whole, however, a fairly consistent pattern of strategic policy points is addressed to audiences abroad. Some of these points are variations on familiar themes; others appear to reflect new considerations. At the time of writing, the general pattern of the external discourse seems largely related to the critical and trying period through which the Soviet leaders have passed during the last year and a half.

During this period, difficulties plaguing Soviet agriculture and the economy made it harder to deal with the competing military and economic claims upon available resources. Within the communist bloc, the dispute with China grew increasingly bitter, as China called into question Soviet leadership of the world communist movement, while at the same time the European satellites displayed an urge for a greater measure of autonomy. Above all, in their politico-strategic relationship with the United States and the West, the Soviet leaders during this period faced some soul-searching crises of decision, the most dramatic of which was the Cuban missile showdown. These dilemmas clearly left their imprint on the strategic discourse with the West, the main lines of which have come to reflect an evident Soviet awareness of the need to adjust Soviet policy to the changing character of the strategic environment. Some particularly interesting features of recent Soviet discourse, to which we shall give further attention in ensuing chapters of this book, can be summed up as follows:

First, there is a persistent effort to enhance the credibility of the Soviet strategic deterrent in Western eyes. This theme, argued with greater technical sophistication than previously, is coupled with an attempt to disabuse the United States of any idea that it can count on a successful first strike or draw political advantage from its strategic position vis-à-vis the Soviet Union. In a sense, this double-barreled "message" seems to be the military concomitant to the political policy of détente. In effect, it warns the West not to try to stretch the limits of détente to its advantage.

Second, there is a general Soviet effort to propagate the idea, not always clearly spelled out, of mutual nuclear deterrence at the strategic level and to give an impression of doctrinal rigidity at this level by rejecting such concepts as controlled strategic warfare. This trend in Soviet discourse may relate to a sense of growing doubt among the Soviet leaders as to whether missile-blackmail diplomacy, which once looked highly promising, can in fact be used successfully to force withdrawal of the West from its stubbornly held political and strategic positions around the world.

Third, in notable contrast with the tendency to rigidify the Soviet doctrinal stance at the strategic level, there appears to be a tentative endeavor to project a less rigidly doctrinaire image than formerly with regard to the escalation potential of local conflicts. This suggests that the Soviets may wish to see the "escalation threshold" raised, perhaps in order to provide greater flexibility for local use of military power below the nuclear level and to disarm Chinese criticisms of Soviet failure to give vigorous support to "national liberation" struggles. Rather curiously, while this trend would seem to allow greater freedom of action for Soviet political strategy in the under-developed world, more support for softening the customary doctrinal line on "inevitability" of escalation seems to have come from military than from political spokesmen.

Fourth, related to the apparent desire in some Soviet quarters to communicate an image of greater flexibility in the support of local conflicts, there is a new suggestion in Soviet discourse that in certain potential third-power conflicts, such as local hostilities involving West Germany and Eastern Europe, the Soviet Union might try to avoid expanding the conflict by withholding nuclear attacks against the United States in return for U.S. abstention. This suggestion seems to relate to a general Soviet concern to reassure the United States against the possibility of a Soviet first strike under borderline conditions in which the question of pre-emption might arise. At the same time, the Soviet position on this point remains somewhat ambivalent. There is still the veiled hint in other Soviet utterances, perhaps intended to reinforce the Soviet deterrent image, that under some circumstances the Soviet Union may entertain what would be in fact, if not in name, a pre-emptive strategy.

Finally, the Soviet voice in the strategic dialogue seems to reflect uncertainty whether the Soviet Union's best interest lies in asserting superiority over the West, at the risk of stimulating greater Western exertions and prematurely jeopardizing the atmosphere of détente, or in settling for a second-best position. Soviet policy on this question is complicated by many factors. For example, not only is the Soviet Union at a relative disadvantage in resources but, as experience shows, it has managed to live for a considerable period in a position of strategic inferiority to its major adversary without being subjected to the "imperialist attack" so often predicted.

Chapter IV

GENERAL IMPORT OF THE NEW SOKOLOVSKII VOLUME

The revised Soviet edition of the Sokolovskii work, *Military Strategy*, offers an unusual opportunity to compare both changes and continuities in Soviet thinking on a wide range of strategic and military-political issues during the eventful period between the two editions. For this reason it would appear useful, before taking up in detail the various questions with which the Soviet strategic thinking and policy seem most concerned today, to comment briefly on the general import of the new Sokolovskii volume.

One of the first things to be said about the revised edition is that it did not register any radical changes in Soviet military doctrine or strategic concepts since the original volume appeared fifteen months earlier in the late summer of 1962.[1] While textual alterations were fairly numerous and the original version was expanded by approximately 50 pages, many of the revisions related to political questions and seemed designed more to bring the book into harmony with shifts in Soviet foreign policy than to advance major new formulations on military questions as such. The revised volume nevertheless represented the most substantial single addition to Soviet military literature since its predecessor, and as such has contributed further insight into the process of Soviet adaptation to the strategic environment of the nuclear-missile age.

With regard to the Soviet military policy debate, the revised Sokolovskii edition gave evidence that a number of issues remain unresolved and that doctrine is still in flux on various questions. Some of the matters still at issue or ambiguously treated were: the duration of a future war; the size of the armed forces; the likelihood of a war outbreak in the 1960's;

the feasibility of wartime mobilization under nuclear conditions; the role of pre-emption in modern war; the danger of escalation of local conflicts; the prospects for effective active defense against nuclear attack; the military uses of space; and, above all, the question of finding a strategy for victory in a possible future nuclear war when the usefulness of war itself as an instrument of policy is increasingly in doubt.

On a number of other military questions, a large measure of consensus can be found in both editions. Included in this category were such matters as: the primacy of strategic nuclear weapons in modern warfare; a target philosophy which emphasizes destruction of both military and urban-industrial targets and rejects the concept of strategic targeting restraint; recognition of the economic difficulty of maintaining large enough standing forces in peacetime; emphasis on the need for qualitative and quantitative superiority; a theater warfare doctrine calling for extensive nuclear strikes with follow-up and occupation by ground forces; and an image of the West as a militarily formidable opponent, still held in check mainly by fear of the consequences of Soviet retaliation.

There was a third category of military questions, namely those upon which a new degree of emphasis was placed in the revised edition of the Sokolovskii work. Among such matters were: more attention to limited war; an increased confidence in the ability of early-warning and other measures to reduce the chances of successful surprise attack; greater stress on the hardening and mobility of strategic weapons; an upgrading of the strategic role of missile-launching submarines; more emphasis on antisubmarine operations and amphibious landing capabilities; some downgrading of heavy bomber prospects for the future but an upgrading of the bomber's role against targets at sea; and the importance of developing both antimissile and antisatellite defenses.

Another interesting new feature of the revised Sokolovskii volume was an analysis of the U.S. "counterforce" or "city-sparing" strategy, accompanied by arguments against its feasibility. This typified Soviet resistance to what the authors described as "some sort of suggestion to the Soviet Union on 'rules' for the conduct of nuclear war."[2] The new volume did not specifically revive Khrushchev's 1960 notions on the substitution of missile firepower for man power, but it did reflect the increasing emphasis placed by Khrushchev and the modernist school on the strategic missile forces as the main element of Soviet military power.

Throughout the revised Sokolovskii volume, as in most expositions of Soviet strategic thought, there was marked ambivalence concerning the military path to victory in modern war, especially against a powerful overseas opponent. In the new volume, as in its predecessor, the concept of winning through the shock effect of strategic nuclear attack alternated with the traditional concept that victory can only be secured by combined-arms operations to seize and occupy the enemy's homeland. A variant line of thought in Soviet military theory of the past year, which placed emphasis on the possibility of Soviet victory in a protracted war through superior political-morale qualities and economic organization, found a slight reflection in the revised Sokolovskii work, but was not taken up as a major new theme.

The revised Sokolovskii volume bore the imprint of political trends both in Soviet domestic affairs and in foreign policy. The new volume supplemented other evidence of unresolved tensions in political-military relations inside the Soviet Union. The revised edition displayed a strong tendency to reaffirm the primacy of the political leadership in military affairs, a trend that appeared in Soviet military writing after publication of the first Sokolovskii edition. There seems to have been a general internal reaction to efforts by the military to claim a larger share of influence in the formation of national security policy.

The signing of the test-ban treaty was acknowledged in the new volume as an important step in reducing international tension, but the new "spirit of Moscow" by no means pervaded the whole work. Indeed, commenting on the test-ban treaty, the authors cautioned against "relying on the 'goodwill' of the imperialists," rather than on "the might of the socialist camp," to prevent a new war.[3]

A certain amount of minor political face-lifting was evident in the new text. The two uncomplimentary references to the Yugoslavs that appeared in the original version were omitted in the new one.[4] This change reflected an improvement over the past months in Soviet-Yugoslav relations. The new volume, like the old, maintained a discreet silence on the Sino-Soviet quarrel. It referred to the Chinese only once, and then indirectly. The reference occurred in a statement on the struggle "against revisionism," to which " . . . and dogmatism" was added in the new text.[5] The dogmatists, in the current Soviet lexicon, are of course the Chinese. This treatment of the Chinese issue stands in contrast to other Soviet writing on military affairs, which often makes polemical attacks on Chinese misrepresentation of Soviet defense policy and strategy.[6] The reason for neutralizing the Sokolovskii volume on the question of China is not clear.[7] Possibly the authors anticipated some improvement in Sino-Soviet relations and did not want to burden their work with invidious references on this delicate issue.

Like the first Sokolovskii edition, the revised work was doubt-less intended to help meet a felt need within the Soviet Union for up-to-date internal communication and instruction in the field of military doctrine and strategy. The numerous reviews of the first Sokolovskii volume in Soviet military periodicals gave evidence that the book was considered professionally significant within the Soviet Union. So, too, did the preface to the second edition where the authors noted that their book was discussed at "the Academy of the General Staff, at military-scientific societies of the Main Staff of the Ground Forces, at the M. V. Frunze Central House of the Soviet Army and in a number of other institutions."[8] The book also was apparently discussed widely in Soviet military units in the field, as was indicated by comment in a Soviet military journal in October 1963.[9]

At the same time, the revised volume clearly was designed to have an impact on external audiences as well. One gets the impression that the second edition was prepared with a somewhat more deliberate eye to audiences outside the Soviet Union than its predecessor.[10] This was perhaps to be expected in the light of the attention given the first volume in the West. While the later version, like the earlier, cannot be regarded as an "official" Soviet policy document, it obviously serves as a medium through which various strategic policy "messages" are directed at audiences abroad. Chapter III briefly indicated the general pattern of such messages, as they are found in the new Sokolovskii work and other Soviet utterances. It is now time to turn to a more detailed examination of the Soviet views revealed in the military debate both internal and external.

Chapter V

THE CREDIBILITY OF THE SOVIET DETERRENT POSTURE

Soviet strategic writers today insist that Soviet military strength and readiness to employ it in the event of aggressive Western moves against the Soviet bloc should be taken seriously in the West. While this is by no means a new Soviet theme, it has become more pronounced since the fall of 1962. A further change of emphasis may be found in the present tendency to argue with somewhat greater technical sophistication than previously that the Soviet Union is militarily capable of retaliating after a nuclear attack. Let us consider the developments that have led to this current effort to reinforce the credibility of the Soviet deterrent posture.

DETERRENCE AND FOREIGN POLICY

In the eyes of the Soviet leadership, one of the prime values of Soviet military power has long been its presumed deterrent effect upon the capitalist countries. To appreciate the weight of this factor in Soviet thinking it is necessary to recall that until quite recently the Soviet leaders took it for granted that sooner or later the capitalist states, seeking to preserve their system against the march of "history," would make war upon the Soviet Union. Accordingly, from the earliest days of the Soviet regime Soviet policy constantly sought to postpone what was expected to be the inevitable military collision of the capitalist and communist systems until the Soviet Union could make itself stronger than any forces that might be arrayed against it. Temporary partnership in arms with some capitalist states in World War II did not alter this long-term policy.

In the Soviet view, the reluctance of the United States to exploit its nuclear monopoly after the last war was less the result of American good intentions than of restraint imposed by Soviet military power. In the first postwar years, the burden of restraining the United States from exploiting its nuclear predominance fell mainly on the large theater ground forces with which the Soviet Union, in a sense, was able to hold Western Europe "hostage." The durability of this indirect restraint, however, was not at all certain in the age of nuclear technology. A major endeavor of Soviet policy in the first postwar decade, therefore, was to ensure that the United States would not retain a nuclear monopoly for long and to provide the Soviet armed forces with at least nominal nuclear capabilities to strengthen their deterrent value. After the Soviet Union began to acquire modern weapons and delivery means, the prime deterrent role shifted gradually but not wholly to Soviet strategic forces whose "reach," as Marshal Biriuzov put it recently,[1] had come to extend beyond Europe to the United States itself. The Soviet theater forces continued to provide an element of indirect deterrence and the PVO, or air defense system, together with the strategic forces, became a direct deterrent to nuclear attack from the West.

For the Soviet leadership, the maintenance of a military posture sufficiently credible to deter the opponent presented many problems. Some of these were technical and operational, since they related to the development of the necessary Soviet forces. In building up its own forces, the Soviet Union also had to take into account the size and posture of U.S. military forces, which did not remain static, particularly after the impact of the Korean War on American defense policy. Other problems grew out of the shifting criteria for effective deterrence, and out of the closely linked demands of the political strategy that Soviet military power was expected to support.

The Soviet military posture that evolved during the later 1950's and early 1960's was doubtless more than adequate to deter an outright attack on the Soviet Union, short of extreme provocation, but its deterrent value was still uncertain in situations where the vital interests of the West were at stake. The Cuban crisis, for example, seems to have brought home vividly to the Soviet leadership the possibility that deterrence might fail if its own policies were sufficiently provocative.

With regard to the needs of Soviet political strategy, Soviet military power in this period was perhaps sufficient in the Soviet view to inhibit dangerous Western initiatives and to bring the United States to reconcile itself to Soviet gains already made. But was it also adequate to support an assertive forward policy that would force the West into retreat on major outstanding political issues? The Berlin experience may well have suggested that a military posture adequate to deter an unprovoked attack can be less effective in supporting an aggressive political strategy. There was also the larger problem of what would happen should deterrence break down. Military forces that looked ample for deterrence were not necessarily strong enough to win a war if it should come to that. Judging from the history of the military debate in the Soviet Union, the Soviet political and military leaders did not see eye to eye on this question.

Developments of the late 1950's and early 1960's appeared to demonstrate that both the deterrent value and the political worth of the Soviet military posture left something to be desired. Indeed, the balance of military forces, as understood by the world at large, was such in the early 1960's that the Soviet leaders themselves were evidently constrained to exercise caution upon the international scene, to adopt a less assertive policy, and to seek what has come to be described as a détente. At the same time, a new emphasis is being placed today on public declarations calculated to make the Soviet deterrent posture seem more credible.

GENERAL WARNINGS TO THE WEST

Soviet military strength, Marshal Malinovskii said in the summer of 1962, ought to "instill doubts about the outcome of a war planned by the aggressor, to frustrate his criminal designs in embryo, and if war becomes a reality, to defeat the aggressor decisively."[2] Such vague warning statements, of course, have long been the stock in trade of Soviet spokesmen, but today there is a somewhat greater tendency to spell out the message. The new Sokolovskii edition, for example, makes explicit a point merely implied in the first edition, namely that the book's comprehensive discussion of war and strategy is intended as a warning to the West against entertaining any thoughts of an outright attack on the Soviet bloc, and against attempts to gain political advantage at Soviet expense.

In a special preface to the second edition, the authors noted that the first edition of their work had caused "repercussions" in the West. They accused the "political and military ideologists of imperialism" of wanting to see the Soviet Union "defenseless before the threat of attack in order to pursue their aggressive policy and dictate their will" to others. Asserting that the communist countries, for their part, "do not intend to attack anybody," the authors stated that these countries nevertheless "will not leave the enemy with any illusions that they are unprepared to rebuff him."[3] The authors next quoted from a pamphlet by Marshal Malinovskii to the effect that in Soviet eyes the best means of defense is not an attack, but rather "a warning to the enemy about our strength and readiness to destroy him at the first attempt to carry out an act of aggression."[4] Then they explained: "That is why we, rather than hide our views on the nature and means of waging a future war, have revealed them in the book *Military Strategy*."

A large Soviet literature has grown up around the theme of Soviet missile power as the mainstay of deterrence. This theme dates back to the late 1950's when Khrushchev claimed that the Soviet Union had "organized the series production of intercontinental ballistic missiles" and that it possessed "the means to deliver a crushing blow to the aggressor at any point on the globe."[5] While most of the literature has avoided specific assertions of Soviet numerical superiority in missiles, it has dwelt heavily on the qualitative edge allegedly enjoyed by the Soviet Union by virtue of greater warhead weight, global range, and so on.[6] After testing very-large-yield nuclear weapons in late 1961, the Soviet Union widely advertised the destructive attributes of weapons in the 50- and 100-megaton class.[7] Making the most of this new element in the Soviet deterrent image, Soviet spokesmen frequently reminded the West that it possessed no weapons of this kind.[8] Upon occasion, they have dropped hints that the Soviet Union might have up its sleeve "even more formidable" weapons, as in 1960 when Khrushchev spoke of a "fantastic weapon" under design by Soviet scientists,[9] and in 1963 when Malinovskii mentioned the possibility of a "fundamentally new weapon."[10]

In the fall of 1963, the Soviet general and military press renewed and intensified its emphasis on the strategic missile forces. A spate of articles, mostly in a popular vein, appeared at this time in connection with the military parade in Red Square on November 7 and the observance of Artillery Day in the latter part of the month. These articles were notable on several counts. First, they bore down hard on the theme that, thanks to Soviet possession of modern weapons, which "the military parade on Red Square [had] visually confirmed,"[11] the Soviet Union now possessed a retaliatory capability that had helped to "solve the country's security problem."[12] Second, the deputy commander of the strategic missile forces himself reacted to Western estimates of Soviet inferiority in the size of strategic delivery forces with a claim that the Soviet Union would respond to an attack of any size with "a still greater number of missiles."[13] Third, some articles dwelt on the capabilities of the strategic missile forces and on the exceptional qualities of Soviet missile personnel, in a manner that may have been meant to pave the way psychologically for further reductions in the more traditional branches of the Soviet armed forces. Khrushchev subsequently indicated, at the close of the Central Committee's plenum in December 1963, that he had such a reduction in mind. Finally, Soviet military spokesmen stressed not only that Soviet nuclear weapons and missiles provided a "reliable shield" for their country, but also that, in the event of Western aggression, "our hands will not falter in using them."[14] Subsequently, when it came time to observe the 46th anniversary of the Soviet armed forces on February 23, 1964, the central theme in the press again was that the "rocket-nuclear might of the USSR" deterred the imperialists and provided "an 'indestructible shield' for the socialist camp."[15]

SOVIET TENDENCY TO ARGUE MORE OBJECTIVELY AND PRECISELY

Soviet emphasis on the Soviet Union's retaliatory might, despite its intensity, has not been particularly persuasive. As a rule, the Soviet case has rested on broad assertions that tend to gloss over many of the problems involved in assuring a successful retaliatory strike. For example, as indicated by some of the remarkably candid disclosures of Secretary of Defense Robert McNamara concerning the state of Soviet defenses, the USSR apparently began only quite recently to adopt measures like hardening its strategic missile forces.[16] Without such measures the chances of their survival to deliver a retaliatory blow would seem quite dim, however suitable these relatively vulnerable forces might be for a *Soviet* first strike. Soviet discourse generally has been along such broad-gauge lines as to brush over the significance of military-technical considerations of this sort. However, there now seems to be growing Soviet recognition that refinement of the Soviet line of argument is needed if the Soviet Union is to propagate a convincing image of certain retaliation to a strategic attack. It is not altogether clear whether this reflects residual concern over the credibility of the Soviet deterrent posture after the Cuban confrontation, or a new sense of confidence growing out of remedial defense measures that the USSR may have undertaken since that time. At any rate, a new note of objectivity has begun to enter Soviet discourse.

A typical example of this can be found in the Glagolev-Larionov article in the November 1963 issue of *International Affairs*, to which reference was made earlier. This article advanced a more precise argument than usual in seeking to establish that the Soviet Union is militarily in a sound position to carry out a second-strike retaliatory policy. While the assertions it contained concerning the Soviet posture were not to be taken without some reservation, the article at least addressed the second-strike problem more explicitly than had been customary hitherto in Soviet literature.[17] It is therefore worth looking at the points on which the Glagolev-Larionov argument rested.

The argument was prefaced by the assertion that "foreign military analysts" are "talking through their hats" when they contend that "Soviet nuclear rocket weapons are highly vulnerable and are designed for a first and not a counterstrike."[18] Couched as a rebuttal to Western analysis of the Soviet military posture, this remark suggests an awareness that actual military dispositions and arrangements sometimes speak louder than words and that it is correspondingly important to shape the opponent's interpretation of these arrangements. The authors then went on to make their first point, namely that Soviet measures to disperse, harden, conceal, and otherwise reduce the vulnerability of their strategic forces make it impossible for an enemy to knock out all these forces simultaneously:

It is obvious that even in the most favorable conditions, an aggressor would be unable to destroy all the counterstrike means with his first salvo, for these means—rockets, bombers, submarines, etc.—are dispersed. A considerable part of them is constantly on the move. Another, even greater part, such as bombers on airfields, are in a state of almost instant readiness to take off. It is physically impossible not only to knock out all the counterstrike means simultaneously, but even to pinpoint their location as the first salvo missiles reach their targets.[19]

Apart from inferring that camouflage and mobility would complicate the problem of target location, Glagolev and Larionov did not specifically point to the target location problem as one that would bear significantly on the success of an attack. By contrast, in a new discussion of U.S. counterforce strategy in the second edition of the Sokolovskii book, as will be noted in more detail later, the target location question received great emphasis. (The Sokolovskii volume's negative assessment of the prospects for a U.S. counterforce strategy, incidentally, served to bolster the argument that the Soviet Union now possesses a secure second-strike capability.)

The next major point of the Glagolev-Larionov argument in *International Affairs* rested on the claim that modern warning techniques make it possible for the defender to avoid being taken by tactical surprise. Besides including a rather novel claim for very early Soviet detection of missile launchings, and implying that Soviet strategic missiles can react with extreme rapidity,[20] the article here reflected a trend, also observable in the new Sokolovskii edition, to re-evaluate somewhat the factor of surprise. It stated:

The element of surprise, rather important in past wars, now has a different character. Even such weapons as instant-action rockets, launched at any time of day or night and in any weather, can be detected in the first section of their flight path by ever vigilant radars and other instruments. In this age of radioelectronics and targeted ready-to-fire rockets, a counterstrike will follow the first strike in a matter of minutes.[21]

The above paragraph concluded with a passage on the defender's ability to get off his missiles before the attacker's weapons arrive, suggesting a notion very close to pre-emption, which we shall take up presently. The authors then argued that an attacker would be limited to a small first strike if he wished to achieve even a degree of surprise. Presumably U.S. bomber forces would not be regarded as a factor in an initial attack, on the ground that their use would sacrifice the advantage of surprise.

If the attacker is to achieve a measure of even relative surprise—an advantage of a few minutes—he would have to use in his very first salvo a small but most efficient part of his means of attack. Thus, existing bombers, whose speed is only a fraction of that of rockets, would hardly produce any element of surprise, in the modern sense. On the other hand, after the aggressor's strike the attacked could discount the element of surprise and would use all his counterstrike means set in motion before the first explosions on his territory or remaining intact after the start of the enemy's nuclear bombardment.[22]

Stating finally that Soviet forces are maintained in a state of heightened readiness to deliver "an instant counterblow, which would be equivalent in power to thousands of millions of tons of TNT," the Glagolev-Larionov article then drew the conclusion that

an aggressor cannot now derive any economic or political advantages from nuclear war, for it merely puts the seal on his own destruction . . . The basic change in the world balance of forces and the new properties of the weapons at the disposal of the Soviet Union are a powerful deterrent to the unleashing of another war by the most aggressive circles of imperialism.[23] [Italics in the original.]

THE QUESTION OF PRE-EMPTION

It has been customary in both public and private Soviet discourse to picture the Soviet strategic forces as a second-strike retaliatory instrument. The possibility that these forces might be used in a first strike has been assiduously disavowed. With regard to a third possible use—for what is described in technical parlance as a pre-emptive or forestalling attack[24]—the Soviet position has been characterized, perhaps purposely, by a great deal of ambiguity.

The question whether the Soviet Union might want to adopt a pre-emptive strategy remains pertinent for at least two sets of reasons. Soviet calculation of the consequences of a nuclear attack, if war should come about, cannot help but recognize that pre-emption might be necessary to keep Soviet losses within survival limits. With regard to practical consequences, there is a very great difference between a policy of attempting a pre-emptive strike, which would be intended to break up or blunt an enemy attack that was about to be launched, and a policy of a purely retaliatory strike, which would be mounted only after having absorbed the unimpeded weight of the enemy's initial blow. Moreover, the deterrent and political values of Soviet forces are to some degree affected by the opponent's view of their pre-emptive role. If the Soviet Union chooses to pursue a forward political policy, for instance, and manages to make convincing its intention and ability to pre-empt, it may stand a better chance in a crisis of forcing retreat or compromise upon the United States. While the possibility of Soviet pre-emptive action in the 1962 Cuban crisis failed to pass the credibility test, the Soviet leaders might come to feel that if they had succeeded in deploying a missile force in Cuba and had thereby improved their pre-emptive capability there would have been less chance of an effective American response, not only in Cuba but perhaps in Berlin and elsewhere.[25]

While a pre-emptive policy might convey a politically useful warning to the West and help to reinforce the Soviet deterrent image, it also creates difficulties. Besides the military requirements of a pre-emptive capability, such as high readiness, quick reaction, and unequivocal warning, there is also the difficulty that a manifest pre-emptive stance may in some situations prompt the other side to make pre-emptive preparations on its own account and thus increase the risk of an unpremeditated nuclear exchange. Moreover, a declaratory pre-emptive policy also has undesirable political overtones in that it mars the image of the Soviet Union as the champion of peaceful coexistence and as a country that would never initiate war under any provocation short of an actual attack. For all these reasons, pro and con, the Soviet attitude on pre-emption has been and remains ambiguous.

Soviet rhetoric customarily proclaims the practical gains to be expected from a pre-emptive strike against an adversary caught in the act of preparing to attack, but at the same time disclaims the possibility that the Soviet Union would ever contemplate making a strike that was other than retaliatory. The resulting uncertainty as to where the Soviets really stand on this question may be precisely the impression they wish to create. This was brought out graphically in the comments on the question of a pre-emptive strike by four of the Sokolovskii authors in their *Red Star* article of November 2, 1963, responding to Western commentary on the first Sokolovskii edition.

Adverting to remarks made by Marshal Malinovskii at the 22nd Congress of the CPSU in October 1961, the Soviet authors denied that Malinovskii was thinking in terms of a pre-emptive strike when he spoke of "the readiness of the Soviet Armed Forces to break up a surprise attack by the imperialists." Without specifying precisely what Marshal Malinovskii may have had in mind, or what their own rendering of his remarks in their book was meant to convey, the Soviet authors declared that "the very idea of such a blow is totally rejected by the peace-loving policy of the Soviet state." They also bridled at the suggestion that relative strategic weakness might account for Soviet resort to ambiguous warnings of pre-emption, as a device to enhance the Soviet deterrent posture.[26]

While the four Sokolovskii authors plainly went to some pains in their *Red Star* article to deny that statements of Soviet readiness to break up an enemy attack are meant to imply pre-emption, it is interesting that the second edition of the Sokolovskii book still adheres to a formula no less ambiguous than that found in the first edition. The pertinent passage in the new edition, essentially unchanged from the previous text, reads as follows:

Since modern weapons permit exceptionally important strategic results to be achieved in the briefest time, *the initial period of the war will be of decisive significance for the outcome of the entire war.* Hence, the main task is to work out methods for reliably *repelling a surprise nuclear attack,* as well as methods of breaking up the opponent's aggressive plans by dealing him in good time a crushing blow.[27] [Italics in the original.]

Variations on the theme of Soviet "readiness to break up the enemy's attack and his criminal designs" continue to appear regularly in Soviet discourse, without ever specifying just what conditions are envisaged.[28] Perhaps the closest Soviet writers have come recently to suggesting that the Soviet Union contemplates a strategy approximating pre-emption, in fact if not in name, was in a previously mentioned passage in the Glagolev-Larionov article in *International Affairs.*

The first rockets and bombers of the side on the defensive [i.e., the Soviet side] would take off *even before the aggressor's first rockets, to say nothing of his bombers, reached their targets.*[29] [Italics in the original.]

If this description is taken at face value, a very fine line indeed separates the Soviet conceptions of a pre-emptive and of a retaliatory strike. The passage seems meant to convey the notion that the Soviet response to warning of a strategic attack would be instant and automatic, and that it would not be delayed until there was incontrovertible evidence of an attack against Soviet targets. The impression of a "hair-trigger" Soviet posture has been heightened, whether by design or otherwise, by recurrent statements that, surprise being fundamentally important in modern war, Soviet forces must "skillfully apply surprise"[30] and seek "to take the enemy unawares."[31]

SOME REASONS FOR THE PRESENT SOVIET CONCERN

Several reasons may account for the efforts described above to enhance the credibility of the Soviet deterrent posture. The Soviet leaders may have some doubts, growing perhaps out of the Cuban experience, about their actual military posture. These doubts may be compounded by frequent Western expressions of confidence in the margin of Western strategic superiority. For this confidence presumably rests in part on Western intelligence assessments that imply some diminution of the secrecy barrier behind which Soviet military preparations customarily have been carried out. The Soviet leaders also may still retain an ingrained suspicion of Western intentions, despite the fact that the West showed no inclination to make war upon the Soviet Union even when it enjoyed a nuclear monopoly.

No doubt the frequent assertion of the impregnability of Soviet defenses offers some reassurance to the home front. Similarly, it may serve to reassure satellite regimes that they need no longer fear overthrow or "rollback" through Western actions. Paradoxically, however, the safer the satellite regimes feel, the more they may be inclined to pull away from the Soviet Union's protective wing and to seek wider intercourse with the West.

Repeated emphasis on the power of the Soviet military to deter war and guarantee the peace may serve a useful psychological function within the military establishment itself. Stress on the role of deterrence may be a device for encouraging the Soviet soldiery to stick to their knitting in an age when many of the traditional contributions of the military profession are being called into question and the political utility of war itself is increasingly in doubt.

Finally, the Soviet leaders, in seeking to project an image of unassailable military power, may still entertain a residual hope that the West can be forced into political retreat. At least they appear to feel that a formidable military stance is a necessary backstop for the kinds of political and ideological struggle called for by the policy of peaceful coexistence. Indeed, a renewed emphasis on Soviet military strength and readiness may seem to the Soviet leaders a prudent concomitant of the détente overtures they have been obliged by the circumstances of the early 1960's to make to the West.

Chapter VI

THE QUESTION OF WAR
AS AN INSTRUMENT OF POLICY

The view is frequently heard in the world today that the scientific-technological revolution, in the words of an American scientist, "has made wars irrational and deprived diplomacy of its most important tool—plausible war threats."[1] Whether the Soviet leadership has gradually come around to such a view— whether it has come to feel that Soviet policy must not only avoid the danger of a major military conflict with the West but also eschew threats of Soviet military action—is a question upon which the final returns are not yet in. However, it seems clear up to this point that Soviet political and military thought has not escaped the profoundly unsettling implications of the idea that it may prove impossible to win a nuclear war in any meaningful sense.

SYMPTOMS OF THE EROSION
OF CLASSICAL DOCTRINE

Ever since Malenkov's short-lived thesis in 1954 that a nuclear war could result in the "mutual destruction" of capitalist and communist society,[2] the Soviet leadership has lived with an unresolved doctrinal crisis over the question of war as an instrument of policy. One symptom of this crisis was the revision by Khrushchev in 1956 of the long-held communist dogma on the inevitability of an eventual war to the death between the capitalist and communist systems.[3] Another symptom has been the gradual erosion of the dogma of inevitable communist victory, should a new world war occur, although this dogma dies hard and has by no means disappeared from Soviet thinking. It seems to find the most currency among Soviet ideologists and military people. As pointed out in the first chapter, increasing doubt as to its validity has evidently seeped into the consciousness of the top leadership and helped to alter their perspectives on fundamental problems of war and peace. A third symptom of the doctrinal crisis over the question of war as an instrument of policy has been the disagreement about it in the many-sided quarrel between Moscow and Peking.

In the Sino-Soviet polemics, understandably, a certain amount of distortion has crept into each disputant's allegations concerning the other's views of the relationship between war and politics. The Soviet side has tended to assert more categorically than the facts may warrant that China is for war and the Soviet Union for peace. It has accused the Chinese of risking a nuclear holocaust by dogmatic interpretation of Lenin's views on war as an instrument of policy. The Chinese, on the other hand, have accused the Soviets of forgetting Lenin's teaching that war is a continuation of politics. They have somewhat overdone the charge that the Soviet Union has permitted itself to be awed into "capitulationism" toward the West through fear of nuclear war, and that it has failed to exploit its military power in a political sense to advance the interests of the communist camp as a whole. Polemics aside, the chances are that neither party to the dispute is any more eager than the other to invite a nuclear war, but that they differ in their estimates of how far it is safe to go in exerting pressure upon the West without serious risk of precipitating war.

INTERNAL SOVIET DEBATE OVER LENIN'S DICTUM

In the post-Cuba period of sharpened polemics with the Chinese, the argument over war as an instrument of policy has become a matter of internal debate within the Soviet Union. Discussions are carried on in the public media, and the discussants fall into two roughly delimited groups, one dominated by political spokesmen, the other by military spokesmen. Khrushchev's own occasional remarks on the implausibility of erecting communism on the radioactive rubble of a nuclear war[4] have set the tone for statements from the political side which have brought into question Lenin's dictum—adapted from Clausewitz—that war is a continuation of politics by violent means. Others have repudiated Lenin's aphorism more outspokenly, for example the political commentator Boris Dimitriev, who has changed the formula to: "War can be a continuation only of folly"[5]

On the other hand, military writers with few exceptions have persistently defended the doctrinal validity of Lenin's formulation. They have continued to assert that war must be regarded as a continuation of politics and an instrument of policy. The new edition of the Sokolovskii work, for example, reaffirmed:

It is well known that the essential nature of war as a continuation of politics does not change with changing technology and armament.[6]

The Sokolovskii authors, in fact, went beyond their original treatment of this question by introducing elsewhere a new quotation from Lenin that has the effect of emphasizing the role military operations play in changing the political landscape.

For a correct understanding of the nature of war as the continuation of politics by *violent means* with the aid of *military operations,* the following thesis from Lenin is of great importance: "War is the continuation by *violent means* of the policy pursued by the ruling classes of the warring powers long before the war. Peace is the continuation of that same policy, with registration of those changes of relationship between the antagonists brought about by military operations.[7] [Italics in the original.]

Not all Soviet military writers have ranged themselves in defense of Lenin's formulation. One conspicuous exception is retired Major General Nikolai Talenskii, a prominent military theorist who has written widely on the character of nuclear warfare and its implications for international politics, and who also has been a regular participant in the informal "Pugwash" meetings of scientists on disarmament questions. Talenskii, whose published views have tended to parallel those of Khrushchev rather closely,[8] broached the notion as early as 1960 and again in 1962 that "the time has passed" when war can any longer be regarded as an instrument of policy.[9] Even Talenskii, however, seems not to have made up his mind fully on this question. On the one hand, unlike some Soviet ideologists and many military writers, he has expressed a quite negative view of a country's prospects of recuperation and mobilization after suffering a nuclear attack. This attitude seems to place him with those who feel that there is little likelihood of anyone's emerging the winner in a nuclear war. On the other hand, he has also identified himself with the view that the communist system could expect to do better in a nuclear war than the other side. He has said, for example:

In the final analysis . . . the outcome of a nuclear war . . . would depend on such decisive factors as the superiority of the social and economic system, the political soundness of the state, the morale and political understanding of the masses, their organization and unity, the prestige of the national leadership.[10]

In these respects, according to Talenskii, the Soviet system is superior to the capitalist system "beyond any doubt," and hence a third world war would spell the doom of the latter. Which of the two viewpoints expressed by Talenskii reflects his own convictions, and which comes closer to the real outlook of the Soviet elite, remains unclear. However, assertions that the Soviet system would meet the test of war better than the capitalist system do not necessarily reflect solid confidence in the outcome. They probably can be regarded more as patriotic reassurances, intended to serve morale and propaganda purposes.

Some Soviet military writers have sought a formula that would reconcile the Leninist doctrine with the apparently contradictory proposition that nuclear war represents an impractical path toward the attainment of political goals. Thus, one writer whose stature as a military theorist has been on the rise in the past few years, Colonel P. Trifonenkov, asserted that "the thesis on war as a continuation of politics can never be called into question by any Marxist-Leninist,"[11] but also observed in effect that the validity of this thesis need not be tested, since great nuclear losses have made world war "unrealistic" and the strength of the Soviet camp makes the prevention of war possible.[12]

A somewhat similar view was presented in an article of December 1963 by Marshal Sergei Biriuzov, Chief of the Soviet General Staff, whose entry into the discussion of war as an instrument of policy suggested that this issue had become more than a matter of doctrinal hairsplitting. Marshal Biriuzov cautioned that the Leninist definition should not be "interpreted dogmatically, without due consideration for the worldwide historical changes that have taken place." Having dissociated himself in this way from the Chinese "dogmatists," Biriuzov reaffirmed the principle that even nuclear war remains an instrument of policy, at least for potential opponents of the Soviet Union, but added that "aggressive circles" would be rash to act on the principle:

Nuclear war, like any war, is also an instrument of policy, but of a rash, senseless policy, because its utterly devastating character cannot guarantee to aggressive circles the achievement of their reactionary goals. Mankind faces a dilemma: either to avoid a new world war or to find itself in a position whose consequences are difficult to foresee in full.[13]

Elsewhere in his excursus on war and politics, Biriuzov observed that "the nuclear form of the continuation of politics" would be enormously destructive. This seemed to imply that in Biriuzov's view there might still be room for nonnuclear forms of warfare in the pursuit of political goals without incurring the charge of rashness, but this point was not developed. The main emphasis of Biriuzov's article was on the need to prevent a war from breaking out: "The more powerful our armed forces are and the better they are equipped, the more reliable they will be as guarantors of lasting world peace."

The continuing ferment in Soviet thinking on the relationship of war to politics was underscored in early 1964, when two military writers, Major General N. Sushko and Major T. Kondratkov, published a tortuous theoretical article on the subject.[14] This article, too, represented a rather painful attempt to have it both ways. On the one hand the authors asserted that "the Marxist-Leninist thesis on war as a continuation of politics by violent means retains its validity with regard to thermonuclear war," and on the other hand that "thermonuclear war cannot serve as an instrument of policy." The latter view was accentuated by the statement that modern weapons had "made war an exceptionally dangerous and risky tool of politics."[15]

Two features of this article were of particular interest. One was a heated attack on "the fabrications of bourgeois theorists" to the effect that nuclear weapons "had 'deprived' war of its political meaning,"[16] and "had made 'obsolete' the thesis of war as a continuation of politics."[17] Under the guise of such criticism, the article charged, "a rabid attack was being conducted against Marxist-Leninist teaching on war." These remarks may have been aimed more at Soviet critics of the Leninist dictum on war and politics than at "bourgeois theorists." This supposition is strengthened by the fact that Sushko and Kondratkov also charged "bourgeois theorists," somewhat inconsistently, with "propagandizing the inevitability and 'acceptability' of rocket-nuclear war."[18] It hardly makes for consistency to argue that bourgeois thinking regards nuclear war as "obsolete" and at the same time as "acceptable."

The second point of special interest in the Sushko-Kondratkov article was the position it took with regard to "national liberation wars." In addition to restating the customary Soviet view that such wars are "just" and "permissible," the article also stressed their "inevitability" and went on to say that in such wars "it is fully understood that the question of rocket-nuclear weapons being used will not arise."[19] Here the Soviet authors seem to have been associating themselves with a trend toward greater tolerance of the thesis that small wars can be waged without danger of nuclear escalation. This subject will be taken up more fully in a subsequent chapter on limited war.

IMPLICATIONS OF THE SOVIET DEBATE ON WAR AND POLICY

To some extent, the surface contradiction between Soviet political and military utterances on the question of war as an instrument of policy may arise from differences of institutional outlook. The political spokesmen, looking for fresh ammunition in the polemics with Peking, have chosen to stress the irrationality of war in contrast to the virtues of peaceful coexistence. In the process, they have dealt with Lenin's dictum in a rather cavalier way. The military, on the other hand, professionally concerned with how to wage wars successfully if they should occur, are naturally disposed to assume that some useful purpose is served by their efforts to ensure victory in any future war. In rallying to the defense of Lenin's dictum, they seem to have sensed that to abandon it might call into question the very basis of their profession and its contribution to the nation's life.[20] The Soviet military, however, have also seized upon the argument, as Marshal Biriuzov's statement on the senselessness of war suggests, that if the military man's *raison d'être* can no longer be found in waging and winning wars, it can rest on the function of preventing them.

However, this explanation alone does not exhaust all the implications of the internal Soviet discourse over Lenin's prescription on war and politics. Practical questions that go to the heart of the problem of Soviet security appear to lie below the surface. The issue hinges not only on the question whether war has lost its meaning as an instrument of policy, but also on what the limits of military power in the nuclear age are understood to be. And it also involves the question whether the Soviet Union can continue to live, as it has for some time past, in a position of strategic inferiority to its major adversary.

If on the one hand there were still a prospect that war could be won or lost in a meaningful sense, then it might be worth the effort to strive for a war-winning strategy and for superior forces commensurate to this task. Undesirable as a nuclear war might be, there would still be a sense in which "nuclear war does pay." But if on the other hand there should no longer be anything to choose between victor and vanquished in a nuclear war, then the course to take might look quite different. So far as Soviet military policy is concerned, a second-best solution might be readily rationalized as the best solution. That is to say, the Soviet leadership might settle indefinitely for a strategy of deterrence and accept Soviet strategic forces sufficient to maintain credibility but still clearly inferior to those of the adversary.

Apart from deterrence of nuclear war, there is also the problem of defining the useful limits of military power in a nuclear world. In a sense, the Soviet leadership seems for some time to have been feeling its way from one potential crisis to another as if probing to find out what these limits are. Can the use of military power, or the threat of its use, enable one side to alter the political situation to its advantage, or can it do no more than prevent the other side from gaining an advantage? And if it appears that power relationships are to become increasingly stable on the strategic level, what are the prospects that military power at other levels of conflict may help to restore some fluidity in the political situation? If, ultimately, the limits of military power require a kind of formal acceptance of the permanence of "peaceful coexistence,"[21] how is communism to replace capitalism in such a world?

These are the kinds of problems that seem to underlie the doctrinal crisis over the question of war as an instrument of policy. It is probably safe to say that neither the political nor the military leaders of the Soviet Union have yet made up their minds how to deal with these problems, if indeed they have posed the issues in this way at all. However, life itself, as Khrushchev sometimes puts it, is likely to place these matters on the agenda in some form. When this happens, Soviet policy can be expected to pass through a crisis of uncertainty and turmoil. To some extent, if we have read the signs correctly, some such process may already have begun. At present it is cloaked—and understandably so—by renewed emphasis on both the credibility of the Soviet deterrent posture and the doctrine of Soviet military superiority. The latter is the next question to which we shall turn.

Chapter VII

THE DOCTRINE OF MILITARY SUPERIORITY

No issue relating to Soviet military-economic policy seems more subject to misconstruction than the Soviet position on the question of military superiority. There are certain discrepancies between Soviet assertions and the manifest facts of international life, and expressed Soviet views show internal inconsistencies, perhaps because of uncertainty in the minds of the Soviet leaders themselves as to what stand should be taken on this question. Broadly, the present Soviet position on military superiority is as follows. There is, first, a rather long-standing public commitment to a doctrine calling for military superiority over the West. Soviet military and political spokesmen have clearly favored such a doctrine. There has been a tendency for military leaders to emphasize the theme, perhaps to draw attention to military needs. During most of 1963, when internal defense-economic competition for resources was apparently intense, there was a notable increase in Soviet propaganda on the military superiority theme, emanating for the most part from military spokesmen. On the other hand, toward the end of the year several prominent military leaders joined in approving the "détente budget" that had been announced, and there was at least a temporary softening of the customary attitude on military superiority.

Most Soviet discussion of military superiority has tended to leave an ambiguous impression as to whether quantitative or qualitative superiority is considered the more important and the more feasible. This issue, which bears overtones of the traditionalist-modernist debate, is often avoided by advocating both quantitative and qualitative superiority, although a present trend toward emphasis upon the latter is discernible.

Soviet discussion of military superiority is also frequently inconsistent about the question whether superiority is to be understood as already achieved, or merely as a goal of future policy.

A certain amount of ambiguity on the question of military superiority also carries over into the East-West strategic discourse, much of which has been devoted to the claims of each side that the military power balance leans in its own favor. The Soviet voice occasionally wavers between assertions that Soviet superiority is incontestable and suggestions that a state close to parity exists between the United States and the Soviet Union.

SOVIET COMMITMENT TO A POLICY OF MILITARY SUPERIORITY

If one judges solely by the volume of utterance on the subject, the Soviet belief in the need to achieve military superiority over the West is unshakable. This commitment probably rests, in general, upon an underlying assumption, as old as the Soviet regime itself, that the Soviet Union must surpass its leading capitalist rivals in the military, economic, and political elements of power if it is to nudge history toward a communist future. In a more immediate sense, Khrushchev himself more than once has made plain that the present policy of peaceful coexistence rests on the premise that the Soviet bloc countries, as he puts it, "have a rapidly growing economy and surpass the imperialist camp in armaments and armed forces."[1] In the Soviet view, of course, the USSR remains the hard core of bloc military strength, and upon it falls the main burden of attaining superiority over the West. In the last two or three years, however, there has been a marked shift of emphasis in Soviet discourse toward the joint strength of the "socialist commonwealth" (*sodruzhestvo*), particularly the Warsaw Pact countries.[2]

The Soviet military have long been committed to the doctrine of military superiority. A recent major Soviet work, for example, in a discussion dealing with the development of Soviet military theory in the 1920's and 1930's, pointed out that the Soviet policy of that period was directed toward "the strengthening of the country's economic potential by every possible means, so as to guarantee the uninterrupted supply of the Armed Forces with all types of arms and equipment for attainment of quantitative and qualitative military superiority over the probable enemy."[3] In the recent past, military emphasis on the superiority theme picked up steam in the fall of 1962, probably as a kind of reflex reaction to events in the Caribbean,[4] and continued to grow throughout the spring and summer of 1963. A typical military expression of this concern was the following statement by Marshal Andrei Grechko, Soviet First Deputy Minister of Defense and Commander of the Warsaw Pact forces:

The Communist Party and the Soviet government base their military policy on the fact that as long as disarmament has not been implemented, the armed forces of the socialist commonwealth must always be superior to those of the imperialists.[5]

A few days later this statement was followed by a leading editorial in *Red Star,* on the eighth anniversary of the Warsaw Pact, which stressed the same point.[6] The Grechko policy declaration continued to receive attention into the fall of 1963. It was repeated in almost identical form in a September *Red Star* article dealing with the Marxist-Leninist position on war and peace.[7]

It is interesting that while, in 1962–1963, military emphasis on the Soviet commitment to military superiority was running high, Khrushchev gave rather restrained expression to his views on the subject. For example, in a December 1962 speech defending his conduct in the Cuban crisis, he twice referred to the fact that the Soviet Union had "a sufficient quantity" of intercontinental missiles to repel aggression. This wording represented something less than a boast about Soviet superiority.[8] Khrushchev and the military leaders have seemingly differed before on the military superiority question. For example, in January 1960 and again at the 22nd Party Congress in October 1961, Khrushchev emphasized Soviet military superiority, evidently to reinforce his position that Soviet defenses were in good shape.[9] By contrast, Marshal Malinovskii's report to the Party Congress failed to advance specific claims of Soviet military preponderance over, or even of equality with, the United States.[10] To the extent that the military superiority issue serves as a touchstone of differing military and political views on Soviet military preparedness, it is possible that Malinovskii in the fall of 1961 may have been conveying a subtle reminder to the Soviet political leadership that the Soviet armed forces were not adequately prepared for a military showdown over Berlin, toward which Soviet policy at that time may have seemed to be veering.

The new Sokolovskii volume, which reached the public in November 1963, reflected a commitment to the doctrine of military superiority no less insistent than that found in the first edition almost eighteen months earlier.[11] Not only were key passages on this theme retained, such as the statement that "the main thing is to maintain constant superiority over the enemy in the basic branches of the armed forces, weapons and ways of waging war,"[12] but some additional points were made in the same vein. For example, in discussing the factors upon which the Soviet expectation of victory in a future war would rest, the authors added a new paragraph:

One of the basic problems is to ensure qualitative and quantitative superiority in the military-technical sphere over the probable aggressor. This demands a suitable military-economic base and the broadest application of scientific-technical resources to solution of the problem.[13]

Military emphasis on the superiority doctrine began to show signs of wavering only after the budget announcement of December.

RELATIVE IMPORTANCE OF QUANTITATIVE AND QUALITATIVE SUPERIORITY

While the revised Sokolovskii volume placed great emphasis on quantitative and qualitative superiority in some passages, it also remained somewhat ambiguous elsewhere as to their relative importance. There were several indications in the revised volume, however, that the qualitative route to superiority might enjoy a slight edge in the authors' current thinking. For example, the following statement from the first edition was retained: "At the present time, in gaining superiority in nuclear weapons, their quality and the technique for their employment are more important than their number."[14] Another passage, which stressed "the need for a large number of nuclear weapons to attain decisive results in destroying the enemy's economy,"[15] was omitted from the second edition.

Differences over the relative importance of quantitative and qualitative superiority seem to be symptomatic of an underlying debate concerning the best use of available resources. This problem has lain at the root of the dispute between modernists and traditionalists.[16] The former have leaned toward the idea that, today, a large investment of resources and scientific effort in research and development offers the prospect of a long-term "qualitative" payoff. Such an investment, therefore, will help to compensate for the margin of U.S. economic superiority. The traditionalists, on the other hand, by advocating the maintenance of large forces-in-being, have implied that these deserve priority in the allocation of presently available resources. The idea that qualitative advance is an important element of superiority is, of course, common to both modernist and traditionalist schools, but the latter group has tended to take the view that qualitative innovations must be translated into the availability of weapons on a massive scale before becoming a significant factor.[17]

The sharpening of the resource allocation problem within the Soviet Union in the past year or two seemingly has worked against the traditionalist position. The acute pressures on available resources have strengthened the argument that military superiority can best be achieved by qualitative improvements, that is, by more intensive research and development efforts that would permit deferment of difficult procurement decisions until later. This course has undoubted appeal for hard-pressed political leaders. It also offers the rationale that the translation of qualitative advances into quantitative dimensions will come later, when the Soviet economic base is in better shape.[18]

A tendency to shift the emphasis in Soviet discourse from numbers to quality of weapons became particularly evident in the pamphlet by Marshal Malinovskii which appeared in the fall of 1962 shortly after the Cuban crisis. Variations on the theme of Soviet military superiority were prominent in this pamphlet, and they tended to focus on qualitative rather than quantitative superiority, as in the following passage:

Our country has improved military equipment at its disposal, fully satisfying the requirements of defense under modern conditions. In the competition for quality of armament forced upon us by aggressive circles, we are not only not inferior to those who threaten us with war, but, in many respects, superior to them.[19]

Malinovskii also stressed Soviet determination not to fall behind in the arms-development race. After asserting that the "development by our scientists of superpowerful thermonuclear bombs and also global rockets" was an index of Soviet superiority over probable enemies, Malinovskii went on:

Let them know we do not intend to rest on our laurels. This common vice of all victorious armies is alien to us. We do not intend to fall behind in development, and we do not intend to be inferior in any way to our probable enemies.[20]

As indicated in our earlier discussion of the Soviet deterrent image, the implication conveyed by current Soviet discourse is that very large yield weapons in the 50- to 100-megaton range, which constitute "qualitative" superiority in the Soviet lexicon, make up for any U.S. numerical superiority in other categories of weapons. Even so, some Soviet spokesmen do not hesitate upon occasion to make rather sweeping claims of numerical superiority. Malinovskii himself, writing in early 1963, responded to an earlier statement by the U.S. Secretary of Defense with the assertion that the Soviet Union would answer "McNamara's 344 missiles with several times more."[21] Some months later, Colonel General V. F. Tolubko, Deputy Commander of the Soviet strategic missile forces, repeated Malinovskii's warning:

To the number of missiles with which we are threatened we will respond with a simultaneous salvo of a still greater number of missiles of such power that they will raze all industrial and administrative targets and political centers of the United States, and will completely destroy the countries on whose territories American military bases are situated.[22]

In both cases, the Soviet claims were not confined to ICBMs, but apparently took into account the substantial numbers of medium-range Soviet missiles that would be aimed at countries less distant from the Soviet Union than the United States. Even while he warned of "a still greater number of missiles,"[23] General Tolubko claimed only a capability to deal with urban-industrial targets. Thus he left us to infer that the Soviet Union may not be in a position to carry out simultaneous attacks against a large number of military or "counterforce" targets as well.

SUPERIORITY—ACCOMPLISHED FACT
OR POLICY GOAL?

The Soviet position, as we have seen, tends to waver between claims that superiority over the West is an accomplished fact and statements implying that such superiority is desired but by no means yet assured. A notable example of Soviet wavering on this question was provided by an interview with Marshal Malinovskii published in *Pravda* on January 24, 1962. The interview dealt explicitly with the balance of military strength, but nevertheless managed to leave an impression of considerable ambiguity. Malinovskii first cited as "more or less correct" an earlier statement at Vienna in 1961 by President Kennedy to the effect that the U.S. and Soviet military strengths were equal. Malinovskii said it "was high time" for American military leaders to draw the appropriate conclusions from this admission. In his own opinion as Soviet Defense Minister the socialist camp was stronger than the United States and its NATO allies; however, "in order to avoid stirring up a war psychosis," he would be willing to call both sides equal. Before the interview was over, Malinovskii once more asserted that the Soviet side was militarily superior. Khrushchev, upon occasion, also has wavered between claiming Soviet superiority and insisting that the United States has acknowledged Soviet strategic power to be equal to its own.[24]

More recent Soviet discourse has continued to intersperse flat claims that "the Soviet Union has military superiority and won't relinquish it"[25] with statements on the need to strengthen the Soviet armed forces, and with other comments that suggest far less assurance about the margin of Soviet advantage. In the revised Sokolovskii volume, for example, the contention was repeated that "we consider our superiority in nuclear weapons over the Western bloc to be indisputable,"[26] and the new claim was added that:

The Soviet Union has achieved superiority over the probable enemy in the decisive means of warfare—in missiles and in the yield of nuclear warheads.[27]

On the other hand the new volume, like the old, continued to urge that the Soviet policy of strengthening "the world socialist system" must include "an unremitting increase in

Soviet military power and that of the entire socialist camp."[28] The new volume also contained an amplified description of Western military power that seemed calculated to serve as a rationale for strengthening the Soviet military posture. The revised Sokolovskii volume retained the greater part of an earlier discussion suggesting that something like a state of strategic parity existed between the United States and the Soviet Union.

The generally mild claims of both editions of the Sokolovskii book regarding the strategic balance stood in rather interesting contrast to customary Soviet claims of outright superiority. While the estimate of approximate equality was attributed to "American strategists," the implication seemed to be that the Soviet authors were not in disagreement. The main argument was that American strategists, recognizing the existence of a "balance" in strategic weapons and "Soviet superiority in conventional armed forces," had come to the conclusion that "mutual deterrence" now operated. Nevertheless, this argument was somewhat emasculated in the revised text by the omission of a passage from the first edition which referred to the prospect of "complete mutual annihilation" in a nuclear war and which stated further that "the greater the stockpiling of weapons of mass destruction, the greater becomes the conviction that it is impossible to use them. Thus, the growth of nuclear-missile power is inversely proportional to the possibility of its use." The effect of this omission was to suggest that large stockpiles of weapons on each side do not necessarily foster stability. The original argument, however, was retained in a less categorical form:

A "nuclear stalemate," to use the Western expression, had arisen; on the one hand a tremendous increase in the number of missiles and nuclear weapons, and on the other hand, the incredible danger of their use. Under these conditions, according to the evaluation of American and NATO political and military circles, both sides have attained the position of so-called "mutual deterrence."[29]

One is left uncertain by this statement, as perhaps its authors intended, whether "mutual deterrence" is accepted in Soviet military thinking as a durable concept or regarded merely as a passing phenomenon.[30]

On the whole, the treatment of the question of military superiority in the Sokolovskii work, as in Soviet military literature generally, conveys the impression that Soviet military theorists, at least, are not yet prepared to write off the prospect of altering the military balance in their favor, and by implication of upsetting the state of mutual deterrence.

LIABILITIES OF A DOCTRINE OF MILITARY SUPERIORITY

While Soviet military thinkers are evidently agreed on the desirability of attaining across-the-board superiority over the United States, it would seem that the Soviet leadership as a whole remains in doubt both as to how this might be accomplished and whether the results would justify the effort involved. There are some obvious liabilities in professing a policy of military superiority. If the Soviet military posture is made to look excessively formidable, the result may well be simply to spur the West to greater efforts and to leave the Soviet Union relatively no better off in a military sense and perhaps a good deal worse off economically. For a country whose resources already seem strained by the high cost of arms competition, this is a serious consideration. Indeed, Soviet cultivation of a détente atmosphere indicates recognition of this problem, for it is aimed in part at moderating such competition. Furthermore, in a tactical sense, undue and untimely emphasis on the military superiority theme could jeopardize other immediate goals which détente seems meant to serve, such as wheat purchases abroad, Western technical and credit support for the chemical expansion program, and so on.

Some tentative signs of wavering on the wisdom of proclaiming a policy of military superiority appeared in Soviet discourse toward the end of 1963. One of these indications was an article by the same Marshal Grechko who had spoken categorically six months before for a policy of military superiority. In this article he voiced approval of Khrushchev's December plenum line, with its emphasis on the chemical industry. Singling out remarks by U.S. Secretary of Defense Robert McNamara at the NATO Council meeting in December on "the number of American long-range missiles and the number of bombers on air alert,"[31] Grechko said that Western military preparations were meant "to attain military superiority over the Soviet Union." Instead of responding, in his former vein, that the Soviet Union intends to maintain forces superior to those of the West, Grechko adopted a notably restrained tone. The Soviet Union, he said, "has sufficient means to restrain any aggressor, no matter what kind of nuclear power he may possess." Further, said Grechko, the Soviet Union is not "in the least interested in an armaments race," but merely intends to maintain its defense "at the level necessary to insure peace."[32]

Whether this restraint connoted merely a temporary softening of the Soviet line on military superiority or a deeper process of reassessment of its pros and cons is still to be seen. Several articles in professional military journals in late 1963 and early 1964, however, seem to indicate that the doctrine of military superiority has by no means been shelved. In one of these articles it was observed that Stalin was guilty of formulating a false "objective law" that the aggressor would always be better prepared than the defender. If the Soviet Union were to acknowledge such a law today, it was argued, perhaps for the ears of Stalin's successor, then the Soviet armed forces would not be in a position to defeat an aggressor. This curious reminder of one of Stalin's alleged errors was followed by a pointed reference to a statement by Malinovskii that if the arms race is not terminated, Soviet "superiority will be still further increased."[33]

In another article it was stressed that preservation of peace today was due to Soviet "superiority in the military field over the imperialist camp," and that it was the economic and scientific-technical task of the Soviet government to insure the "maintenance and further increase of military superiority of the Soviet Union over the imperialist camp."[34] An especially forceful statement was made by Marshal Biriuzov, Chief of the General Staff: "The maintenance of our superiority over probable enemies in the field of new weapons and military technology is one of the most important tasks in development of the armed forces at the present time."[35] Biriuzov noted that victory in modern war would go to the side that "not only masters the new weapons, but takes the lead in producing missiles."[36] This view would seem to be an indirect challenge to those members of the Soviet hierarchy who may wish to rest their case on "sufficient" rather than superior numbers of missiles.

Whatever the future of theoretical arguments concerning military superiority, the practical question of how a significant military superiority is to be achieved over a powerful opponent like the United States—given its relative advantage in resources and a disinclination to rest on its laurels—is likely to remain a vexing problem for Soviet policy-makers.

Chapter VIII

SIGNS OF STRESS IN
POLITICAL-MILITARY RELATIONS

Political-military relations in the Soviet Union have been characterized by a number of built-in tensions and controversies since the beginning of the Soviet regime. Basically, these tensions have grown out of the process by which the Party has sought to integrate the armed forces into the totalitarian structure of the state and to prevent them from developing a separate identity. The fact that the military establishment possesses a *de facto* power of coercion far beyond that of any other element in the apparatus of the Soviet state naturally has sharpened the concern of the Party to keep it an acquiescent instrument of political authority.

The Soviet military command, while not disposed to challenge the basic policy-making powers of the Party, has tended to seek a greater measure of autonomy in matters within its professional competence and to look upon excessive Party-political intrusion into military affairs as a threat to military effectiveness. In a sense, therefore, the history of Soviet political-military relations can be described as the search for a formula to reconcile political control with professional military efficiency, played out against the background issue of what the proper extent of military influence should be upon the formulation of Soviet policy and strategy.[1]

Recent developments, especially since the Cuban crisis of October 1962, have furnished revealing testimony to the continuing vitality of many of the old problems of political-military relations, and have suggested the emergence of new difficulties from the politics and technology of the nuclear-missile age. While it is important to bear in mind that a basic consensus

still binds the various elements of the Soviet leadership together, the present signs of stress in Soviet political-military
relations are not without interest as evidence that no stable
solution of this relationship has yet been worked out.

REAFFIRMATION OF POLITICAL PRIMACY
IN MILITARY AFFAIRS

One of the symptoms of underlying tension in Soviet
political-military relations evident in the past two years has
been the conspicuous reassertion of political primacy in military affairs. While the need to re-emphasize this time-honored
assumption of Soviet political life may spring from deeper
sources of ferment in Soviet society, we are here concerned
mainly with the relative weight of the military and political
leadership in the development of military doctrine and strategy,
and with the tendency of some elements of the military elite to
overemphasize military professionalism at the expense of
ideological values.

A noticeable trend toward reassertion of political primacy
became evident on the heels of the Cuban missile crisis, when
critical second thoughts about the Soviet handling of the
crisis presumably were circulating within the Moscow hierarchy.[2] Among the first signs of a new campaign to reassert
political primacy in unmistakable terms was an article in *Red
Star* for November 17 by Marshal Chuikov, Commander of the
Soviet ground forces. The Chuikov article, which took the
form of an interview, repeatedly stressed the dominant role of
the Party in military affairs and used the rather transparent
device of citing a hitherto unpublished exchange of messages
between Stalin and Lenin in 1920 to refute the notion that
"our diplomacy sometimes very effectively spoils the results
achieved by our military victories."[3] Chuikov criticized unnamed fellow officers for failing to "maintain proper attitudes
and opinions," and seemed to be reminding the military leaders

that it would be unwise to question decisions of the political leaders, who were in a better position to see the larger policy picture. The delivery of this "message" by a high-ranking military leader avoided the embarrassment of any open confrontation between the Party and the professional military.[4] Indeed, one of the interesting features of the Soviet campaign to reassert political primacy in military affairs and to stress the importance of Marxist-Leninist attitudes among military personnel has been the fact that top-ranking military leaders have taken on the task of setting their own colleagues straight. While the impetus for the campaign may have come from the political authorities, there is also a possibility that the military leaders may have embarked to some extent upon a process of self-catharsis in order to ward off stronger measures of the sort that Khrushchev felt obliged to administer in the Zhukov case in 1957.

Another important military leader to lend his prestige to the Party primacy campaign was Marshal Malinovskii, the Soviet Minister of Defense. A pamphlet over Malinovskii's name, as mentioned earlier, was sent to the press in late November 1962.[5] One of the conspicuous features of this document was its assertion of the complete dominance of the Party generally and of Nikita Khrushchev personally in military affairs and in the formulation of military doctrine. Stressing explicitly that "military doctrine is developed and determined by the political leadership of the state," the pamphlet emphasized Khrushchev's personal role in this process. It stated that his January 1960 speech represented "the first developed exposition" of modern Soviet military doctrine "from both a political and a technical standpoint."[6] This tribute was the more conspicuous because no specific mention was made of Malinovskii's own major formulation of the new military doctrine at the 22nd Party Congress in October 1961. While Malinovskii may have written the November pamphlet on his own initiative to deflect Party criticism of the military, the character of the document suggests that more than one author may have been involved. It is not implausible, for instance, that the Party and Khrushchev may have had in hand a pamphlet in search of an author, and that their choice fell upon Malinovskii.[7]

The trend toward stressing political pre-eminence in the military field gathered momentum in 1963. In February, General of the Army A. A. Epishev, Chief of the Main Political Administration of the Ministry of Defense and presumably the Party's principal voice in the armed forces,[8] published an article that emphasized the leadership of the Party in developing military doctrine and policy, and in strengthening the Soviet military posture.[9] Early in 1963, several Soviet reviews of the Sokolovskii book on military strategy sounded a similar reaffirmation of Party supremacy. In contrast with earlier reviews of the book, which had not dwelt on the subject, one of the 1963 reviews criticized the work for its failure to follow Lenin's injunction to "subordinate the military point of view to the political," and charged that the book had broadened the scope of military doctrine and strategy at the "expense of politics," whether the authors "meant it or not."[10] Another review suggested that the Sokolovskii authors had overstated the military leadership's role in the determination of strategy. It said the book tended to overlook Frunze's words, "strategy is not the prerogative solely of the military command." It should be borne in mind, noted the reviewer, that the government leadership "determines the final and interim goals of warfare . . . and the means of attaining them," while the job of the military command "comes down mainly to carrying out concrete operations to attain these goals."[11]

While these reviews took the Sokolovskii book to task for exaggerating military prerogatives in *strategy* formulation, other Soviet military writings of 1963 raised the issue of Party supremacy frequently in connection with the formulation of *military doctrine.* There was little doubt that the new guide-lines on this question had been laid out. While an under-current of resistance persisted, many military writers found it expedient to fall in line with the new trend. Thus, a con-ference on Soviet military doctrine held in Moscow in May 1963 (but not reported until October)[12] unanimously found, among other things, that "Military doctrine is developed and determined by the political leadership of the state."[13] The same point was underscored even more explicitly in May 1963 in a brochure, *Soviet Military Doctrine*, by Colonel General N. A. Lomov. A year earlier, another article by the same author in a Soviet military journal had advanced a claim for signifi-cant military influence on policy formulation, in the following words:

The formation of our military world-view has taken place in a creative atmosphere . . . and is the result of the common efforts of military theorists and practical military people. Thanks to this, we have developed a body of unified, theoretical views, on the basis of which has been carried out a broad state program to prepare the country and the armed forces for the defense of the Fatherland.[14]

This passage was conspicuously missing from the Lomov bro-chure on the same subject published a year later. The brochure of May 1963 offered a new formula:

The foundations of military doctrine are determined by the country's political leadership, for it alone has the competence and the juris-diction to solve the problems of developing the armed forces . . . . [15]

The journal *Communist of the Armed Forces,* which is the organ of the Main Political Administration of the Ministry of Defense, was especially diligent in reminding its audience that the Party is both the creator and the leader of the armed forces. A particularly notable exposition along this line was an article by Colonels S. Baranov and E. Nikitin in April 1963, which quoted the following from Lenin:

The policy of the military establishment, like that of all other estab-
lishments and institutions, is conducted on the exact basis of general
directives issued by the Party Central Committee, and under its
control.[16]

In the fall of 1963, the political-military issue took on new
interest when Soviet commentary began to display marked
sensitivity to foreign interpretations of the original Sokolovskii
edition as a document reflecting a conflict of views and interests between the Soviet political and military leaders. The
Glagolev-Larionov article in the November issue of *International Affairs* noted, for example, that Western writers had
sought to use the Sokolovskii work as evidence of "glaring"
contradictions between Soviet foreign policy and military
thinking.[17] Four of the Sokolovskii authors themselves, in the
highly unusual *Red Star* article dealing with foreign commentary on their book, conceded that the work had been a
forum for "theoretical discussion" of varying viewpoints, but
vehemently denied that this betokened any conflict of views
over military doctrine, strategy, or defense appropriations.
Controversy over such matters is rife within imperialist countries, they charged, but not in the Soviet Union, where

All these questions are decided by the Central Committee of the
CPSU and the Soviet government on a scientific basis . . . with full
support from the people, the army, and the navy.[18]

Concurrent with this riposte to foreign commentary on the
first Sokolovskii edition, the second edition appeared in
Moscow bookstores, a scant fifteen months after its predecessor.
It is not unreasonable to assume that such an early republica-
tion of this substantial work was undertaken, at least in part,
because the editors felt some need to treat the political-military
issue more circumspectly. Interestingly enough, however, although some effort obviously was made to bring the book into
line with the prevailing emphasis on Party primacy, the Soko-

lovskii authors gave ground rather grudgingly. Most of the changes they introduced in this area were relatively minor. For example, in one place the authors dropped a sentence which, Western commentators had speculated, might be aimed indirectly at Khrushchev. The sentence read:

Military doctrine is not thought out or compiled by a single person or group of persons.[19]

In its place, the authors substituted the currently favored formula:

The basic positions of military doctrine are determined by the political leadership of the state.[20]

At another place, where the discussion concerned the relations of strategy to policy, the first edition, after citing Engels to the effect that policy must not violate the laws of military strategy in wartime, went on to say:

In wartime, therefore, strategic considerations often determine policy.[21]

The new edition addressed itself to the same question by first inserting the caveat that Engels did not intend to emphasize "the independence of strategy from politics." It then substituted a new sentence:

In wartime, strategic considerations often reflect and in turn influence policy.[22]

Here the Sokolovskii authors appeared to be making some concession to criticism that they had failed to "subordinate the military point of view to the political." However, they retained in the new edition a sentence stating unequivocally:

Cases even arise where the military factor not only predominates, but even acquires decisive significance.[23]

97

MILITARY PROFESSIONALISM VERSUS POLITICAL
INDOCTRINATION—OLD ISSUE WITH NEW CURRENCY

The Party traditionally has held the view that the armed forces not only should provide an effective military capability but also should be a "school for communism."[24] A good deal of friction in political-military relations has been generated by failure to reconcile fully these two objectives. One of the transgressions laid at Marshal Zhukov's door was that he had "underestimated" and tried to "liquidate" indoctrination and other activities of political workers in the armed forces.[25] Concurrently with revival of the Party supremacy campaign, this issue also took on new currency. Various Soviet media found it expedient to cite the unhappy fate of Zhukov and to recall that he had "followed a line of ignoring and doing away with Party-government leadership and control of the armed forces,"[26] and had sought "to tear the army away from the Party and the people."[27]

As if to steer clear of his predecessor's mistakes, Marshal Malinovskii, at a military conference in Moscow in October 1963, sounded a warning to military cadres to avoid thinking too exclusively in professional military terms and "to develop their skill in analyzing phenomena and facts from a Marxist-Leninist position."[28] His admonition came in the wake of a year-long dialogue in which one side argued in effect against spending too much time on propaganda and political orientation activities in the armed forces when the increasing complexity of the new military technology demanded more time for intensive training,[29] while the other side bore down on the tendency of high-ranking officers to give superficial attention to ideological and Party matters, and thus to set a poor example.[30] The Party's concern to channel this dialogue in the right direction was made evident in late 1962 and early 1963 by a flurry of meetings designed to investigate the ideological health of the officer corps and to devise ways to improve the work of political organs within the military establishment. At one of these meetings, Epishev, the Party watchdog in the Ministry of Defense, urged political organs to "inquire deeply into the activities of generals, admirals, and officers, and to evaluate their professional and political-morale qualities on the basis of their activities."[31]

This warning apparently was not fully effective, for complaints from some high-ranking military figures about excessive political interference in military affairs and in the private lives of officers continued to find their way into print. For example, Colonel General Tolubko, Deputy Commander of the strategic missile forces, took occasion in January 1963 to criticize political organs for "burdening officers" with political requirements that interfered with their military duties.[32] There was also other military criticism of political workers in the armed forces.[33] Malinovskii's urging some months later in October 1963 that military professionalism should not be overdone at the expense of political indoctrination, therefore, merely underlined an old and apparently unresolved dilemma. Further testimony to the failure to find a happy balance between the requirements of military-technical training and those of political indoctrination was furnished by another lengthy excursus on the subject by Marshal Malinovskii in *Red Star* in March 1964. In this article, which capped a series on the need for "unity of theory and practice," Malinovskii took both military professionals and political workers to task for not working together closely enough. The commanders and professional staff officers should seek more help from Party workers in detecting shortcomings in training and indoctrination, Malinovskii said, while the political workers on their part should acquire a better knowledge of modern military affairs and technology if they were to make a useful contribution to preparing the armed forces for the tasks of modern warfare.[34]

A new facet of the old conflict between military professional-ism and Party work in the armed forces deserves note. It relates to the rise of a new generation of "military specialists" associated with advanced technology in the missile forces and other branches of the Soviet military establishment.[35] Evi-dently, an unusual amount of tension has arisen between these officers, who urge release from political activities to devote more time to their complex military tasks, and the Party ap-paratus in the armed forces. This is suggested by the fact that Party workers' complaints have tended to single out the "mili-tary technologists," along with some "staff officers," as the main source of "obstructionism" and resistance to Party activ-ities in the military forces.[36]

THE QUESTION OF MILITARY INFLUENCE ON POLICY

On the practical side, the political primacy issue boils down to the question of what the proper limits of military influence should be in the area of strategy and national security policy. Notwithstanding the cooperative role that the Soviet military hierarchy has found it expedient to assume in the Party supremacy campaign, it is evident that an effort has been quietly under way at the same time to resist the narrowing of the military's sphere of influence. Before turning to some ex-amples of this effort of the military professionals to hold their ground, it may be useful to distinguish somewhat more pre-cisely the areas in which military influence on Soviet policy comes into play, at least potentially. One may distinguish three such areas, or levels. The first is the level of Party-state policy formulation. The second is the level of military-technical con-siderations relating to the development and management of the military establishment itself. A third area in which the in-fluence of the military is of actual or potential moment is that of internal Soviet politics.

With respect to the Party-state policy level, the *direct* formal influence of the military traditionally has been minimal, even concerning questions affecting the country's defense arrangements. There has been little disposition in the past on the part of the Soviet military—either as individuals or as an institution—to challenge the dominant role of the political leadership in this area. Neither the case of Tukhachevskii in the 1930's nor that of Zhukov in the 1950's seems to constitute a genuine exception to this rule. In the Soviet scheme of things, such basic policy questions as the share of national resources to be devoted to the armed forces and the uses to which military power is to be put have been determined by the political leaders. The role of the military at this level has been to furnish professional advice and to assist in the process of integrating military doctrine and strategy with state policy, rather than to participate in the policy-making function itself. Whatever the indirect influence of the military may have been from time to time, the absence of military figures at the summit of the Soviet policy-making structure—except for Zhukov's short-lived tenure on the Party Presidium—attests to the formal primacy of the political leadership at this level.

At the level of military-technical policy, in the planning and direction of purely military activities the military professionals have tended over the years to enjoy considerable autonomy. Over most of the past decade, for example, the Minister of Defense has been a bona fide soldier, and at virtually all levels the Ministry of Defense is staffed by professional military men rather than civilian authorities. This is not to say, of course, that the military leadership has ruled supreme in the professional realm. Not only have the missions of the armed forces and the general policies for their development been laid down by the political leadership, but political and secret-police controls have pervaded the armed forces themselves. At the same time, as we have already noted, the attempt to maintain close

CARL A. RUDISILL LIBRARY
LENOIR RHYNE COLLEGE

political control within the armed forces without impairing their professional effectiveness is a long-standing problem to which an ultimate solution apparently has not yet been found.

In the third area, that of internal Soviet politics, the Soviet military leadership has tended—almost in spite of itself—to become a potential political force of some consequence in the post-Stalin period. In a sense, disunity and maneuvering for position among the political leaders after Stalin's death drew the military into the political arena as a kind of "balancer." At the time of Beria's arrest in 1953 and again in Khrushchev's struggle with the "anti-Party group" in mid-1957, one internal political faction apparently sought military support against another, and the generals' intervention proved important.[37] Zhukov's downfall, which seems to have been at least partly related to Khrushchev's concern that he might intervene politically on someone else's side in the future, brought a decline in the political influence of the military. However, the pattern of military involvement in political affairs has been established. Should Khrushchev's position be seriously challenged by other political leaders, or should a succession crisis follow his departure from the scene, it seems likely that the support of the military would again be courted by one faction or another. The known ability of the military to influence internal Soviet politics may tend to increase their authority in matters of state policy and fundamental strategy.

The Soviet military has evidently been trying, by a process of silent encroachment, to extend its influence in a gray area lying between the military-technical level and the Party-state level of policy concern. There have been two principal avenues of advance into the terrain traditionally reserved to the political leaders. The first of these, so far as the visible evidence enables one to judge, has been a military bid for greater influence in the formulation of military doctrine and strategy, both of which impinge upon the area of state policy to a greater or lesser extent, depending on how they are defined. According to the

presently prevailing Soviet definition, doctrine is more fundamental than strategy. The former represents "the officially
accepted expressions of state views . . . on questions of war
and the country's defense"; the content of military strategy,
though a legitimate concern of the generals, is in a sense pro-
visional until approved by the political leadership.[38]

Generally speaking, the broader the accepted scope of military doctrine and strategy, and the greater the acknowledged
share of the military in their formulation, the more room there
is for the military leadership to exert influence on policy—
whether to advance the national interest as the generals perceive it or to serve more parochial military interests. This helps
to explain why the Party supremacy issue has tended to center
so frequently on the question of "jurisdiction" over military
doctrine and strategy. Unless the Party has sensed an implicit
challenge from this direction, it is difficult to account for the
concerted effort to re-establish a point that has generally been
taken for granted—namely, that primacy in the formulation of
military doctrine and strategy belongs to the political leadership.

The second avenue of quiet military encroachment upon the
traditional prerogatives of the political leadership has been
the more or less subtle assertion that the military-technological
revolution of the nuclear age has put a higher premium than
ever before upon professional military expertise and thus enhanced the contribution that the professional officer corps is
fitted to make to the complex and many-sided task of assuring
the country's defense. This is a modern version of older claims
based on military professionalism. The force of the argument
has been somewhat weakened by the modernist-traditionalist
debate within the Soviet military establishment itself. The advocates of modernism have had to look to Khrushchev and the
Party to combat the military conservatives and the outworn
concepts apparently still dear to them. Another factor that has
tended to smudge the line of argument based on the special

qualities of the military leadership as a whole has been the emergence of the so-called "Stalingrad group" of military leaders. The careers of these men have been closely linked with Khrushchev's, and they occupy many of the top positions in the military hierarchy at the expense of officers whose earlier service did not bring them into close contact with Khrushchev. By and large, Khrushchev has rewarded the Stalingrad group well, and in return has expected their support for policies that may have been unpalatable to large sectors of military opinion.[39] Nevertheless, despite the internal military factions, there has been a perceptible tendency for the military leaders as a group to seek leverage upon policy by claiming to perform unique functions beyond the capacity of the political leadership.

"REAR GUARD ACTIONS" IN DEFENSE OF MILITARY INFLUENCE

In the period since the latter part of 1962, when political primacy in military affairs has been reasserted, the Soviet military professionals appear to have conducted a number of rear guard actions, as it were, in order to keep alive the question of what the proper limits of military influence should be in the area of defense policy. On the issue of military doctrine and strategy, as the previous discussion has indicated, the military case suffered a perceptible setback. Even so, while giving way on some points, the military held their ground on others. An interesting example of this was provided by the revised Sokolovskii edition.

In the preface to the revised edition, the authors bowed to criticism that they had failed to accord enough weight to the role of the political leadership in the formulation of strategy. They did so by the interesting device of saying that some Soviet critics had found fault with them for defining strategy on a class-oriented basis "in contradiction with its objective character as a science." This criticism, they said, took an "objectivist position" with which they could not agree, for the "dependence of strategy on politics" and its "party character" were incontrovertible.[40] After thus clearing themselves of any leaning toward a nonpolitical or purely professional view of strategy, however, the authors went on to indicate that they were not prepared to "exclude" from the scope of military strategy the "study of problems of leadership in preparing the country for war," as other critics had suggested. This suggestion, they said, was founded on the notion that military strategy "should deal with questions of leadership concerning the armed forces alone," while preparation of the country itself in a military respect was "a political matter." The authors then asked:

Is it possible to separate so mechanically the two interrelated aspects of the indivisible process of leadership?[41]

Answering this question in the negative, they pointed out that the defense capability of the country was inextricably bound up with the combat readiness of the armed forces themselves, and therefore,

in addition to questions of leadership of the armed forces, the task of Soviet military strategy must also include study of the problems of leadership involved in preparing the country itself to repulse aggression.[42]

Regarding the claim of the Soviet military for a larger share of influence upon policies governing the country's defense preparations, the Sokolovskii authors in this passage appeared to be taking back with one hand what they had conceded with the other. As previously noted, they also did much the same thing with regard to the relationship of political and strategic considerations in wartime. They softened their original position somewhat, but at the same time reminded the political leadership that in wartime there are occasions "when the military factor not only predominates, but even acquires decisive significance."[43]

Attempts to shore up the military side of the political-military balance by emphasis on the unique contributions of the professional officer corps have found expression in Soviet discourse periodically, even during the campaign to reassert Party supremacy. A typical example of this was furnished in the brochure *Soviet Military Doctrine* by Colonel General Lomov, published in mid-1963. Discussing the command cadres of the armed forces—and noting in the process that almost 90 per cent of the officer corps consists of Party and Komsomol members, which in itself was a way of inferring that the political health of Soviet officers need not be questioned—Lomov stressed that the regular officer corps has a special role to play in the era of a revolution in military technology. "Preparation of the officer corps has an especially important significance," he wrote,

for they are the backbone of the armed forces, the creator and the bearer of the military art and the teacher of the soldiers in the ranks.[44]

Lomov then went on to emphasize the high level of technical competence required of the officer corps in a modern military establishment.[45] These passages, which incidentally did not appear in Lomov's earlier article of May 1962 on military doctrine, came close to being a reminder that the professional officer corps serves a function for which the Party by itself is no substitute. Much the same point was made again by Lomov in a January 1964 series of articles in *Red Star,* where he also introduced the theme that even the best technology is not good enough in war without well-trained commanders and troops to employ it. This theme, developed concurrently in other Soviet military writing,[46] has overtones broader than the issue of Soviet military-political relations alone. It has been introduced into Sino-Soviet polemics by the Chinese, who for reasons of their own have charged Khrushchev with "nuclear fetishism" and one-sided emphasis on technology rather than on man.[47] In *Red Star,* Lomov said:

Qualitative changes in military personnel, changes in the "human materials," as Engels would say, particularly in the command cadres of the Soviet armed forces, are a most important feature of the revolution in military affairs. Marxism-Leninism teaches that man is the main factor in war, since warfare is waged by people mastering weapons. The equipping of modern armed forces with the most modern weapons and equipment has even further enhanced the importance of man and the role of his many-sided qualities in attaining victory over the enemy.[48]

The revised edition of the Sokolovskii work also contributed its bit to sustain an image of the Soviet military elite as an asset that no amount of harping on Party supremacy should be allowed to obscure. It carried over virtually intact from the first edition a lengthy exposition on the role and qualities of the top Soviet professional military leadership. This included a passage making the point that history affords no examples of an army "led by inexperienced military leaders successfully waging war against an army led by an experienced military leader."[49]

Another set of arguments drawn from history, which seems to have had at least an oblique bearing on political-military relations, was introduced into Soviet discourse in late January and early February 1963, around the time of the anniversary of the Battle of Stalingrad (now Volgograd). Several articles by prominent military men assigned responsibility for planning and organizing this key victory of World War II in a way that suggested the authors' views about the relative weight of military-political influence in a more current context.[50] One group, including Marshals Eremenko, Chuikov, and Biriuzov, paid tribute mainly to local Party and military authorities at Stalingrad.[51] This meant giving a large share of credit to Khrushchev, who was the political commissar of the Stalingrad Military Council at the time. The second group, which included Marshals Voronov, Rotmistrov, and Malinovskii, singled out professional officers of the *Stavka,* or military high command in

Moscow, as the main architects of the Stalingrad plan for victory.[52]

Malinovskii's *Pravda* article of February 2 was perhaps the boldest in taking a line that emphasized the professional military ingredient over the political leadership one, for he revived the name of Marshal Zhukov, along with Marshals Vasilevskii and Voronov, as the *Stavka* representatives who played key roles in conceiving and planning the Stalingrad operation. Why Malinovskii chose on this occasion to slight Khrushchev's Stalingrad role and to make favorable public reference to Zhukov, whose name had become synonymous with professional military flouting of Party supremacy, remains one of the minor mysteries of internal Soviet politics. It should be noted, however, that Malinovskii's position with respect to the subtle and touchy problems of political-military relations has never been altogether clear and consistent. In a figurative sense at least, he has seemed to suffer a split personality, being at once the titular guardian of military interests within the Soviet bureaucracy and the chief executor of Khrushchev's policies within the armed forces. While himself a member of the "Stalingrad group," he has not always gone out of his way to pay special tribute to Khrushchev, as witnessed by the 1963 anniversary article.[53] His gruff presence at Khrushchev's elbow during the abortive 1960 "summit" meeting in Paris was widely noted, but whether he wielded real influence there or was merely brought along as a bemedalled symbol of Soviet military might has never become clear. Further, though Malinovskii often has spoken out against military conservatism, outmoded thinking, and ideological backsliding among Soviet military people, yet at times he has seemed to defend essentially conservative positions.

His views on the qualities of Soviet military leaders have served as a rallying point for those emphasizing the unique professional contributions of the military. An example is offered by a review in December 1963 of a two-volume work, *A History of Military Art*, edited by Marshal Rotmistrov. The reviewer, Major General E. Boltin, drew on a statement by Malinovskii to illustrate his main point, namely that the Rotmistrov book, which stressed the value of applying the lessons of the past to today's military problems, was a worthy testimonial to the creative qualities of Soviet military leaders. Referring to Malinovskii's description of military art as the application of military science and theory in actual warfare, the reviewer then quoted Malinovskii as follows:

The creative minds of military leaders and commanders and the initiative of military personnel exert tremendous influence on the practical application of military-theoretical knowledge. This is not a mere craftsman's trade—it is an art.[54]

While it would seem unwarranted to suppose that the conflicting views and interests of military and political leaders in the Soviet Union are anywhere near getting out of hand, the evidence generally available does seem to support the proposition that no stable solution to the problem of Soviet political-military relations has yet been worked out. The old difficulty of balancing military professionalism and efficiency against political interference remains alive. New problems have arisen as the military-technological revolution of the nuclear age has put a higher premium on professional military competence and hence tended to strengthen the position of the military leadership vis-à-vis the political elite. At the same time, judging from the trends examined here, it would also seem true that the Soviet military as an elite group is still far from being in a position to exercise dominating influence on Soviet policy-making as a whole.

Chapter IX

NATURE AND LIKELIHOOD
OF A FUTURE WAR

The architects of Soviet strategic policy face a task which is not fundamentally unlike that set before the leadership of any great power in the world today. First, they must decide what sort of strategic posture within the country's means will best prevent the occurrence of a nuclear war and support the country's political strategy generally. Second, they must consider how the country would conduct a war if one should occur, and what forces and measures would be required for this purpose.

In their own way, in order to orient themselves and provide a theoretical foundation for the multiplicity of practical decisions involved, the Soviets have tended to place much emphasis on development of a unified body of doctrine on the problems of war and strategy. As indicated in the previous chapter, the formulation of Soviet military doctrine has certain important implications for political-military relations within the Soviet Union. But quite apart from this, it also has in Soviet eyes an inherent value of its own "of great scientific and cognitive significance."[1] This doctrine involves the blending together of Marxist-Leninist theory, political policy, military-technical factors, and other considerations. While one may properly question whether a happy blend of these ingredients is ever actually achieved, or whether the resultant doctrine will necessarily govern Soviet decision-making to a significant degree when pragmatic factors happen to bear heavily on the situation, nevertheless, a doctrinal underpinning appears to be important to the evolution of Soviet strategic policy.

Among doctrinal questions of cardinal importance in the Soviet view is that of making a correct theoretical analysis of the nature of a future war. As Marshal Malinovskii once put it:

Soviet military doctrine—based on the policy of our party and resting its leading recommendations on the conclusions of military science—helps us to penetrate deeply into the nature of nuclear war and its initial period, helps us to determine the most suitable modes of operation in it, and points out the path for development and preparation of our armed forces.[2]

Only from the starting point of such doctrinal analysis, in the Soviet belief, can proper policies be developed to prepare the armed forces and the country for the possible eventuality of war. Soviet military strategy today, as indicated by the two Sokolovskii editions and other Soviet literature on the subject, "assumes the theoretical possibility" of three types of wars—general world war, imperialist wars, and national-liberation wars.[3] The main focus of attention in Soviet military literature and general discourse on the question of war continues to be on the first category, world war, although there are currently some interesting shifts of emphasis concerning the latter two categories of wars which will be taken up presently when we discuss the question of limited war.

With regard to the nature of a future world war, which in the Soviet view would see the "imperialist and socialist camps" pitted against each other, there is a large area of agreement among Soviet military theorists. At the same time there are also some significant differences of view which appear to remain unresolved. These pertain in part to the nature of a possible future world war, particularly to the question whether it would be short or protracted, but on the whole they center more on the methods and requirements for conducting a general war, and upon the differing criteria for peacetime deterrent forces and those needed to fight a war. Differing Soviet views on these questions will be examined in subsequent chapters.

THE SOVIET IMAGE OF A FUTURE WORLD WAR

Among the basic features of a future general war upon which a large measure of consensus is to be found in Soviet military literature are that it would be global and nuclear in character; that missiles would be the main means of nuclear delivery; that it would be a war of coalitions with a group of socialist states ranged together on one side for the first time in history; and that it would be fought for unlimited ends, namely, the existence of one system or the other. The possibility that some non-communist countries might range themselves on the side of the Soviet bloc in the course of the war is also recognized.[4] Another agreed feature of a future world war is that it would be highly destructive, with nuclear attacks being carried out not only against military targets, but against industrial, population, and communication centers as well. The idea of adopting measures to limit the destructiveness of a nuclear war if one should occur has no public backing among Soviet military theorists or political spokesmen, and current Soviet doctrine remains inhospitable to such concepts as controlled response and restrained nuclear targeting. In addition to these aspects of a future war, Soviet thinking is agreed upon the special importance of its initial period, which in the general Soviet view may have a decisive influence on both the course and the outcome of the war.[5]

Detailed scenarios of the possible ways in which a future world war might run its course are singularly lacking in Soviet military literature, despite the large amount of attention given to the subject in general and the special importance attached to "thorough scientific analysis" of the nature of war. In part, this may be due to the many unpredictable factors that would affect Soviet strategy for a general war, as well as reluctance to discuss details bordering upon Soviet war plans. However, from the open literature available, one might reconstruct the typical Soviet image of a future world war along the following lines.

With regard to the circumstances of war outbreak, the favored Soviet view remains that a future war would start with a surprise nuclear attack upon the Soviet Union, probably during a period of crisis. Escalation from a local war is another possibility in Soviet opinion, as is war by miscalculation or accident.[6] Soviet literature is quite hazy on the expected train of developments at the immediate outset of a war, although it recognizes that a war begun by surprise attack and one arising from the escalation of a local conflict have widely different implications.[7] The questions of warning and pre-emption also serve to cloud the picture at this point.

On the matter of warning, Soviet views are divided. During the latter 1950's, the prevailing view was that since war would be likely to come after a period of crisis, the Soviet Union should receive sufficient strategic warning to make preparations to deal with an attack. In the last few years the validity of this assumption has been questioned, and there is at least one school of thought that an aggressor might try to mount an attack from the blue with no advance period of crisis, which—given the constant high state of readiness of strategic delivery forces— might mean war outbreak without signs of mobilization and other traditional preparations.[8] On the other hand, there is apparently a growing belief among some Soviet circles that modern warning methods, plus other factors which were discussed in Chapter V, have reduced Western confidence in the feasibility of a successful surprise attack, and hence lowered the prospect of war outbreak in this fashion.[9]

As for pre-emption, the ambiguity of the Soviet position on this question also has been discussed earlier. In view of Soviet statements on the serious consequences of a nuclear first-strike, which some Soviet authorities have said could place their country "in an exceptionally difficult position" and even "lead to defeat,"[10] one is perhaps warranted in supposing that the Soviet scenario for the initial period of a future world war would include an attempt to pre-empt and blunt any initial nuclear attack that the other side might seek to launch. This was certainly the implication given by the arguments of one Soviet military writer in 1963 against the notion of adopting a strategically defensive posture in the initial period of a modern war, which he said, "means to doom oneself beforehand to irreparable losses and defeat."[11]

Whatever the outbreak circumstances might prove to be, however, in the Soviet view a future war would involve an initial nuclear exchange by both sides "not only in the first days, but even in the first minutes of the war."[12] Most of the strategic forces-in-being are expected to be consumed in the initial phase of the war,[13] which would bring heavy mutual destruction but which probably would not—at least in the most frequently professed Soviet view—end the fighting capacity of the major contestants then and there. While the Soviet concept of the decisive character of the initial period admits the possibility that the war might come to a sudden and abrupt close, the general tendency is to hedge at this point and assume that the war would now move into a second phase. The majority of Soviet military writers suggest that the initial round of strategic attacks would be followed by theater campaigns in Europe and elsewhere on land, sea, and air. These would be fought with both nuclear and conventional weapons, and would vary in intensity from bitterly contested battles involving strong combined armed forces to mop up operations.[14] The rapid occupation of Europe and its isolation from U.S. support by Soviet operations against sea and air lines of communication between America and Europe are regarded in Soviet literature as among the major strategic tasks to be accomplished in these campaigns.[15] The participation of the Warsaw Pact countries in the European campaigns is foreseen in Soviet writing,[16] but nothing similar is mentioned with respect to Sino-Soviet collaboration in the Far Eastern theaters of any future global war.

At this point, having pictured a two-phase war consisting of initial strategic strikes followed by widespread theater campaigns, the Soviet literature of general war becomes quite vague as to the character of any further military operations or how the war itself might be terminated. For those countries in the enemy camp within the reach of Soviet theater forces, the expectation is that occupation of their territory and probably the overthrow of their governments with the help of internal "peace forces" would bring a political settlement of the war favorable to the Soviet Union.[17] The United States, however, would pose a different problem. Soviet literature is silent on the strategic course to be pursued against the American continent in this phase of the war. Unless the U.S. will to continue the war had been broken, the Soviet Union would now be confronted with a long-drawn-out war of uncertain outcome. If Soviet capabilities permitted, it might attempt a military assault against the United States, although Soviet military theorists on the whole do not appear to be very optimistic that the capabilities left over after a period of nuclear exchanges would permit such an undertaking. Or the Soviet Union might expect to do no more in this phase of the war than to discourage any American attempt to assemble forces for a counteroffensive against Soviet-held areas. The only Soviet clew as to what might be expected from here on are the suggestions by some Soviet writers that in a "class war" of rival systems for organizing society, they would expect their system to prove the more durable in a badly disrupted world, bringing about an eventual margin of communist superiority before which the opposition would ultimately decide to give in.[18]

THE SOVIET POSITION ON THE LIKELIHOOD OF WAR

From the utterances of Soviet political and military leaders on the likelihood of war, it is difficult to judge what the real rock-bottom Soviet estimate of this danger actually is. In a sense, charges that the West is preparing for a "preventive" war and a surprise attack on the Soviet bloc have been a constant prop of Soviet foreign and domestic policy for so long that, even though they may wax and wane with the immediate exigencies of the situation, they have ceased to throw much light on what the Soviet leadership considers the prospect of a major East-West military collision to be.

The danger-of-war issue, moreover, has certain controversial implications in Soviet internal politics. The more real the danger can be painted, the stronger is the case of those who feel it necessary to put more resources into the defense establishment —a point on which, as we have previously indicated, Khrushchev and the military have not always seen eye-to-eye. The issue is also enmeshed in a very complicated way in the dispute between Moscow and the Chinese Communists. The Soviet tactical position in the dispute calls for both minimizing and accentuating the danger-of-war issue, depending on the context in which it is argued. On the one hand, the Soviet leaders need to play down the danger when defending themselves against Chinese charges that they are neglecting the defense of the communist camp against predatory imperialist designs. On the other hand, the Soviet side is obliged to raise the specter of war and its destructive consequences when arguing that adventurous Chinese policies could provoke a capitalist attack.

In current Soviet discourse, an ambiguous position on the likelihood of war continues to be evident. The general Soviet line, consonant with efforts to cultivate an atmosphere of détente in East-West relations, is that the danger of war has abated somewhat, thanks largely to respect in the "imperialist camp" for Soviet military might. While there has thus been some tendency to tone down earlier stress on the growing danger of war,[19] the issue still comes up with the persistency of a well-learned reflex, particularly in military writing. The revised edition of the Sokolovskii book illustrates both tendencies. Preparing their new edition at a time when general Soviet policy was being shaped toward a limited détente with the West, the Sokolovskii authors seem to have searched for a slightly moderated formula on the likelihood of war in the current period. Thus, a statement which previously read that "at the present time (in the 1960's) the danger of a world war breaking out has become particularly real,"[20] was altered in the revised text to read ". . . more real than earlier."[21]

At the same time, the new Sokolovskii edition is still permeated by standard references to the danger of Western attack on the Soviet Union, "despite the growing influence of factors ensuring the preservation of peace."[22] In this connection, the revised volume includes a new reference to President Kennedy's statement in an interview in early 1962 that under certain conditions the United States might initiate the use of nuclear weapons.[23] This, said the Sokolovskii authors, provided

a direct indication that the United States is preparing for the surprise use of nuclear weapons in unlimited fashion against the socialist countries.[24]

Like the Sokolovskii authors, most military writers have tended to give the benefit of the doubt to the assumption that the danger of war is ever-present,[25] whereas the political leadership has seemed less constrained to do so. Although the "official" views of the Soviet political leaders on the danger of Western attack and the likelihood of war have been by no means temperate and relaxed, their impromptu remarks sometimes have implied a lower measure of concern, as when Khrushchev suggested in the spring of 1962 that threats of war from both sides had the effect of cancelling each other out and stabilizing things, which, as he put it, "is why we consider the situation to be good."[26] It can be argued, in fact, that if the Soviet political leadership had consistently entertained a really high expectation of war, it would probably have sanctioned considerably larger military budgets and programs in the past few years than appears to have been the case.[27]

Chapter X

LIMITED WAR

The relatively meager treatment customarily given in Soviet military literature to the question of conducting limited wars is in marked contrast to the attention bestowed on general nuclear war. In one sense, the elaboration of a voluminous doctrine on the nature and conduct of general war probably reflects the Soviets' concern for the contingency they fear most. In another sense, the Soviet doctrinal image of such a war—emphasizing its violent, global character and rejecting any notion of limitation on its scope and destructiveness once it has begun—doubtless serves a deterrent function in the strategic discourse by suggesting an unqualified and automatic Soviet nuclear response in any warfare at the strategic level between the nuclear powers. Similarly, on the question of the link between small wars and global war, Soviet doctrine has also been marked by a rather high degree of rigidity, exemplified by the much-repeated escalation formula to the effect that any armed conflict will "develop, inevitably, into a general war if the nuclear powers are drawn into it."[1]

This attitude toward the escalation potential of local wars seemingly represents both a genuine Soviet concern and a Soviet political stratagem for discouraging the West from using military power against "national liberation" movements. A considerable body of Soviet literature, dealing not with Soviet views on how to conduct limited wars, but rather depreciating the possibility of localizing war under modern conditions, has accumulated in the past decade or so.[2]

Today, however, there are some signs that the Soviet doctrinal position with respect to local and limited wars may be undergoing change. There is still a good deal of ambiguity and inconsistency in the Soviet treatment of the subject, and no unified doctrine of limited war applying to Soviet forces has by any means yet emerged in the open literature. However, more attention is being given to the possibility of local wars, and there seems to be some evidence of less rigidity toward the question of escalation in areas of local conflict. These tendencies are somewhat more evident in military writings than in the pronouncements of political spokesmen, who have upon occasion continued to stress the danger of escalation, as in Khrushchev's January 1964 New Year's message to heads of state.[3]

SIGNS OF A DOCTRINAL SHIFT ON LIMITED WAR AND ESCALATION

One should preface this discussion of recent signs of change in the Soviet doctrinal position on limited war by making clear that Soviet writing still gives predominant emphasis to the danger that small wars may expand into general war. The revised Sokolovskii edition is a case in point. Although it gave increased recognition to the possibility of local wars, it also furnished few reasons for suggesting that small wars might be kept limited. Thus, for example, an expanded section of the book dealing with Western theories of limited war was devoted largely to rebutting the points on which Western limited war doctrine allegedly rests. In this section, which incidently followed closely the treatment of this subject by General A. Nevsky in the previously mentioned *World Marxist Review* article,[4] the Sokolovskii authors argued that U.S. political and strategic objectives in small wars were not limited, despite claims of their modest character; that setting geographic limits to local wars is "complicated" by the Western alliance system; that a distinction between tactical and strategic targets is infeasible; and that nuclear weapons, if employed, cannot be limited to tactical types or according to yield.[5] The Sokolovskii authors also linked

Western theories of limited war with the U.S. strategy of "flexible response" as an "adventuristic" attempt of American theorists to find a safe way "to wage war on other people's territory."[6]

The trend of this new section was to assert that "the concept of limited war contains many contradictions," and that the danger of escalation to general nuclear war remains very high, particularly if tactical nuclear weapons were used, which would involve "unpredictable political, military, and psychological consequences."[7] Previous references to the danger of escalation were also retained in the revised volume, including a statement that "an aggressive local war against one of the nonsocialist countries that affects the basic interests of the socialist states" is among the cases that "will obviously lead to a new world war."[8]

By contrast with this recurrent stress on the prospects of escalation, however, the new Sokolovskii volume also contained some discussion of local or limited wars that suggested a Soviet interest both in military preparations for conducting such wars and in raising the threshold at which local conflicts might be expected, according to Soviet doctrine, to escalate to general nuclear war. The first point, on the need to prepare the Soviet bloc armed forces for local wars had also been made in the original Sokolovskii volume.[9] It was carried over to the new edition in two virtually unchanged passages, one of which is given below:

While preparing for a decisive struggle with the aggressor in a world war, the armed forces of the socialist countries must also be ready for small-scale local varieties of war which the imperialists might initiate. The experience of such wars, which have broken out repeatedly in the postwar period, is that they are waged with different instruments and by other methods than world wars. Soviet military strategy therefore must study the methods of waging such wars, too, in order to prevent their expansion into a world war and in order to achieve a rapid victory over the enemy.[10]

An even more specific statement on the need for the Soviet armed forces to be prepared to fight a conventional-type war of local character, while keeping nuclear weapons ready for instant use should the enemy employ them, occurred in a Soviet military journal in May 1963, during the interval between the two Sokolovskii volumes. The author of the article, Major D. Kazakov, after speaking of the likelihood that the "imperialists" would launch any future war with a surprise nuclear attack, then turned to the possibility that the Soviet Union might be confronted first with a local war. Here he said:

One ought not to lose sight of the fact that the imperialists, fearing an inevitable retaliatory rocket-nuclear blow, might launch against us one form or another of war without employing nuclear weapons. From this comes the practical conclusion—our armed forces must be prepared to deal an appropriate rebuff also with conventional means, while keeping rocket-nuclear weapons in the highest state of readiness.[11]

This statement suggests an escalation threshold at a fairly high level, at least up to the point when nuclear weapons might be introduced. Likewise, a new passage in the revised Sokolovskii volume also appeared to place the escalation threshold for at least some local war situations at a somewhat higher level in Soviet thinking than before. It went beyond anything in the previous volume to suggest the possibility of limited war being fought on a rather large scale under theater conditions. The new passage, inserted in the midst of a discussion of strategic operations in a world war, gave a description of local war in the following terms:

In a local war events would develop differently. First of all, in such a war military operations will be conducted in land theaters and also in naval theaters. Operations will be directed against military forces, although one cannot exclude attempts to hit targets in rear areas with the help of aviation. Offensive and defensive actions in land theaters will be carried out by ground and air forces. Military operations will be characterized by maneuver and by greater mobility than in the last war, because ground and air forces have undergone fundamental changes in comparison with the last war.[12]

This description presumably envisages a local war fought with conventional forces. The possibility of tactical nuclear weapons being used by both sides in such a local war is recognized in a subsequent passage, stating:

In the course of a local war, it may happen that the belligerents will employ tactical nuclear weapons, without resorting to strategic nuclear weapons.[13]

The introduction of nuclear weapons, however, apparently marked the limit at which the Sokolovskii authors were prepared to set the escalation threshold. At this point, they reverted to the standard argument that use of nuclear weapons in any form would mean escalation to world war:

However, the war would hardly be waged very long with use of tactical nuclear weapons only. Once matters reach the point where nuclear weapons are used, then the belligerents will be forced to launch all of their nuclear power. Local war will be transformed into a global nuclear war.[14]

On the question of tactical nuclear employment, a slight lapse from this standard escalation argument has been discernible upon occasion in other Soviet commentary over the past year or so. For example, the Lomov brochure on *Soviet Military Doctrine* in mid-1963 included an almost casual reference to the possibility that nuclear weapons might be employed in local war, without adding the usual caveat that this would mean escalation to general war.[15] In an article in the English-language newspaper *Moscow News* in early 1963, Marshal Rotmistrov spoke categorically of the readiness of the Soviet armed forces to conduct conventional or nuclear operations at any level of conflict in local as well as general war, which seems to indicate a possible new direction in Soviet thinking. Rotmistrov said:

"The Soviet Army has at its command an absolutely new arsenal of weapons, with well trained men able to wage both atomic and conventional warfare, on a large or small scale, in any climate and on any territory."[16] Another sign of Soviet interest in the employment of tactical nuclear weapons, though not confined to the context of local war, was an article in November 1963 by a Soviet general commenting on the desirability of small-caliber nuclear weapons for battlefield use.[17]

Such straws in the wind do not necessarily mean that a basic shift has occurred in the Soviet attitude toward using tactical nuclear weapons in a local war. The tendency is still to single out the use of tactical nuclear weapons in local war as the point at which escalation is likely to occur. Witness, for example, the flat statement by Marshall Malinovskii in November 1962 that: "No matter where a 'tactical' atomic weapon might be used against us, it would trigger a crushing counterblow."[18] At the same time, other factors may be at work which could bring a gradual change in the Soviet view. The possibility that Soviet supplies of nuclear material for tactical weapons may be more ample in the future than hitherto and a Soviet conviction that mutual deterrence had become more stable at the strategic level are two such factors which might alter the customary Soviet view on the feasibility of tactical nuclear use at the local war level.

Perhaps the most interesting evidence of an effort to redefine the customary Soviet doctrinal position on limited war and escalation is to be found in the *Red Star* article of November 2, 1963, by four of the Sokolovskii authors. In this article, the Soviet authors went to rather unusual lengths to make the point that Soviet doctrine does not preach the "inevitable" escalation of limited war into general war. Taking issue with the U.S. editors of their book, the Sokolovskii authors said they had merely warned that a local war "can grow into a world war." They cited some 70 limited conflicts since World War II as proof that escalation was not inevitable, and charged that the U.S. editors had deliberately ignored an important proviso in their book linking escalation with the participation of the nuclear powers in local conflicts.

In point of fact, this charge amounted to setting up and demolishing a straw man, for the U.S. editors in question had quoted in full from the pertinent passage in the Sokolovskii volume, which stated:

One must emphasize that the present international system and the present state of military technology will cause any armed conflict to develop, inevitably, into a general war if the nuclear powers are drawn into it.[19]

The Sokolovskii authors then resorted in their *Red Star* article to the curious step of misquoting themselves in order to reinforce the point they were interested in making. In citing the above passage from their book, they omitted the key word "inevitably."[20] This omission, along with generally denying the inevitability of escalation, represents a notable shift in the usual Soviet argument. While not necessarily indicating that the Soviet Union has suddenly developed a fresh interest in waging local wars, the new trend of argument suggests that the Soviets are at least seeking to hedge their argument on the inevitability of escalation. One reason for this may be to reduce their vulnerability to Chinese charges that a rigid line on escalation immobilizes support of national liberation movements. They may also wish to deter the West from feeling that it has greater freedom to take the initiative in local situations because of excessive Soviet fears of escalation.

SUPPORT OF NATIONAL-LIBERATION WARS

The Soviet doctrinal position on limited wars has long been complicated by the political necessity to demonstrate that the Soviet Union is a strong supporter of so-called national-liberation wars. While arguing on the one hand that local wars involve the danger of escalation and should therefore be avoided, Soviet policy-makers from Khrushchev on down have at the same time pledged Soviet support of "national-liberation struggles."[21] Since the latter may appear indistinguishable in many respects from local wars, this ambiguous formula has given rise to considerable doctrinal confusion,[22] and has placed the Soviet Union in the rather awkward position of having made a pledge whose logical outcome—by its own definition—could be the expansion of a local conflict into global nuclear war.

As a practical matter, the Soviet Union has sought to resolve this contradiction by making a careful distinction between inter-governmental wars (which by Khrushchev's definition are "local" wars)[23] and national-liberation wars, or what might be called wars by proxy. The former, involving possible formal confrontation between U.S. and Soviet forces, are dangerous and should be avoided if possible, while the latter may be pursued with less risk by lending moral support and other forms of aid to guerrilla and proxy forces. In the light of events, it would seem that this formula may fall somewhat short of Soviet expectations, and that competition with the Chinese for influence over national-liberation movements may be forcing the Soviet Union to reappraise its position and to seek ways of rendering more effective support to national-liberation wars.[24]

A suggestion that the issue here may involve the question of how much and what kinds of armed support the Soviet Union is prepared to furnish can be found in the noticeably defensive tone taken in Soviet statements on the subject. Khrushchev's comments to a group of editors from Ghana, Algeria, and Burma in Moscow on the day when Chou En-lai began his visit to Algiers in December 1963 is a case in point. In the course of defending the Soviet record against standing Chinese charges of timid and ineffective support of the national-liberation movement in Asia, Africa, and Latin America, Khrushchev asserted specifically for the first time that the Soviet Union had "dispatched large quantities of weapons to the Algerian patriots free of charge."[25] Numerous statements both defending the past Soviet record for providing aid and pledging firm Soviet support in the future to the national-liberation movements were frequently voiced by other Soviet sources, particularly in the military press, during the latter part of 1963 and early 1964.[26]

It is worthy of note, however, that Soviet commentary has remained deliberately vague on the central point whether the kind of material support the Soviet Union is prepared to render may include the use of Soviet forces in military situations growing out of the national-liberation struggle. The revised Sokolovskii edition, for example, gave slightly strengthened Soviet assurance of support to national-liberation movements and was a bit more specific as to its nature. Whereas the earlier edition had said only that the Soviets ". . . consider it their duty to support the sacred struggle of oppressed nations and their just wars of liberation,"[27] the revised version specified that:

The Soviet Union fulfills its duty consistently and steadfastly, helping nations in their struggle against imperialism not only ideologically and politically, but also in a material sense.[28]

While seeming to go slightly further than the previous version with regard to support of national-liberation struggles, the new Sokolovskii edition still failed to define the kind of material support envisaged, and specifically, whether this might include the use of Soviet armed forces.

Other Soviet spokesmen have remained equally reticent on this point. For example, in December 1963 Marshal Biriuzov, Chief of the General Staff, noted that "the Soviet people are not against any war" and that "they know how to fight" if necessary in a just war. However, while placing national-liberation wars in the category of "just wars," Marshal Biriuzov carefully avoided a specific pledge of military support to national-liberation wars.[29] Another matter germane to Soviet thinking on local war problems, which Soviet sources have sedulously avoided bringing into open discussion, concerns the various questions arising from the presence of Soviet military personnel in such places as Cuba, Indonesia, and some parts of the Middle East. Although ostensibly present to instruct and assist host country forces in connection with Soviet military aid programs, Soviet military personnel have been in a position where they could well become involved in local military action. Any development of Soviet doctrine and policy covering these situations presumably is somewhat too delicate for discussion in an open forum.

THE QUESTION OF THIRD-POWER CONFLICTS AND ESCALATION

The apparent Soviet desire to convey an image of greater flexibility for support of local conflicts has tended to stop short of Central Europe. As a Soviet radio commentator put it in 1957, the Soviet attitude for many years has consistently been that little wars would be impossible to contain "in the center of Europe, along the frontiers between the NATO powers and the members of the Warsaw Pact."[30] Again in 1964 in his New Year's message to heads of state, Khrushchev voiced a similar notion that a local war "in such a region as Europe" would pose great danger of expansion into global nuclear war.[31]

However, while Soviet spokesmen still decry the possibility of keeping a local war limited in the heart of Europe, some thought is apparently now being given to the possibility of isolating certain third-power conflicts so as to dampen the chances of escalation to the level of a U.S.-USSR strategic nuclear exchange. Evidence of a somewhat tentative character pointing in this direction was introduced into the strategic discourse by the Sokolovskii authors in their *Red Star* article of November 2,

1963. Commenting on a statement by the U.S. editors of their book to the effect that Soviet doctrine seems to imply a first strike against the United States in the event of Western action against another member of the Soviet bloc, the Sokolovskii authors denied that this was a valid interpretation of the Soviet position.[32]

In their book, the Soviet authors said, they were dealing simply with the case of "an attack by imperialist forces" on a socialist country, and "the United States was not mentioned." Only if the United States were "to carry out such an attack itself"—they noted pointedly—would the Soviet Union be impelled to deliver a retaliatory blow, "in which case the United States would have been the aggressor."[33]

The circumlocution displayed here suggests more than a semantic sidestep to dodge the implication that there are circumstances under which the Soviet Union might strike first. Rather, the Soviet authors seemed to be trying to convey the thought that there are some situations, as in Central Europe, where the Soviet Union is anxious to lessen the possibilities of automatic escalation by distinguishing between the United States and third powers in the event of local conflict. Soviet thinking as to the locale of such a conflict is suggested by Khrushchev's recent references to the high escalation potential of a local clash between countries in the heart of Europe,[34] and by statements elsewhere that West Germany might start a local war against East Germany on its own initiative.[35]

If the Sokolovskii authors are to be understood as thinking of possible hostilities involving West Germany and Eastern Europe, their intent may have been to suggest that in such a case the Soviet Union would try to avoid expanding the conflict by withholding any strategic attack against the United States in return for U.S. abstention. Besides offering the United States reassurance against a Soviet first strike under borderline conditions in which the question of pre-emption might arise, a Soviet approach along these lines would presumably be meant to convey the political "message" that the United States should not let itself be drawn along by West Germany should the latter attempt to pursue an "adventurous" policy of its own. Whether in fact these purposes can be associated with the commentary by the Sokolovskii authors is, of course, a question which perforce remains uncertain.

Chapter XI

THE SHORT-VERSUS-LONG WAR ISSUE

In the context of internal military discussion and debate in the Soviet Union, certain questions have tended to become charged with broader policy implications than their intrinsic nature might suggest. The short-versus-long war issue is one of these. Positions taken one way or the other on this issue have often tended to signify either sympathy or resistance to Khrushchev's general military policy approach. The issue has also sometimes served as a kind of key to the differences between modernist and traditionalist schools of military thought. And in a further sense, the short-versus-long war issue probably has touched upon a still deeper stratum of considerations involving such fundamental matters as the prospect for survival and viability of Soviet society under the conditions of nuclear warfare.

As indicated in Chapter II, the military debate of the early 1960's left the short war-long war issue, along with such closely related questions as the decisiveness of the initial period and the size of the armed forces, in an essentially unresolved state. In Soviet military discussion over the past year or so, this has continued to be the case.

Two differing lines of thought on the short-versus-long war issue have been evident. Both begin from the proposition, now thoroughly embedded in Soviet doctrine on general war, that the initial period of a future war will have decisive influence on its course and outcome. However, the two lines of thought diverge here over the still ambiguous question whether the initial period will be "decisive" enough to bring the war to a quick and conclusive termination. The first view places major stress on the *decisive* character of the initial period and the need to prepare the Soviet armed forces and economy for bringing war to a conclusion "in the shortest possible time, with minimum losses."[1] The second pays more heed to the possibility of a protracted war, with consequent need to make strenuous preparation economically, militarily, and psychologically for it.

THE DEBATE ON THE DURATION-OF-WAR THEME

It would be difficult and perhaps misleading to conclude from recent Soviet discourse that a strong trend is running in favor of one or the other of the above-mentioned viewpoints. To the extent that these viewpoints can be identified with pro or con attitudes toward Khrushchev's military policy, one might say that the Khrushchevian view seems to have gained ground slightly at the expense of the long-war, big-army thesis favored by many military conservatives.

Early in 1963, after a period of relative silence on the question, Khrushchev himself strongly reaffirmed his conviction that a new war would be likely to end quickly after an initial nuclear exchange, in fact, "on the very first day."[2] This view was adopted by a number of military writers and commentators. An article in a Soviet military journal in April 1963, to which earlier reference has been made, spoke of the readiness of the Soviet armed forces to deal "a lightning blow in order to topple and destroy the enemy on the very first day of the war."[3] The following month an article in the same journal, giving added momentum to the public reiteration of Khrushchev's January 1960 strategic ideas, emphasized the radical changes in military affairs that were tending to make strategic nuclear attacks more significant than ground offensives in long-drawn-out wars of the past.[4] Later in the year, similar themes, emphasizing the Soviet's capability of "routing the enemy on the very first day of the war," appeared in some of the Soviet commentary on the anniversary parade in Red Square on November 7th.[5]

Meanwhile, the published views of several prominent military leaders revealed a shift toward Khrushchev's line of argument. Those of Marshal Malinovskii were of particular interest for their gradual evolution in this direction. In October 1961, Malinovskii had avoided the duration-of-war issue in his Party Congress report, although as pointed out earlier, his remarks suggested a hedge against the possibility of protracted war. In his November 1962 pamphlet, *Vigilantly Stand Guard Over the Peace,* Malinovskii stressed the prospect of "decisive military results" in the initial period of a war, stating: "No one can now deny the possibility that a war may quickly run its course."[6] While he noted that Soviet doctrine takes into account the possibility of a protracted war, he did not elaborate on this point.[7] A year later, in an interview with a group of editors of Soviet military newspapers and journals, Malinovskii omitted altogether the hedge against the possibility of a protracted war. Rather, he emphasized the radical effect which modern weapons might have on the duration of a war, stating:

New means of warfare are radically changing the character of modern war. . . . Very little time may be required with modern weapons to accomplish the basic missions of the war, perhaps hours or even minutes. All of this has a definite impact on the operations of all branches of the armed forces.[8]

Another military leader who also advanced the view that nuclear weapons were likely to shorten significantly the length of a future war was Colonel General S. Shtemenko, Chief of Staff of the Soviet ground forces. His views were of more than casual interest in light of his role in the ground forces, an establishment tending to lean toward the conservative, long-war view. In a major article in early 1963, Shtemenko wrote that "with such large stockpiles of nuclear weapons and diversified means of delivery, the duration of a war may be substantially shortened."[9] At the same time, while restating the validity of

Soviet combined arms doctrine, he gave no attention in this lengthy article to the prospect of protracted war.

The long-war view, however, was not without its advocates, although most of them argued their case in terms of the need for mass armies rather than on specific grounds of protracted war. One of the more prominent exponents of the long-war viewpoint was Marshal Pavel Rotmistrov, the tank expert, who took a sober view of the heavy losses which widespread enemy nuclear attacks could be expected to inflict on the Soviet Union and its armed forces, and who argued from this that

Soviet soldiers therefore must be prepared for a quite lengthy and bitter war. They must be ready for massive heroism and any sacrifices in the name of victory over the enemy.[10]

Another more extensive and theoretically elaborate argument for the protracted war thesis was made in two books published in the Soviet Union following the first Sokolovskii edition. One of these, which appeared in late 1962, was a book by Colonel P. I. Trifonenkov, whom we have previously mentioned. His work was entitled *On the Fundamental Laws of the Course and Outcome of Modern War.* The other was a symposium volume, the latest in a series published intermittently in the Soviet Union under the title, *Marxism-Leninism on War and the Army,* by a group of twelve military writers. Both books followed in general the main tenets of Soviet doctrine and strategy as found in other current Soviet military literature, including recognition of the decisive influence of the initial period of a war. However, they were no longer tentative about the duration of a war, but assumed that war would very likely extend beyond the initial nuclear exchanges. They also argued for a strategy of protracted war in which the economic superiority of the West could be canceled out because of the West's more vulnerable industry and population. Thereafter, it was argued further, the superior political-morale qualities of the Soviet side, plus its residual economic and military capacities, would operate to insure victory.[11]

Between the two more or less well-defined poles of thought on the short-versus-long war issue, meanwhile, there has also been a body of thought reflecting still other viewpoints. The new edition of the Sokolovskii volume fell into this category, much as did its predecessor. While the predominant view in the second edition continued to be that "missiles and nuclear weapons make it possible to achieve the purposes of war within relatively short periods of time,"[12] slightly more emphasis than before was given to the possibility of a protracted war. Thus, a brief statement in the first edition, that "it is necessary to make serious preparations for a protracted war," was expanded to read:

However, war may drag out, which will demand a prolonged maximum effort from the army and the people. Therefore we must be ready for a protracted war, and prepare our human and national resources for this contingency.[13]

The revised Sokolovskii work showed some signs of being influenced by the views on protracted war in the Trifonenkov book and *Marxism-Leninism on War and the Army*. While the Sokolovskii authors did not go nearly so far in the direction of arguing the protracted war case as these books, they did dwell somewhat more on the political-morale factor and gave a bit more weight to the possibility of a prolonged war than in their original volume.

Among other military theorists whose views on the duration-of-war issue were of some interest was Colonel General Lomov. His assessment over a period of a year and a half shifted first in one direction and then another, typifying the ambivalence on this issue so often encountered in Soviet doctrinal writings. Lomov's mid-1963 brochure on Soviet military doctrine, for example, gave somewhat less weight to the possibility of protracted war than his article on the same subject a year earlier, which had dwelt at length on the importance of preparing the country's economic base for a prolonged war by providing for large-scale wartime expansion of industry.[14] In mid-1963, by contrast, Lomov stated:

On this question, current Soviet military doctrine is guided by the proposition that war objectives can be attained in a short period of time, since powerful surprise blows with rocket-nuclear weapons and effective exploitation of the results by the armed forces can quickly decide the major strategic tasks of the war.[15]

Lomov went on to say in mid-1963 that the prospect of a short war was based on "current realities"—first, on the growing advantage of the socialist camp with respect to the "correlation of forces in the world arena," and second, on the superiority of the Soviet Union over "its probable enemy in the military-technical provision of nuclear weapons to the armed forces." A third factor adduced by Lomov was that the worldwide peace movement, together with modern weapons capabilities, would make it possible to "significantly shorten the duration of a war and to speed up the conclusion of peace." Only after this marshaling of reasons favoring the likelihood of a short war did Lomov add a single sentence to the effect that

it cannot be excluded that under certain conditions a war might take on a protracted character, which will demand of the country and the armed forces a prolonged, maximum effort.[16]

By early 1964, however, Lomov had again shifted ground. In his January *Red Star* series on military doctrine he returned to the importance of preparing the economy for a prolonged war,[17] a point stressed in 1962 but dropped in 1963. While acknowledging the prospects of a short war by citing Malinovskii, Lomov also gave added emphasis in his *Red Star* series to the possibility of a long war. Instead of saying that the possibility "is not excluded," he now declared:

It is absolutely clear that, depending on the conditions under which the war begins . . . warfare will not be confined to nuclear strikes.

It could become protracted and demand of the country and the armed forces a prolonged, maximum effort.[18]

What may have prompted Lomov to swing back in the protracted war direction is not clear. Nor is it necessarily of any consequence, except to suggest that while Khrushchev's short-war view may have gained headway among the Soviet military, it had not apparently won over at least some military opinion, which continued to favor a more conservative position. Lomov's change of heart on the duration-of-war issue was apparently related also to the fact that his January *Red Star* series as a whole seemed intended to offer support for a quiet military lobbying effort against Khrushchev's December 1963 forecast of impending man-power cuts in the Soviet armed forces. This is a subject to be taken up in the next chapter.

THE COROLLARY ISSUE OF VIABILITY UNDER NUCLEAR WAR CONDITIONS

A corollary aspect of the short-versus-long war issue in Soviet military literature has been for some time a running discussion as to whether the country can count only on forces-in-being and resources mobilized and stockpiled in advance of a war, or whether it will still be possible under nuclear conditions to generate significant additional strength in trained military man power and new production during the course of the war. Hidden below the surface of this debate, and seldom given explicit attention except in occasional formulary utterances by political and military leaders on the general destructiveness of nuclear warfare, is the larger question of the prospect for survival of a viable Soviet society in the event of nuclear war. As suggested elsewhere in this book, real doubt is at work in the minds of many Soviet leaders, and has found its way into both their public and private discourse, whether any meaningful outcome might be salvaged after the damage the Soviet Union would suffer in a nuclear war. Nevertheless, in the Soviet case as in others, this nagging question has been set to one side, so to speak, while professional preoccupation continues with the problems of managing a war if it should occur.

The opinions of the professional military about force mobilization and industrial build-up after the start of a nuclear war were exhibited in the first Sokolovskii edition and further illuminated in the second edition. With regard to mobilization of the armed forces, the Sokolovskii authors in both editions concluded that peacetime forces-in-being would be inadequate to attain the goals of the war. This view, to which Soviet military opinion has somewhat reluctantly come around, as will be discussed in the next chapter, is based on the proposition that it is beyond the economic capability of the Soviet Union or any other country to maintain sufficiently large forces in peacetime to meet wartime needs.[19] The logical way out of this impasse is to assume that the necessary force build-up would be carried out after the start of the war in accordance with mobilization plans.[20] Here, however, Soviet military theory runs into two obstacles.

One of these is the view that the length of the war and its outcome may be determined "by the effectiveness of the efforts made at its very beginning,"[21] rather than by the old method, as Malinovskii once put it, of "stepping up one's efforts gradually . . . in the course of a prolonged war."[22] This means that forces-in-being are the critical factor, and if they are to be limited by peacetime economic constraints, the prognosis in case of war may look very poor. The second obstacle is Soviet recognition of the great difficulty and uncertainty of mobilizing and deploying additional forces under nuclear conditions.[23] In general, however, Soviet military theorists have not drawn the pessimistic conclusion that wartime mobilization efforts are likely to prove futile, as Khrushchev's occasional remarks suggest that he may have done.[24] Rather, military writers have continued to concern themselves with such matters as methods of mobilization,[25] and have seemed to draw some comfort from the prospect that the enemy would face problems similar to their own. In this connection, both Sokolovskii editions contained a passage which stated:

Under conditions where missiles and nuclear weapons are used, both belligerents will be subjected to attacks in the very first hours of the war, and it can be assumed that both will find themselves in approximately the same circumstances as regards techniques of carrying out mobilization and moving troops to the theater of military operations.[26]

On the question of industrial viability after the initial blows of a nuclear war, Soviet military theorists likewise have tended to express a less somber view than may be found in some political utterance. This is particularly true in the case of military spokesmen identified with the traditionalist viewpoint, or even the centrist position, for their general conception of a world war that would develop into widespread theater campaigns by mass armies after the initial nuclear strikes is partly contingent upon continuing wartime production. The modernist school, on the other hand, may have come to its conception of a quite different kind of war, most likely short but brutal, partly out of the conviction that the issue would be settled by the means in hand at the outset.

All schools of Soviet military thought, however, agree on the importance of peacetime preparation of the economy and armed forces so as to be ready at the outset of a war to apply "the full might of the state, stockpiled before the war," for the attainment of victory.[27] The principal new trend in recent doctrinal discussion has been to expand earlier arguments that the significance of economic potential has been enhanced under nuclear war conditions, not only for a long war, but even in a short war. The revised Sokolovskii edition offered a formula which sums up the general view as follows:

There is no doubt that economic preparation of the country in advance of a future war has now taken on exceptionally great importance. At the same time, even during the course of the war, even a short war, the role of the economy will not only remain but will increase.[28]

Chapter XII

DEBATE OVER THE SIZE
OF THE ARMED FORCES

The question of the size of the Soviet armed forces has been at the center of the debate on military policy in the Soviet Union since Khrushchev in the late 1950's began preaching to the more conservative-minded elements of the Soviet military elite that modern technology should make it possible to pare down an oversized traditional military establishment and free some resources for other urgent needs without endangering Soviet security. On this touchstone issue, as on the question of a short versus a protracted war, somewhat more is involved than first meets the eye. Both the economics and the politics of Soviet defense have been so intimately interwoven with this question that it can scarcely be regarded as a mere technical problem of determining what the appropriate size and composition of the armed forces should be to meet Soviet military requirements. Controversy over the problem of resource allocation among the Soviet leadership, for example, probably has bubbled up more often around the issue of the size of the armed forces than around any other issue in the military policy debate.

In the idiom of internal Soviet debate, the claims of the military establishment for its share of national resources have often been made not only in terms of the general need to keep the armed forces strong or to insure their superiority over the enemy, but also in terms of attitudes taken on certain doctrinal questions. One of these is the question whether "mass, multi-million man" armies will be needed any longer in the nuclear age, to which is closely related the question whether victory can be had only through "combined-arms" operations. The question of short-versus-long war, which we have just discussed, is another. In a sense, the debate on these issues has served as a substitute for more direct, but politically unsettling, arguments bearing on the allocation of resources among various claimants.

Generally speaking, the claims of the military for a larger cut of the resources cake have taken the form of advocating the "multimillion man" and "combined-arms" doctrines. However, the military has not presented a wholly united front here vis-à-vis the political leadership. In the modernist-traditionalist dialogue over doctrine, strategy, and force structure, the modernist outlook has often leaned toward Khrushchev's position, with its emphasis on missile forces over very large theater ground forces. The modernists, therefore, have shown less concern over measures affecting the size of the armed forces than the traditionalists, who are more or less closely identified with the interests of the theater ground forces, and whose ox stands to be gored more severely when troop reductions are made than in the case of the less "manpower intensive" strategic missile and air defense forces, submarine forces, and so on. Indeed, the "multimillion man" doctrine has tended to become the cachet of the traditionalist position in the internal dialogue. At the same time, however, the modernists—whose needs may be smaller for man power but not necessarily for other forms of resources—have had a common interest with the traditionalists in sustaining a high priority for the over-all military claim on national resources; hence, they too have been willing to some extent to put the military case under the doctrinal rubric of "multimillion man" forces and "combined-arms" operations. Further, while both modernist and traditionalist representatives have lent lip service to Soviet proffers of troop reductions as a ploy in the East-West disarmament dialogue, neither has seemed to do so with an excess of enthusiasm.

THE ARGUMENT FOR "MULTIMILLION MAN" ARMED FORCES

After Khrushchev's January 1960 program for a reduction of the Soviet armed forces from an announced figure of 3.6 million to 2.4 million men was suspended and the Soviet military budget was increased by 500 million rubles under the pressure of events in the summer of 1961,[1] Khrushchev noted on several occasions that these measures were "temporary" and "in the nature of a reply" to various U.S. moves.[2] The implication was that Khrushchev might return to his former program should an easing of international tensions be achieved. By the end of 1963, a state of limited détente between the United States and the Soviet Union had progressed to the point where Khrushchev again announced a military budget cut of about the same amount as the 1961 increase, and indicated that man-power reductions might soon be resumed.[3] In the interval between these developments, there was a quiet but insistent lobbying effort by some influential elements of the Soviet military—whose case received a temporary boost of sorts from the Cuban events of 1962—to demonstrate the need for the Soviet Union to "strengthen its armed forces" and to "maintain massive armies."[4] Although this effort fell short of carrying the day against Khrushchev's policy and its supporters, there were signs in early 1964 that at least certain elements of the Soviet military had not given up trying. Some features of the running argument on massive armies down to the time of Khrushchev's December 1963 hint of impending troop reductions are reviewed below.

The first Sokolovskii volume in late summer 1962 tended to come down on both sides of the multimillion man doctrinal argument, although on balance, judging from traditionalist criticism of it for having neglected the role of ground forces in particular, it probably gave no great comfort to exponents of the large-army case.[5] In the military press, the massive-army formula continued to receive favored treatment in the fall of 1962 and early 1963,[6] though the top man in the military hierarchy, Marshal Malinovskii, was notably not among its ardent advocates. In fact, in his widely circulated pamphlet of November 1962, he singled out for mention the "special care shown by the Presidium of the Central Committee for the missile forces, the air forces and the submarine fleet" in a way which seemed to indicate a shift in priority from forces involved in traditional land warfare to those with newer tasks.[7] Later, on Armed Forces Day in February 1963, Malinovskii noted that the size of the ground forces had been "considerably reduced" from past levels, but that their capabilities had been increased by modern equipment.[8]

The most prominent spokesman for the mass-army view at this time proved to be Marshal Rotmistrov—a one-time "progressive" in military affairs who had gradually become a strong voice for what might be called the "enlightened conservative" outlook in the military debate.[9] In an article in January 1963, notable among other things for its defense of the military role in formulation of military doctrine, Rotmistrov stressed the need to prepare for a long war as well as a short one, and he also called attention to the fact that modern war, despite its nuclear character, cannot be "depicted as a 'pushbutton war' which can be waged without massive armies." Further, Rotmistrov argued, even the bourgeois powers "in practice are following the course of creating multimillion man armies."[10] The latter point, which has tended to become one of the main arguments of the mass-army lobby, was taken up by another writer in an article signed to the press on March 21, 1963. The author, Colonel N. Azotsev, asserted that Lenin's views on the Soviet need for a regular, standing army "as long as the imperialists maintain powerful regular armies" were still valid "under contemporary conditions" —thus pressing Lenin's authority into the service of the mass-army advocates.[11]

In February 1963 a curious sign appeared that the massive-army lobby had gained an unlikely recruit in the person of General Epishev, Chief of the Main Political Administration of the Ministry of Defense and presumably Khrushchev's choice as the Party's principal spokesman within the armed forces. An article by Epishev, which we have mentioned earlier, was published in a Party journal at this time. While in it Epishev indeed stressed the leadership of the Party in military affairs, he took a position on the size of the armed forces which was at odds with that espoused by Khrushchev and generally favored by the modernist school. He wrote that the "views of some theoreticians about the need to stop developing mass armies, and instead to replace manpower by technology, have proved unfounded," and that in fact, "the role of mass armies has grown with the increased importance of technology in modern war."[12] This view by a top Party spokesman was almost immediately contradicted by Khrushchev himself in a major speech in Moscow on February 27,[13] in which, as indicated earlier, he strongly reaffirmed his short-war thesis—which had been the basis of his previous assertions that a future war would be decisively settled "before vast armies can be mobilized and thrown into battle."[14] One can only speculate that at this time an internal leadership crisis over defense policy was being thrashed out, with the issue still in the balance, and that Khrushchev was under Party as well as military pressure to commit himself to larger military allocations. Indeed, the over-all tenor of his speech indicated that he had moved in this direction, in which case his emphasis on short war could have been meant to serve notice that if more rubles were to be spent, they should go into newer arms like the missile forces rather than the traditional theater ground forces.[15]

In the spring and summer of 1963, as the détente phase of the general Soviet policy line developed and Khrushchev seemed to be making progress in shifting investment priorities toward economic development and a new assault on the agricultural problem,[16] the military debate on the mass-army issue began to reflect a parallel turn in this direction. Two articles several weeks apart in *Communist of the Armed Forces* were particularly notable, as mentioned earlier, for their conspicuous revival of Khrushchev's January 1960 formula that nuclear firepower counts more in determining the strength of the armed forces than numbers of troops. The author of the second article, Major D. Kazakov, credited a qualitative "leap" in weapons, theory, and practice with having strengthened Soviet military capabilities and changed past methods of waging war. He said:

Beyond doubt, the basic methods of waging war today are not offensives by ground forces, as in the past, but the delivery of massed, rocket-nuclear strikes.[17]

The Kazakov article then pursued its point further with the following statement, citing Khrushchev's 1960 doctrinal thesis in the process:

Soviet military science, supported by the *dialectic law of the transformation of quantitative changes into qualitative,* is now resolving in a new way many problems concerned with development of the army. "In our times," emphasized N. S. Khrushchev, "the country's defense capability is determined not by how many soldiers we have under arms or by how many people we have in soldiers' greatcoats. Leaving aside general political and economic factors . . ., the defense capability of a country is determined by the firepower and delivery capabilities available to it."[18] [Italics and elision in original text.]

This revival of the earlier Khrushchevian line on the doctrinal issue of massive armies, with its practical implications for the Soviet defense budget, was of particular interest when viewed against the background of a conference on Soviet military doctrine held in Moscow in May 1963. The proceedings of this conference, as previously mentioned, were not reported until October, which itself suggests that there may have been controversial issues involved. The conference discussed many questions, including the primacy of strategic operations in a future war, the critical nature of the initial period, the continuing importance of theater operations, the relationship between offense and defense, the possibility of local war, and a range of other matters.[19] Curiously, however, the conference proceedings as reported did not mention the issue of massive armies at all, nor the closely-related question of short-versus-long war. Omission of any reference to such touchstone issues would suggest that they may have been considered politically too controversial to be made public.

In the fall of 1963, the revised Sokolovskii edition—that useful barometer of shifts in Soviet thinking—reflected, rather interestingly, a slight new bias toward the mass-army doctrine. Because the book was typeset on April 18, 1963, and sent to press on August 30, 1963, there may not have been time to respond to the mounting emphasis on Khrushchev's formula, or perhaps the Sokolovskii authors themselves remained divided on the mass-army issue. In any event, the new volume continued to be ambivalent on the subject. On the one hand, it argued as before that even in the nuclear age, mass, multimillion man armies would be needed. Indeed, the argument was embellished somewhat. At one place, for example, where both editions repudiated the "notorious" theory of the possibility of waging modern war with small but technically well-equipped forces, the original volume merely stated:

The advocates of such armies fail to consider that the new equipment, far from reducing the requirements of the armed forces for personnel, increases them. For this reason, massive armies of millions of men will be needed to wage a future war.[20]

The revised edition repeated in essentially the same words the first sentence of this argument, but then went on to flesh out the argument in greater detail:

The need for massive armies derives from the fact that enormous simultaneous losses from nuclear strikes require significant reserves to replenish the troops and restore their combat capability. Moreover, the enlarged territorial scope of the war and the creation through nuclear strikes of vast zones of destruction and radioactive contamination require a large number of troops for guarding and defending state borders, rear objectives and communications, and for eliminating the aftereffects of the nuclear strikes. Hence, there cannot be any doubt that future war will involve massive armed forces of millions of men.[21]

On the other hand, along with these and other arguments for large forces scattered throughout the book, the revised Sokolovskii volume also displayed some views that tended the other way. In particular, the new volume gave added recognition to the economic problems involved in the maintenance of large forces.

RECOGNITION OF THE ECONOMIC
PROBLEM OF LARGE FORCES

The Soviet military, as indicated in the preceding chapter, have come gradually to accept the view that economic constraints limit the size and character of the forces that the Soviet Union, or, for that matter, any country, can expect to maintain on a permanent peacetime basis. This view is not entirely welcomed. It can hardly be squared, for example, with the doctrine of military superiority. How can a significant order of superiority in forces-in-being—recognized as an increasingly critical factor in the nuclear age—be attained against the West, particularly when the relative economic foundations are somewhat disparate to begin with? The trauma suffered as a result of the Nazi invasion in the last war also has left its effects. Soviet military men remember uneasily that Soviet unreadiness helped pile one disaster upon another early in the war, and they do not want it to happen again, with probable fatal effects. It is perhaps significant that in the fall of 1961, when there was evidently some concern about where the Berlin crisis might be leading, Soviet military leaders recalled how the country was taken by surprise in 1941 and vowed that it would not happen again.[22] It is interesting also that the historical treatment of the early part of World War II in a recent major six-volume series has dealt explicitly and candidly with the unreadiness of the Soviet military posture.[23] The blame for this is conveniently Stalin's, but the moral is that any political leader bent on disregarding sound military advice may fall into the same error.

These are but some of the factors that help explain why the idea of large standing forces ready for war has a tenacious grip on the Soviet military. Large forces and combat readiness are, of course, by no means synonymous in a technical sense, but in an emotional sense they have tended to merge in the thinking of many Soviet military men. How nearly the actual state of Soviet defenses today may meet the military leadership's idea of what is needed is difficult to say. But certainly the idea of cutting back forces, even forces which may be demonstrably superfluous, has met with a considerable amount of instinctive resistance. It has undoubtedly been one of the major policy and psychological problems of Khrushchev's administration of Soviet affairs to change the traditional conceptions of the Soviet military so as to gain acceptance of a military posture which gives primacy to strategic delivery and air defense forces, while calling for reduction of large standing ground forces in the name of economy.[24]

The state of Soviet military thinking on the economic implications of large forces as seen in the new Sokolovskii edition and other Soviet literature shows a willingness to accept the notion of constraints, which can be regarded as a step in the right direction in terms of Khrushchev's policy necessities. It also reveals a tendency to suggest that there may be ways out of the economic dilemma that ought not to be forgotten. Thus, Chapter Seven of the new volume reiterates that however advisable it may be to have peacetime forces sufficient to fulfill all the tasks "of the initial period of a war without additional mobilization," this is not within the economic capability of "even the strongest state."[25]

At the same time, there is an increased tendency in the revised volume to stress the point that a country with a planned economy and a highly disciplined social system like the Soviet

147

Union can make better use of available resources and distribute them more wisely between the "armed forces and the economy" than can capitalist countries.[26] This line of argument might be interpreted as a subtle reminder from the military to the political side of the house that despite the Western margin of economic strength, the Soviet leadership need not feel compelled to back away from an arms competition with the West. While this discussion was related to peacetime preparations, it was paralleled, as noted earlier, by a suggestion similiar to that of the Trifonenkov book that in an extended war the superior economic organization and political-morale features of the Soviet system might prove decisive over a less durable capitalist system.[27]

Along with acknowledging the economic burden of the Soviet defense program, military writing has tended to reflect growing sensitivity to the need for justifying large military expenditures. The revised Sokolovskii work, for example, noted that military requirements had made it "necessary to divert significant economic resources and large sums of money" from other purposes.[28] Even so, it argued, Soviet military expenditures are less than those of the United States.

Besides citing Western military spending to justify large Soviet investments in defense, the Sokolovskii authors also argued that maintenance by the "imperialist" states of "multi-million man cadre armies" requires the Soviet Union and other socialist countries to maintain strong forces, "part of which must be kept in a constant state of combat readiness." However, as in other public Soviet discourse, they avoided saying exactly how large the Soviet standing forces should be, noting merely that such forces "will not be sufficient to conduct war" and will have to be built up "in accordance with planned mobilization."[29]

Even while recognizing economic limits on the size of peacetime forces-in-being, the Sokolovskii authors, like a good many of their military colleagues, have continued to labor the point that war itself would require a great expansion of the armed forces. This position, needless to say, was somewhat at variance with the revival of Khrushchev's January 1960 theme that a new war fought with missiles and nuclear weapons would end quickly, obviating the need for massive armies.

MILITARY REACTION TO DECEMBER 1963 TROOP-CUT PROPOSAL

In view of the considerations discussed above, it is not surprising that some elements of the Soviet military had their misgivings when Khrushchev announced in December 1963 that the Soviet Union was considering "the possibility of some further reduction in the numerical strength of our armed forces."[30] The announcement, coupled with a move to reduce the military budget slightly for 1964,[31] indicated that Khrushchev's policy line was for the time being in the ascendant but signs were not long in coming that an anti-troop-cut lobby was gathering itself for an effort to bring about reconsideration of the force-reduction proposal.

Military reaction to the proposal took several forms. Top military leaders studiously avoided direct mention of the troop-cut proposal in the Soviet press,[32] although several of them had opportunity to do so in public statements, touching on the companion budget-reduction measure.[33] The military press itself, in its initial editorial comment expressing approval of the budget measure, was silent on the troop-cut proposal,[34] and only mentioned it for the first time, without comment, on December 25.[35] The nonmilitary press several times alluded approvingly to the troop-cut proposal in the first days after its announcement.[36]

The most significant sign of distress among the military came in a major article on December 22 by Marshal Chuikov, Commander of the Soviet ground forces, whose professional domain was the most likely target of any move to reduce the number of men under arms. In this article, entitled "Modern Ground Forces," Chuikov expressed no direct disapproval of Khrushchev's proposal; indeed, he did not mention it at all. However, the article itself was an unmistakable piece of special pleading. The first half expounded the favorite new theme of the mass-army advocates—that the Western countries, while "preparing for a nuclear war, not only are not liquidating ground forces, but on the contrary, are steadily developing them."[37] Chuikov elaborated on his point that the Western countries "are constantly improving their ground forces to accord with modern demands" by citing not only technical improvements but numbers—5 million men in the NATO armies, of which 3.2 million are ground forces; 1.2 million men in the ground forces of the United States alone. And these forces, he said, emphasizing a central point in his argument, are now "in peacetime" concentrated "in the decisive area of Europe." Further, in marshaling his evidence of current Western solicitude for ground forces, Chuikov pointed out that certain "one-sided" foreign theories which had once exercised "a harmful effect on the development of armed forces" had apparently now been abandoned by Western military leaders themselves, who "realize that in a future war, they will not be able to get along without mass armies."

In the second half of his article, Chuikov dealt with the status of Soviet theater and ground forces. Here he described their technical proficiency and fine qualities—as if to warn the West not to let his prior encomium go to its head—but he gave no figures on Soviet numerical strength. The main emphasis here was on the continued validity of Soviet combined-arms doctrine, and the indispensable role of ground forces in a future war. While offering a one-sentence obeisance to the idea that "a decisive part in achieving the main aims of a war will be played by the strategic missile forces," he capped his thesis by declaring:

Therefore, in modern conditions, the ground forces continue to be not only a mandatory but also a highly important integral part of the armed forces.

Other military commentary by lesser figures followed the lead laid down by Chuikov, pointing to Western endorsement of the concept of mass armies and actual large-scale Western maneuvers with "million-strong armies"[38] as a warning against tampering with Soviet ground forces. In early 1964, Major General Lomov's *Red Star* series on Soviet military doctrine furnished additional support for the lobbying effort by stating, among other things, that despite the nuclear-age revolution in military affairs, victory against a strong adversary still "requires the efforts of a multimillion man nuclear army."[39] However, as the spring of 1964 approached, there were signs that this campaign of special pleading had failed to stay Khrushchev's proposal for a reduction in the size of the Soviet armed forces. At the same time, the campaign may have scored at least a few points by making it necessary for Khrushchev to allay military concern that economic development priorities might adversely affect the Soviet defense posture.

This became evident from Khrushchev's remarks on defense problems in a major speech at the close of the Central Committee plenum session on agriculture in mid-February. Here Khrushchev repeated that the Soviet Union "is embarking upon certain reductions in military expenditures and in the numerical strength of the armed forces." Significantly, however, he then added:

But we realize that economizing in this respect must be reasonable. In present conditions when the imperialist countries have created powerful armed forces and equipped them with nuclear weapons, it is impossible to reduce the size of appropriations for armaments and the army to a degree that would allow the imperialists to surpass us in armed strength and thus impose their will and policy on us.[40]

This reassurance that defense requirements were not to be slighted was reinforced by a statement reminiscent of Khrushchev's comment a year earlier that satisfaction of consumer demands would have to be postponed in favor of defense needs.[41] Referring to criticism from unnamed quarters that "too little" was being done about the housing program, Khrushchev said: "If we accepted an unreasonable reduction of military expenditures, if we started to build more housing and forgot about defense, we would be like blind men who cannot assesss the real situation correctly."[42] In light of these words, there was a palpably hollow ring to Khrushchev's denial in the same speech that the Soviet Union was being "forced to reduce armaments and armed forces because of difficulties in economic development."

How much ground Khrushchev might actually yield on the troop-reduction issue was left unclear by this speech. That some concession may have been made to military opinion was suggested by increasing public references by military spokesmen, beginning around mid-February, to both the reduction in military expenditure and in troop strength. These references were accompanied by the admonition that foreign foes should not "nourish any hopes" that weakening of the Soviet armed forces or economic difficulties were implied by the budget and troop reduction measures.[43]

To the outside observer of this ongoing phase of the Soviet military policy debate, one factor was conspicuous by its absence. The case of Soviet mass-army advocates was made to depend on ground force trends in the West, but nowhere was there a public hint that Soviet military leaders might also have had an eye on developments to the East. It does not strain credibility, however, to suppose that another element of concern may have been the potential threat of China. The old Soviet military problem of being prepared for trouble at both ends of the vast Soviet land mass may well have increased the forebodings of many Soviet military men as they contemplated the prospect of their forces being reduced.

Chapter XIII

THE PRIMACY OF STRATEGIC
FORCES AND OPERATIONS

Perhaps the most striking change in the Soviet military outlook over the past decade and a half has been a gradual but
basic shift from almost exclusive preoccupation with continental
land warfare to a new emphasis on the problems of global
strategic war. In essence, this trend has paralleled a growing
appreciation of the enormous impact of strategic nuclear
weapons upon the outcome of war. It also has reflected a
growing differentiation in Soviet thinking between two quite
different military problems—that of conducting a continental
war, especially in the European theater, and that of dealing
with an adversary whose strength and influence extend to the
far corners of the world and whose main bastion lies beyond
the confines of Europe.

The latter problem has moved gradually toward the center
of Soviet attention, although it has by no means displaced the
importance in Soviet eyes of the European theater problem and
seems unlikely to do so in the foreseeable future. As indicated
in the preceding chapter, the heritage of a continental military
tradition still runs strongly through Soviet strategic thinking.
The emphasis given today to the strategic missile forces and to
the influence of strategic operations upon war's outcome has
not meant a corresponding decline in the role of theater forces
and operations. These are still viewed as essential within the
framework of general war, and a large share of Soviet defense
resources and planning continues to be devoted to the theater
warfare problem.

It has not been easy to adjust Soviet military thinking and
practice so as to find a happy medium in dealing with the

respective problems of theater warfare and global strategic war. Much of the tension evident between the professional Soviet military and Khrushchev since he took up the reins of Soviet power in the latter 1950's has come from this process of adjustment.[1] And, as will be brought out in this chapter and a subsequent one dealing with Soviet views on the military path to victory, there still seems to be a military debate under way on the relative weight to be given these two basic problems in Soviet strategy.

THE DOCTRINAL SHIFT TO STRATEGIC PRIMACY

From a doctrinal standpoint, there is no longer any question about the primacy accorded nuclear weapons and strategic missiles in Soviet thinking, by traditionalist as well as modernist schools of thought. The shift in this direction did not take place dramatically at any single point along the route which Soviet strategic thinking has traveled in the past eight or ten years. Already in the mid-1950's doctrinal ferment over the significance of nuclear weapons had begun to find expression in the Soviet Union.[2] However, it was a question then mainly of how to harness these destructive new weapons to familiar Soviet concepts. Nuclear weapons were regarded most often as *supplementary* to the operations of the traditional forces, whose primacy was not questioned. The idea that nuclear weapons might prove strategically decisive was not sanctioned, since it seemed to violate the stern injunction in traditional Soviet doctrine aginst "one-weapon" theories.

The extent of the shift in outlook may be gained by comparing a few typical expressions of the mid-1950's with representative statements today. In 1954, Marshal K. Moskalenko, then a general, wrote that "Soviet military science decisively rejects any arbitrary fabrications . . . that one could, as it were, achieve victory by employment of one or another new weapon. There are no such weapons which possess exceptional and all-powerful qualities."[3] The same year Major General B. Olisov said: "Strategic atomic bombs, which are a source of great danger to cities and civilian populations, have little effect on the battle-field. Strategic bombing will not decide the outcome of war, but the soldiers on the battlefield."[4] A year later, Major General G. Pokrovskii, a prominent military expert and at the time one of the leading Soviet authorities in the field of advanced military technology, wrote:

Atomic and thermonuclear weapons at their present stage of develop-ment only supplement the firepower of the old forms of armament. Artillery, small arms, tanks, aviation and other armaments were and remain the basic firepower of the army.[5]

By contrast, Major General Lomov's January 1964 *Red Star* series on Soviet military doctrine, which represented a rather middle-of-the-road presentation in terms of modernist-tradi-tionalist positions, stated unequivocally that "the most important tenet of Soviet military doctrine is the recognition of rocket-nuclear weapons, and above all strategic missiles and nuclear weapons, as the decisive means of repelling imperialist aggres-sion and completely crushing the enemy."[6] On an earlier occa-sion in 1963, Lomov had underscored the importance attached in his thinking to nuclear weapons and missiles by saying that "one can scarcely imagine at the present time anything which could take the place of these weapons." He went on to say that under today's conditions, a country cannot expect to make up for nuclear deficiency with other forces, as in the past one might "compensate for inferiority in one type of force with strength in another type."[7] A colleague, Major General P. E. Varezhnikov, projected Lomov's appreciation of nuclear weap-ons into the future, stating at a military doctrine conference in May 1963 that "the possibilities of further improvement of nuclear weapons are limitless."[8]

Another representative statement in 1963 from a Soviet naval officer, Captain Y. V. Kolesnikov, illustrated explicitly how far

Soviet doctrine had moved from the conceptions of 1955. "Soviet military doctrine," he said, "must look upon missiles and nuclear weapons as the principal means of victory over the enemy." Further, to make the point clear:

> We emphasize that these are the principal means, not a reserve, nor a supplement, nor a means of exploiting success achieved through employment of conventional weapons. On the contrary, the latter have become the secondary, supplementary and sometimes reserve means.[9]

Even such currently staunch champions of the traditional mass-army and combined-arms doctrine as Marshals Chuikov and Rotmistrov have associated themselves without apparent reservation with the view that nuclear weapons have a decisive role in modern war and that strategic missiles constitute the main striking force of the Soviet Union. The latter, for example, said in 1963: "Of course, we do not deny, but on the contrary, emphasize the decisive role of nuclear weapons . . . the strategic missile forces have become the main branch of our armed forces. At the same time, we do not belittle the role and significance of other types of forces."[10] This statement, giving first place to strategic missile forces but without depreciating more conventional forces, probably reflects the present doctrinal understanding shared by most Soviet military leaders.[11] Rotmistrov, however, as we shall point out more fully later in this chapter, has since qualified his views somewhat in a way suggesting that he does not wholly approve the massive shift of emphasis upon strategic missile forces that has occurred in Soviet doctrine in the past few years.

If one were to seek the principal factor on which this doctrinal shift hinged, it was probably the Soviet Union's acquisition of advanced weapons and the means of their delivery in sufficient numbers to make a strategy for their employment something more than an academic matter. In the Soviet case, this occurred in the latter 1950's, coincident with Khrushchev's assumption of political power. Prior to this, when the Soviet nuclear stockpile was still very limited, the main focus of doctrinal discussion was, understandably, on how to adapt the new means of warfare to traditional Soviet concepts. Afterward, particularly with the advent of intercontinental ballistic missiles, the problem became one of radical revision of Soviet doctrine, along with reorganization and re-equipment of the armed forces themselves.[12]

There are numerous indications, many of which already have been discussed in this book, that Khrushchev's ideas and policies met with resistance from various elements of the military bureaucracy. The Soviet decision to carry on with a major program in the field of ballistic missiles, around which Soviet doctrine and forces have since been reoriented, apparently was one of the issues on which Khrushchev encountered opposition. An interesting bit of testimony on this point was furnished by Fidel Castro, in a rambling television interview in Havana on June 5, 1963, after returning from his first trip to the Soviet Union. While lauding Khrushchev, among other things, for "understanding the need for the Soviet forces to have the maximum fighting preparation in order to face the possibility of war," Castro said:

We must keep in mind one thing: The fact that the Soviet government, the Soviet leadership and Comrade Khrushchev have shown great interest—I had a special opportunity to see it in my talks with the Soviet officers on strategic matters—in the decision to build missiles. This was a decision in which Khrushchev contributed with his leadership. He defended this policy consistently, that is, the development of missiles—a weapon that has made it possible for the USSR to face, from a military point of view, the danger of imperialist aggression.[13]

Against whom Khrushchev found it necessary to defend his missile policy was not made clear by Castro, but other evidence suggests that critics were, and perhaps still are, to be found among military men. For example, one of the articles reasserting Khrushchev's strategic line in May 1963 went out of its way to note that "in determining the role of rocket-nuclear weapons various opinions were advanced," and that while some comrades "overvalued" such weapons, others "insisted" that they would only serve "for supporting troop operations." With the latter, Kazakov said, "it is impossible to agree."[14] Another indication of difficulty in establishing proper appreciation of ballistic missiles among some military people was furnished by Colonel I. Korotkov, author of a recent article on postwar development of Soviet military theory. Even in the early 1960's, Korotkov said, after it was widely recognized in Soviet military literature that the ballistic missile had "changed the methods and forms of warfare in a radical fashion . . . some comrades still did not consider the missile a decisive instrument of victory." And to prove their point, he said, "they turned again to the experience of the last war."[15] The revised Sokolovskii edition also took note, as had the first,[16] that some Soviet military people continued to place too much weight on the experience of the past war and to apply it mechanically to modern conditions. The expansion of this point in the revised edition would suggest that while doctrinal obeisance was being paid to the primacy of strategic weapons, resistance to the new line of strategic thinking was still in evidence in some quarters. The expanded passage stated:

The error in such a point of view is that it depreciates the role of strategic missiles and nuclear weapons and underestimates their enormous combat potentialities. This results in an orientation toward the ground forces and toward traditional ways of waging war. But the imperialists do not intend to wage war against the socialist countries with ground forces. Basically they place their stakes on strategic nuclear weapons.[17]

That Soviet strategy has also come to place its stakes increasingly on strategic nuclear weapons is underlined by the amount of attention given in current military literature to strategic operations, as well as to the evolving autonomy of such operations, apart from traditional battlefield operations in theater campaigns.

VIEWS ON THE CHARACTER OF STRATEGIC OPERATIONS

The revised Sokolovskii volume furnished a number of interesting additions to this subject, although in general its discussion of strategic operations followed the pattern of the first edition. On how strategic operations alone may have decisive results in war, the Sokolovskii authors strengthened some of the propositions in their first edition. One of these had said that modern strategic weapons "make it possible to achieve decisive results in winning victory in war sometimes without resort to tactical and field forces and their weapons."[18] In the new edition, the authors said further:

Strategy, which in the past attained its ends through tactics and the operational art, now has the capability to achieve its goals by its own autonomous means—independent of the outcome of battles and operations in other spheres of combat.[19]

In an expanded discussion of strategic operations elsewhere in the revised volume, the interesting point was made that it would be necessary in a nuclear war to coordinate the operation of all branches of the armed forces "according to a single plan and under a single strategic command."[20] This suggests considerable reliance on a fixed form of strategic operations, and might indicate that alternative plans and options have not been devised for a variety of circumstances that might arise. However, this impression is somewhat at variance with another passage in the same discussion, which stressed at some length the many-sided character of a future war and the need to adapt strategic operational planning to a variety of possible developments:

War is always a quite complex and many-sided phenomenon, which will be even more true of a future nuclear war. In working out the forms and methods of conducting a future war one must take into account a number of questions: how will the war be initiated; what will be its character; who is the main enemy; will nuclear weapons be used at the very outset or only in the course of the war; what kind of nuclear weapons—strategic or only tactical, and where; in what region or theater will the main events develop, etc.? By taking these factors into account it is possible to solve concretely the question of the forms and methods of waging a war. One form of strategic operations may take place in a global nuclear war resulting from an enemy surprise attack; a different form of operations may develop in a global nuclear war arising as a result of escalation from a local war, while a completely different form of operations will take place in a local war.[21]

Strategic operations, the authors predicted further, "will unfold on a widespread geographic scale, embracing simultaneously all the continents and seas, while at the same time they will be short-lived, running their course rapidly."[22] However, with a show of cautiousness in marked contrast to more sanguine expectations expressed elsewhere in the book, the authors then added that the outcome of such operations "is difficult at the present time even to imagine."[23]

Like other recent Soviet military writing, the new Sokolovskii work gave no indication that any revision of Soviet targeting doctrine for the strategic forces may be under contemplation. This doctrine has been consistent over the last few years in calling for nuclear strikes against both military and nonmilitary targets deep in the enemy's territory, in order "to deprive him simultaneously of the military, political, and economic capacity to wage war."[24] While *simultaneity* of attack upon both military and nonmilitary target systems has been emphasized in virtually all Soviet military and political discussion of the subject, an order of priority of sorts does seem to emerge in the professional literature. The usual order, found in both Sokolovskii volumes, is to emphasize that the nuclear delivery means of the enemy, "the basis of his military power," constitute the priority target system. Next come other major military forces, the economic base, command and control system, and "other important strategic targets" that support the enemy's capacity to make war.[25] Within the category of nuclear delivery means, strategic forces generally are earmarked as the priority targets, on the grounds that they represent the greatest threat.[26] Both Sokolovskii editions emphasized this point, as stated below:

The decisive weapon in modern warfare is the strategic nuclear weapon. The long-range delivery vehicle for this weapon is located far from the front lines or the borders, at a great distance from the theaters of military operations. Unless these weapons are destroyed or neutralized, it is impossible to protect the country's vital centers from destruction, and one cannot count on successfully achieving the aim of the war even if the [enemy] troop formations deployed in the military theaters are destroyed.[27]

Among the significant implications of this targeting doctrine is that it calls for counterforce capabilities of a very substantial order, well beyond what would be involved for a "minimum deterrent" threat mainly against cities. The doctrine thus seems strangely out of key with the current Soviet tendency described elsewhere in this book to depreciate the feasibility of a U.S. counterforce strategy, and to argue that to have any chance of success such a strategy would require a surprise first strike. One may suspect that a major source of Soviet policy concern and controversy is the question whether Soviet resources can provide the forces required to support such a targeting doctrine.[28] In this connection, a small but significant change appeared in the revised Sokolovskii edition in a discussion of the question whether the main strategic effort would be directed simultaneously against military and nonmilitary targets. The answers in both editions was yes, but in explaining why, the second edition added two words (italicized for identification in the quotation below) which did not appear in the original text:

There is a real possibility *for us* of achieving these aims simultaneously with the use of the military instruments at hand.[29]

This insertion of "for us" may have reflected some feeling by the Sokolovskii authors that Soviet forces had increased in strength sufficiently in the 1962–1963 period between their editions to warrant making the "possibility" of which they spoke more emphatic. What actual changes in the strength of Soviet strategic forces may have occurred is, of course, a matter of conjecture. No subject is more religiously shunned in Soviet discourse than actual figures on Soviet missile strength. General statements abound that "the Soviet Union has strategic missiles in such quantity and of such quality that it can simultaneously destroy the required number of the aggressor's targets,"[30] but these are hardly a suitable basis of judgment as to whether Soviet missile strength is at all adequate to support the kind of targeting doctrine in question.[31]

While the habit of being close-mouthed about Soviet missile strength probably contributes, in Soviet eyes, to their "secrecy stockpile" and is thus regarded as a military asset, Soviet spokesmen are also notably sensitive to the implication that this may imply an inferior strategic posture. One example of this was a parenthetical statement inserted in a February 1963 article by a Soviet Air Force general, who said: "Recently bourgeois propaganda has begun to talk more intensive gibberish about the 'military weakness' of the Soviet Union, alleging, if you please, that it has missile forces without strategic missiles and nuclear warheads for them."[32] A year later, in an interview in *Izvestiia*, the Commander of the strategic missile forces, Marshal N. I. Krylov, displayed unusual anxiety to get across the point that the Soviet Union is numerically strong in missiles, without, however, divulging actual figures. After asserting that Soviet missiles were qualitatively superior in all respects to American missiles, Krylov addressed himself to the quantitative question in the following words:

It should be added that our forces have SUCH A QUANTITY of nuclear warheads and SUCH A QUANTITY of missiles as to permit us, if the imperialists start a war, to destroy any aggressor, wherever he may be located, including an aggressor who has nuclear weapons at his disposal.[33] [Capitals in original.]

This resort to capital letters illustrates the handicap under which Soviet marshals labor in not being free to disclose even approximate numbers of Soviet missiles when trying to hold up their end of the strategic dialogue. In Krylov's interview, incidentally, he spoke only of Soviet ability to destroy cities, ignoring entirely the question of military targets.

ATTITUDE TOWARD STRATEGIC TARGETING RESTRAINTS

Another feature of current Soviet discussion bearing on strategic targeting has been a consistently negative attitude toward such concepts as the controlled use of strategic weapons and damage-limiting restraints in the event a major war should occur. As this writer has observed on a previous occasion, several factors may underlie the lack of Soviet interest in such concepts, which have been widely discussed in the West.[34] One appears to be the doctrinaire assumption that the political aims of the belligerents in any general war would be unlimited, and that neither side could be expected, as Khrushchev has put it, "to concede defeat before resorting to the use of all weapons, even the most devastating ones."[35] Another and perhaps more compelling factor may relate to Soviet reticence about actual figures on Soviet missile strength. For if the Soviet Union knows itself to be in an inferior strategic posture, it may wish to enhance the deterrent value of its strategic forces by professing no interest in ground rules for restrained targeting.

Throughout Soviet discourse there is insistence that only measures to avert war, rather than to limit its destructiveness, are a permissible subject of discussion. This, of course, ignores the question of trying to place limits on the level of violence in case a war unwanted by either side should begin through accident or miscalculation. American statements on the subject of restraints in strategic warfare have been vigorously scored as an attempt to invent "rules for waging a nuclear war" in a way that would preserve the capitalist system.[36] Soviet disapproval of controlled strategic war concepts has also been linked to criticism of U.S. counterforce or "city-sparing" strategy, a subject to be taken up in a subsequent chapter.

At the same time, however, there have been some signs of Soviet sensitivity to Western suggestions that damage-limiting concepts are a fit subject of discussion. The Glagolev-Larionov article of November 1963, to which we have previously alluded, displayed a notably defensive attitude on this question in taking note of Western comment that, as the Soviet authors put it, "the Soviet strategic concept is rigid and does not set any limits on the use of nuclear weapons in the event of war."[37] The article then went on to argue that the Soviet refusal to entertain agreements which would have the effect of "legalizing" nuclear war is actually more "humanitarian" than the position of Western advocates of damage-limiting concepts. Other Soviet commentary has also suggested that at least a propaganda liability is sensed in the Soviet position that no distinction is to be made between military and nonmilitary targets. On various occasions Soviet writers have risen to protest, as did one Colonel Morozov in criticism of a column by Joseph Alsop, that American military doctrine is not "more humane" than Soviet doctrine, simply because of its "stress on the destruction of military objectives only."[38]

On the related question of adopting safeguards of various kinds to reduce the possibility of accidental nuclear war, the Soviet Union has tended to treat the issue polemically without much evidence, with perhaps the conspicuous exception of the 1963 "hot line" agreement, of a serious effort to advance mutual understanding in this area. Certainly, Soviet professional military literature has not seriously discussed the problems and techniques of nuclear safeguards. Again, however, there is some sign that the publicity given to American proposals in contrast with Soviet silence on this subject has touched a sensitive spot. For example, a somewhat defensive note on this question crept into an otherwise boastful article by Colonel General Tolubko, Deputy Commander of the Soviet missile forces, in November 1963. Following a recitation of the readiness of his rocket troops to fulfill their duty, Tolubko took note of "press accounts of 'precautionary measures adopted by the USA against accidental outbreak of nuclear war.'" Such measures might be necessary for the Americans, he said, who have real reason to fear that "a mad man" among them might start a war. But as for the Soviet Union, according to Tolubko, "there is no need to think about such problems," because "Soviet rocketeers have strong nerves . . . and a deep sense of responsibility."[39]

PSYCHO-POLITICAL EXPLOITATION OF THE STRATEGIC MISSILE FORCES

In a purely military sense, much of current Soviet professional discussion of the strategic missile forces, as in the successive Sokolovskii volumes, can be regarded as a stage in the process, under way for the past few years, of adapting Soviet military doctrine and strategy to the potentialities of missiles and nuclear weapons. This process has also involved restructuring the Soviet military establishment to accommodate the new strategic missile forces, creation of which was first confirmed by Marshal Malinovskii in 1961.[40] The professional Soviet discussion of ways and means to employ the strategic missile forces if war should come can be considered—within the limits of such open publications as the Sokolovskii volumes—as a useful contribution to understanding of Soviet strategic thinking and policy.

However, there is another aspect of Soviet discourse on the strategic missile forces that should be distinguished from that noted above. This is what might be called the process of employing these forces against men's minds, rather than against physical target systems. This process, too, is part of the strategic dialogue; it represents the political and psychological exploitation of the Soviet missile forces, as distinct from their contemplated use in any actual war that might occur. This political exploitation of Soviet missile potentialities began as early as the late 1950's, when Khrushchev, on the strength of the first Soviet ICBM tests and sputnik launchings in 1957, set out to persuade the world that the strategic balance of power had shifted suddenly to the Soviet side.[41]

Today, the strategic missile forces bear a special cachet in Soviet discourse. They frequently are described, for example, as a force "from which no aggressor is safe,"[42] or as "the mighty shield standing in the way of the imperialist aggressors."[43] The "special care" which the Presidium of the Central Committee and Khrushchev personally have shown toward development of the missile forces is often mentioned.[44] As discussed earlier in Chapter V, the acclaim bestowed upon these forces has played its part in the East-West strategic dialogue as a device to enhance the credibility of the Soviet deterrent posture. Besides being pictured as the guarantor of Soviet security, Soviet missile forces are also credited with being a major tool of Soviet foreign policy. Thus, for example, an article in November 1963 ascribed a string of diplomatic victories to Soviet missile forces, observing that the Soviet Union had "used its nuclear rocket might to shield Socialist Cuba, to avert aggression against the Chinese People's Republic, and safeguard the independence and freedom of Egypt, Syria and Iraq."[45]

Perhaps the case of Cuba illustrates most vividly the special burden borne by Soviet missiles in the conduct of Soviet foreign policy. Although Khrushchev learned a lesson in the limits of missile diplomacy in the Cuban episode of 1962, he has since then fallen back again on the missile theme to lend authority to Soviet promises of protection to the Castro regime. His remarks during Castro's second visit to the Soviet Union in January 1964 were characteristically missile-oriented, as when he said:

There were people who began to criticize us for placing the missiles and then taking them away. It is true we did emplace them and removed them. But we received the promise that there would be no invasion of Cuba. And we told the enemies of Cuba that if they butted in, our missiles would not necessarily have to be in Cuba. Our missiles will reach you at the farthest corner of the world from Soviet territory.[46]

One of the articles which appeared in the Soviet press in the fall of 1963, at a time when the strategic missile forces were the object of an unusual amount of public attention, deserves particular note for its contribution to the new mystique which the Soviet Union seems to be creating around the strategic missile troops. The article dealt with a day in the life of an unidentified Soviet strategic missile unit, describing the technical competence, readiness for combat, and devotion to duty of the unit's personnel. In this account, there was an extraordinary passage that seemed to be aimed at giving a special identity to Soviet rocket personnel. Remarking first that "a strategic rocketeer" outwardly may not be distinguishable from an officer in any other branch of the Soviet armed forces, the author then said: "But if you knew that here before you stands a lieutenant or a colonel of the strategic rockets—then, word of honor, you would doff your cap in his presence!"[47]

SIGNS OF REACTION AGAINST PREVAILING EMPHASIS ON MISSILES

Interestingly enough, the exceptional emphasis now bestowed on both the military and psychological aspects of the strategic missile forces seems to have generated a certain amount of renewed doctrinal resistance among some Soviet military men. In part, this may represent merely a continuation of the familiar debate in which proponents of Khrushchev's modernist theories and policy are still being resisted by defenders of traditionally oriented interests. However, a new element also appears to have been introduced into the modernist-traditionalist dialogue. Recently, some military writers have begun to suggest that such modernist notions as the absolute primacy of nuclear-missile weapons have been carried too far, threatening to create a "new orthodoxy" that could cripple creative development of Soviet military theory and forces.

The leading voice thus far in challenging the new orthodoxy seems to be that of Marshal P. A. Rotmistrov, who has been cast in a bellwether role previously in his career. This colorful figure, a hero of tank warfare in World War II and a military scholar to boot, was one of the first open critics of Stalinist military doctrine in the mid-1950's. Like some of the other standard-bearers of a "progressive" approach at the time of breaking away from Stalin's outmoded military theories, Rotmistrov later came to find himself taking the conservative side of the argument frequently in the context of the military debate of the early 1960's.[48] While he cannot be described as an outright traditionalist, Romistrov has tended to favor the theme that despite the important role of strategic nuclear weapons, other arms—including his favorite tank forces—still have a vital contribution to make in modern war.[49]

The publication of two articles by Rotmistrov in the spring of 1964 in *Red Star* marked a sharper turn than hitherto in his criticism of modernist trends in Soviet military thinking.[50] These articles ostensibly dealt with the need to improve research and teaching in higher military schools. In fact, however, they came close to being an indictment of the new military concepts and doctrine associated with Khrushchev's name in the past few years. In the first and most significant of the two articles, Rotmistrov opened his attack on the new orthodoxy of the modernist school by charging that some military theorists "express their views as categorically as if they had already been validated by the practical experience of war."[51] Many problems are in fact still unresolved, according to Rotmistrov, "and require further deep research." To accept presently established views as the last word in military theory apparently is one of the modernist vices, in Rotmistrov's opinion.

Suggesting that some of the modernist thinking of the recent past has already become subject to question, Rotmistrov said: "Today, as a result of military-technical research already carried out . . . certain established views and propositions of military art already are beginning to lose their original significance in light of further development of armaments and military technology." While not spelling out the "established views" in question, Rotmistrov later made it amply clear that his criticism was germane not only to the modernist school in general, but also to Khrushchev's own approach to the subject of modern weapons and their influence on warfare:

In defining the roles [of weapons and forces] in warfare, calculations based on the anticipated results of using a single new type of weapon alone can lead to erroneous conclusions.

Castigating further what he apparently regards as one-sided modernist emphasis on new weapons and unverified theories of warfare, Rotmistrov observed at another point:

We should not be diverted by any sort of fruitless theorizing and forget about reality. It should be remembered that an over-estimate as well as an under-estimate, or worse still, a scornful attitude toward old types of forces or toward the old weapons is not only impermissible, but even harmful, especially within the framework of tactical operations, where the need for "old" weapons will continue, evidently, for a significant time.

As the history of war teaches, new forms of warfare replace the old not at one stroke, but gradually, since the new cannot manage without the old for a long time. This situation also pertains to the development of armaments and military technology.

Similar references to the theme that new weapons and forces cannot replace the old all at once have appeared in other recent Soviet military writing. In a book by Colonel S. I. Krupnov, *Dialectics and Military Science,* published in late 1963, two reasons for the validity of this proposition were cited: "First, even old weapons are very expensive, and no government can afford to throw them on the scrap heap until general and complete disarmament occurs; second, no matter how powerful nuclear weapons and missiles may be, they cannot decide all the tasks of modern war."[52]

Not all of the recent reaction against the prevailing emphasis on the strategic missile forces has been specifically critical of modernist tendencies *per se*. It is noteworthy that some critics have complained precisely on the grounds that missile advocates have stopped short, as it were, of exploiting the full potentialities afforded by other forms of modern military technology. Indeed, there is some flavor of this view in Rotmistrov's observations. A better case in point, perhaps, was furnished by a *Red Star* article in April 1964, written by Major General V. Bolotnikov. He clearly established his credentials as a modernist by saying:

Weapons and methods of employing them have changed. The truth is obvious, and most commanders have learned it well. But one still encounters people with peculiar views about modern weapons. To the bitter end they still do not understand that one cannot approach the problem of employing the new weapons with the old yardstick.[53]

The argument developed elsewhere in Bolotnikov's article, which was devoted to the impact on aviation of the revolution in military affairs, was that adaptation to new weaponry should include full exploitation of the potential of aircraft. In common, therefore, with Rotmistrov's thesis, this article pressed the point that in the nuclear-missile era, forces other than the strategic missile forces also retain an important role in modern warfare. Soviet views on the evolving roles of these other forces are to be taken up in the next chapter.

Chapter XIV

EVOLVING ROLES OF
THE TRADITIONAL FORCES

Although the increasing emphasis placed upon the strategic missile forces stands out as the most conspicuous trend in current Soviet military literature, other branches of the Soviet armed forces have not been correspondingly neglected in Soviet thinking. In fact, the impact of the new missile forces upon Soviet doctrine and strategy probably has stimulated efforts to redefine and re-evaluate the roles which other elements of the armed forces may play. In this chapter, we touch upon some of the principal trends in recent Soviet discussion with regard to the evolving roles of the traditional ground, air, and naval forces.

GROUND FORCES

Traditionally, the Soviet ground forces have been expected to carry the main brunt of theater warfare operations. For a considerable time after World War II, as noted earlier, they represented the principal element of Soviet deterrence by virtue of their ability to hold Europe "hostage." Technological developments in the nuclear-missile age have had a strong impact on doctrine for these forces, whose evolving role is clearly undergoing change. Soviet MRBM-IRBM units, for example, which are part of the strategic missile forces, apparently have taken over much of the "hostage" role vis-à-vis Europe. Within the ground forces themselves, the need to mount a dual capability for both nuclear and conventional warfare has further stimulated structural change and helped to keep doctrine in flux. Moreover, as indicated in Chapter XII, the question of the size of the Soviet military establishment has particularly affected the ground forces. While it is clear that the majority of Soviet ground force leaders continue to support the concept that Soviet security is indissolubly linked with the maintenance of massive armies, arguments in the open professional literature for large forces do not specify the relative slice envisaged for combat elements, as distinct from troops required for such functions as interior security, logistic support, and civil defense. It is therefore hard to tell whether Soviet ground force leaders are disturbed by the present balance of combat forces, or by what they would regard as deficiencies in supporting units and large requirements for trained man power to restore order and carry out rehabilitation tasks in the rear during a nuclear war.

The central point stressed in Soviet military discourse today concerning the ground forces, as in Marshal Chuikov's December 1963 exhortation on their importance, is that they still play an indispensable role "in achieving the final goals of the war."[1] Despite this concession to the idea that the initial operations of a war would be dominated by the strategic offensive and defensive forces,[2] a wide range of operations is envisaged for the ground forces in all phases of a war. A picture of the theater ground operations to be expected at the outset of a general war can be found in the following passages from the revised Sokolovskii edition.

In the theater of ground operations, offensive operations will develop along fronts, in the course of which strategic tasks will be accomplished. This will be a theater offensive following nuclear strikes by strategic means, which will play the decisive role in defeat of the enemy.[3]

Following the retaliatory nuclear strikes, airborne landings may be launched in great depth and—depending on the radiological conditions—the ground force formations which are still intact will initiate a rapid advance with the support of the air force, in order to complete the destruction of the surviving armed forces of the enemy.[4]

It is noteworthy that these passages and a similar one elsewhere[5] in the second Sokolovskii edition suggested that the ground operations probably would not begin simultaneously with the first nuclear strikes, but that there might be an interval, with the first follow-up action in depth by airborne troops. Most Soviet military literature has conveyed the impression that ground operations would be timed to begin simultaneously with the initial strategic strikes.

The increased importance of tank forces and airborne troops in a future war is repeatedly stressed by top Soviet military leaders and military writers.[6] The second Sokolovskii edition, interestingly enough, placed even more emphasis than the first on the role of airborne operations, noting that "air landing as well as paratroop operations have taken on a new significance."[7] Among the purposes of airborne operations, according to the Sokolovskii authors, will be seizure of enemy nuclear weapons, airfields, and naval bases.[8] A suggestion that technical improvements in Soviet airborne capabilities may account in part for increased Soviet interest in airborne operations was conveyed by a *Red Star* article in January 1963, in which the author pointed out that the airborne forces now have heavier weapons and equipment, deliverable by airdrop.[9]

The acquisition of nuclear weapons by the ground forces has been one of the major factors affecting their development over the past few years. Soviet military literature makes clear that nuclear weapons and tactical missiles now constitute the "main firepower" of the ground forces.[10] However, there is a certain amount of doctrinal and perhaps organizational uncertainty, tinged with possible rivalry between strategic and tactical missile elements, on the question of nuclear weapons in the ground forces. Signs of this emerge from shifting evaluation placed upon tactical missile units within the ground forces.[11] Marshal S. Varentsov, who was in charge of tactical missile units before his fall from grace because of his connection with the Penkovskii espionage case, wrote an article on tactical missile doctrine in late 1962 in which he laid great stress on the superior value of tactical missiles over tactical aviation and artillery in theater operations.[12] This assessment seemed to be generally (though not exclusively) shared in other military writing, including the first edition of the Sokolovskii book. However, two interesting modifications appeared in the revised edition. One of these changes consisted of dropping a previous statement that the tactical missile troops

will to a considerable degree replace artillery and aviation in bombarding the front; for some purposes they will completely replace artillery and aviation.[13]

The other change occurred in a passage stating that the tactical missile troops "will be the main means used to clear the way for tank and motorized troops."[14] The revised statement dropped the words "main means" and said instead that the missile units of the ground forces will

help clear the way . . . by destroying any important enemy targets and troop formations that may survive strikes by the strategic missile forces . . . [15]

The effect of these changes was to suggest that some re-evaluation of the role of tactical missile units within the ground forces may have taken place in the past year or so, resulting in a downgrading of their contribution to battlefield operations. The expressed expectation that strategic missile forces will play a greater role in "clearing the way" for ground force theater operations contributed further to this impression. However, other Soviet military writing conveys the impression that the use of tactical nuclear weapons in battlefield operations is still very much an open question. As indicated in the discussion of limited war in Chapter X, some Soviet military men show an increased interest in the value of small weapons for tactical purposes. Colonel General Shtemenko, for example, in assessing significant weapons developments in February 1963, took note of Western development of "small- and very-small-yield nuclear weapons," although he was noncommittal as to Soviet activity in this area.[16] A *Red Star* article by Major General Anureev in November 1963 also placed rather unaccustomed emphasis on the value of small weapons, stating:

The necessity for such weapons is dictated by the circumstances themselves. It is difficult to use large-yield nuclear warheads on the battlefield . . . without risking the destruction of one's own forces.[17]

As in other countries with a nuclear potential, the question of maintaining dual capabilities—both nuclear and conventional —in the Soviet ground forces is undoubtedly one of the most complex and troublesome problems with which Soviet military planners have had to contend. It is rather surprising, therefore, that very little professional discussion of the technical and operational problems arising out of this matter has appeared in Soviet military literature. The standard treatment goes little beyond statements that the Soviet ground forces must be prepared to use both nuclear and conventional weapons, and that improvement of conventional weapons will continue along with development of new types of weapons.[18]

The underlying doctrinal assumption in Soviet writing today is that in any general war the use of conventional arms will take place within the framework of operations dominated by nuclear weapons. Some statements, however, suggest the independent employment of conventional forces under a variety of conditions. Both editions of the Sokolovskii work, for example, stated that conventional weapons "will be extensively employed in local and world wars, either independently or in conjunction with new types of weapons."[19] While no doctrine for dealing with a purely conventional war on a large scale currently appears in the open Soviet literature, there have been, as noted earlier, some recent signs of an awakened interest in the question of local wars which might involve conventional operations on a fairly extensive scale.[20]

AIR FORCES

As in the case of the Soviet ground forces, technological change and other factors have had a strong impact on traditional roles and doctrine for the air forces. These forces were less well-entrenched in the Soviet scheme of things than the ground forces. For example, the Soviet air forces were elevated to the same level as the ground and naval forces and so became one of the three basic branches of the armed forces only after the last war.[21] Consequently, the air forces have had perhaps an even more difficult time than the ground forces in holding their own against the competition of missile technology. This was suggested by the first Sokolovskii edition, in a passage stating:

Today, the air forces are in a special situation. In recent years, there has been keen competition between bombers, missiles and air defense weapons. In this competition, air defense weapons have gained the advantage over bomber aircraft . . . consequently, long-range bombers are rapidly yielding first place to intercontinental bombers and intermediate range ballistic missiles.[22]

The impression given by the first Sokolovskii edition that many decisions affecting the future development of the air forces probably were pending or under debate has not been altered by the second edition or other Soviet writing in the interim. The area of principal flux in Soviet air power doctrine seems to concern the role of the long-range bomber, although a zone of contention over the relative weight of tactical missiles and tactical aviation in the conduct of theater operations is also evident.

The case of the long-range bomber, which gave the Soviet Union its first intercontinental delivery capability before the advent of the ballistic missile, is or would be affected not only by competition from other weapons systems, but also by recent disarmament proposals relating to strategic delivery means. These ranged from a U.S. suggestion to "freeze" the present level of all types of strategic delivery vehicles to a Soviet proposal to scrap existing inventories of all bombers.[23] Khrushchev, moreover, has again announced that the Soviet Union has ceased production of strategic bombers, along with surface warships,[24] which no doubt limits the latitude for expressing professional military views on the bomber question.

To judge from the revised Sokolovskii edition and other professional writing, there has been a further trend toward downgrading the worth of strategic bombers in the past year or so, offset to some extent by continued recognition that air-to-surface missiles have given the bomber a further lease on life.[25] For example, the revised Sokolovskii edition, like the first, stated that strategic missions deep within enemy territory can be better performed by ballistic missiles than bombers.[26] Both volumes also noted that the use of air-to-surface missiles can prolong the combat potential of strategic bombers.[27] However, in the second edition, after observing that air-to-surface missiles can "considerably increase the capabilities of long-range bombers" by enabling them to strike "enemy targets, without penetrating his air-defense zone," the Sokolovskii authors then went on to say:

But even in this case, strategic bomber aviation cannot regain its lost significance. Its speed is too low compared to ballistic missiles.[28]

Other signs of backing away slightly from their mid-1962 appreciation of the long-range bomber role were also evident in the 1963 Sokolovskii edition. Thus, in a passage dealing with bomber penetration of enemy airspace, greater stress was put on the difficulty of concealing bomber flights "from modern means of detection."[29] Elsewhere, in a discussion of future aircraft development possibilities, including aircraft not requiring improved airfields, the second edition omitted reference to a statement that development trends promised to increase significantly the capabilities of aircraft operating "in the deep rear" of enemy territory.[30] This omission suggests a somewhat lessened optimism about improving the capabilities of aircraft with deep penetration roles, such as those in the long-range bomber category.

On the other hand, in discussing strategic operations in a general time-frame without specific reference to future trends, the new Sokolovskii volume, like the first, was somewhat more generous to the strategic bomber. In both editions, a standing role was ascribed to long-range aviation, together with the strategic missile forces, as the main instrumentality for carrying out strategic attacks.[31] Moreover, the new volume gave greater emphasis than before to the role of long-range bombers for "independent strikes against enemy targets, especially on the seas and oceans."[32] This emphasis could reflect the increased activity in the past year of Soviet long-range aircraft, which were publicly reported on several occasions to be shadowing U.S. carrier forces at sea.[33] The new volume also added long-range aviation to an enumeration of Soviet forces that would play an important role in disrupting enemy maritime communications.[34]

The ambiguity thus attending the treatment of long-range bombers in the respective Sokolovskii editions has been evident in other Soviet military commentary, particularly as regards evaluation of bombers equipped as air-to-surface missile carriers. Opinion on this subject has not been divided along branch-of-service lines.[35] Various high-ranking non-air force officers, among them Marshal Malinovskii, have endorsed the ASM-equipped bomber in emphatic terms. Malinovskii, for example, said in February 1963:

Important changes have taken place in recent years in the air forces . . . the bomber has been replaced by missile-carrying aircraft which are capable of carrying out—with great accuracy—long-range, nuclear strikes against the enemy, without entering the zone where they are vulnerable to his air defenses.[36]

Other officers, however, have seemed to slight the missile-carrying bomber when discussing air force capabilities. A conspicuous example of this turned up in Major General Lomov's January 1964 doctrine series in *Red Star*. He enumerated several fields of improvement in Soviet aviation which had occurred "simultaneously with the growth of the air forces as a branch of the armed forces," but made no mention at all of missile-carrying aircraft except in connection with naval aviation.[37] The warmest proponents of the ASM-equipped bomber have been found, as might be expected, among air force officers and aircraft designers. One of the latter, the world-famous aircraft designer Andrei Tupolev, publicly argued in 1962 that missile-carrying bombers had some "very important advantages" over ballistic missiles, but there has since been no evidence that this view has gained wide acceptance in Soviet military opinion.[38]

If the long-range bomber has received somewhat lessened support, other elements of the air forces have fared somewhat better in recent Soviet discussion. Tactical or frontal (*frontovaia*) aviation, which traditionally has been the central element of Soviet air forces, has lost some of its functions to tactical missiles. As indicated earlier, however, there are signs of a revived interest in the contributions of this arm, particularly against mobile targets in theater warfare. Colonel General Shtemenko, Chief of Staff of the ground forces, spoke up as a strong champion of tactical aviation in February 1963, noting that there is "no substitute" for it, "especially when independent searching out of targets is required."[39] The revised Sokolovskii edition also stressed the continuing importance of tactical bombers and fighter bombers for use against mobile targets, and suggested that technological improvement of aircraft for battlefield use could be expected:

There are many specific tasks, such as destruction of mobile targets, which can be more effectively carried out by bombers or fighter-bombers than missiles. The future improvement of aircraft-missile technology may significantly increase the operational effectiveness of the bomber air force on the battlefield.[40]

In addition to long-range strategic and tactical support roles, other missions of the air forces also have been under reassessment. The present trend is to foresee an important role for fighter aircraft "in the next years" in the air defense system, and a need for improved fighter performance, including endurance.[41] The importance of aerial reconnaissance has been upgraded, now being described as one of the "more important missions of aviation."[42] In this connection, the revised Sokolovskii volume placed added weight on the need for aerial reconnaissance, both to aid the missile forces and to locate submarine bases and submarine positions at sea.[43] Air force contributions to airborne operations, logistic support, and communications are also described as of growing importance in Soviet military discourse today.[44]

Perhaps the most interesting doctrinal development bearing on the future role of air power in Soviet military thinking has been the recent reaction in some quarters to one-sided emphasis on missiles, which was discussed in the preceding chapter. In his article in April 1964 which seemed to foreshadow a growing dissatisfaction with the new missile orthodoxy, Marshal Rotmistrov—not hitherto known as an especially ardent advocate of the air forces—singled out aviation for special appreciation. Speaking mainly of the use of air power in support of theater operations, Rotmistrov said that "despite the employment of missiles, aviation also will play an important role, especially in operations of tank forces and other strike groups separated from the remaining forces."

In a war of maneuver, aviation will become not only an irreplaceable means of reconnaissance, but also a reliable and adequately effective means for suppression of mobile targets through use of both nuclear and conventional bombs.[45]

Aircraft, Rotmistrov affirmed, will be able to carry out their ground support missions despite the development of surface-to-air missile defenses. "Consequently," he said, "notwithstanding the rapid development of missiles and missile technology in general, aviation in a future war, evidently, will also be given a significant role." By way of advice, Rotmistrov urged that specialists of the air force higher academies should "apply themselves to working out methods for employing aviation under conditions of modern war." Furthermore, he admonished, they should insist on

. . . working out new questions, with real future significance, freeing themselves from fruitless repetition of even the "established propositions" of staff manuals.

In Rotmistrov's argument for the future of aviation, the issue of the long-range bomber versus the strategic missile was largely ignored. Not so in the case of Major General Bolotnikov, whose analysis of the future potential of manned aircraft appeared in *Red Star* at about the same time as Rotmistrov's commentary. Arguing that aircraft are as good as, and in some cases better than, missiles alone in performing essential military tasks, Bolotnikov chose to stress the interdependence between missiles and aircraft, rather than, as he put it, "making an absolute" of one or the other. In a passage directed to this point, he said:

It is easy to destroy airdromes with missiles. It is easier still to strike launching pads with aircraft. Missiles need reconnaissance by aircraft. A peculiar collaboration arises. A clear example is the capability of launching ballistic missiles from heavy aircraft.[46]

Despite his expressed confidence that new paths were being opened for manned aviation by advances in technology and operational techniques, such as development of air-to-surface missiles and "operations at very low levels," Bolotnikov betrayed some concern that this confidence was not shared in all quarters. At several points he commented that there are still "some people strongly attached to the old ways," and in one revealing passage he remarked rather ruefully: "How strange it is that the triumphant demonstration of the almost limitless capabilities of aviation has led to a peculiar pessimism about aviation. Some foreign figures, for example, are inclined to assert that aviation has put itself out of business, that with modern speeds and altitudes the advantage of human presence aboard aircraft is quite doubtful." While attributing these pessimistic sentiments to "foreign skeptics," in the manner often employed by Soviet writers when dealing with controversial questions, Bolotnikov may very well have had in mind some home-grown skeptics also.

NAVAL FORCES

The great change in the strategic landscape brought about by World War II, which left the Soviet Union and its continental satellites facing a global coalition of maritime powers, resulted in a new Soviet emphasis on the importance of naval forces. The Soviet navy had played no major role in the world's oceans in World War II, having been used mainly for support of the seaward flanks of the Soviet ground forces and for defense of Soviet coastal areas. While these tasks remain among the missions of the naval forces, they have been overshadowed by new roles—to interdict American support of Europe in case of war, to combat U.S. carrier and submarine forces, and lately, since acquisition of missile-launching submarines, to share to some extent in the strategic offensive effort.

For several years after World War II, it appeared that the Soviet Union might attempt to create a surface challenge to Western sea power. However, a large program of surface naval construction was cut back,[47] and after Khrushchev consolidated his power, he publicly announced the obsolescence of surface warships, a view he reiterated as recently as June 1963.[48] The main Soviet emphasis went into building a large submarine fleet, and although no carrier program was ever initiated, a substantial land-based air arm consisting mainly of jet bombers and reconnaissance aircraft has been provided for naval tasks.

These are some of the factors which have given the naval forces greater weight today in the Soviet scheme of things than was formerly the case.

Judging from Soviet military literature since the appearance of the first Sokolovskii edition in 1962, a fairly significant re-evaluation of navy roles and missions appears to have been taking place over the past year or two, partly influenced perhaps by reassessment of threats with which Soviet naval forces may have to cope, and partly by changes in the capabilities of these forces themselves. One of the naval tasks upon which new emphasis has been placed is that of antisubmarine warfare. In particular, more stress has been evident on measures for combating Polaris submarines, a problem which had been treated somewhat lightly in the first Sokolovskii edition, as both foreign commentators and Soviet critics pointed out.[49] The second Sokolovskii edition, by contrast, described this problem as "the most important task of the Soviet navy."[50] In an expanded discussion of ASW operations, the Sokolovskii authors noted that such operations must now be conducted at great distances, and that "the former coastal system of ASW is not effective today against missile-launching submarines."[51] A more important role was ascribed to antisub submarines in the new volume, and it was stated that Soviet submarines used for ASW purposes will be armed with "homing torpedoes" as well as missiles.[52] Soviet strategic missile forces, long-range aviation, and naval surface forces were also said to have a role in dealing with the Polaris threat.[53] While taking a more sober view of the Polaris problem than in their previous edition, the Sokolovskii authors repeated the assertion that such submarines are "vulnerable" despite foreign claims to the contrary.[54] In this connection, they said:

Atomic submarines with "Polaris" missiles can be destroyed at their bases by strikes delivered by the strategic missile forces, [also] during transit and in their patrol areas, by antisub submarines, by long-range aviation and by other anti-submarine forces and means.[55]

Other Soviet discussion has indicated differing views on the ASW problem. Some spokesmen, including Admiral S. G. Gorshkov, Commander of the Soviet Navy, have expressed rather sanguine views of the "successes" achieved in Soviet ASW exercises.[56] In October 1963, a Soviet admiral said that "methods and equipment are being improved more each year" in the ASW field, although he noted that "concealment and surprise" might be used as a counter to ASW operations.[57] A comment in July 1963 in a military journal's description of a submarine exercise to penetrate an ASW barrier seemed to suggest an improvement in ASW capabilities by noting that the submarine commander "was very much disturbed by the unprecedented range of an ASW ship" operating against him.[58] In contrast with these expressions on the subject were those of Admiral V. A. Alafuzov in January 1963. In a discussion dealing with the problem of finding surface naval vessels and attacking them with missiles, Alafuzov first observed that this "is not so easy, unless one uses a missile with a super-powerful nuclear warhead whose destructive radius will compensate for all possible mistakes in calculation of the target's location." Alafuzov then added:

It will be even more difficult to detect and destroy atomic submarines which are all the time in a submerged position.[59]

Another problem which has been high on the list of Soviet naval tasks for the past few years is that of dealing with U.S. carrier forces. The revised Sokolovskii volume in 1963 continued to stress the importance of operations against carriers, giving preference to submarines as the best anticarrier weapon when nuclear torpedoes or missiles are employed.[60] An important role in operations against carriers was also mentioned, as before, for units of the naval air arm and long-range aviation.[61] In this connection, the new volume advanced the claim that when such air units use air-to-surface missiles with nuclear warheads, only a small number of aircraft will be required for successful attacks against carrier forces.[62] In general, the new volume expanded somewhat on the vulnerability of carrier forces, asserting that Soviet possession of missile-launching submarines makes it possible to attack carrier forces without having to penetrate their protective screen. At one point in the revised volume, reference was made to U.S. press accounts that nuclear-powered aircraft carriers can operate without a protective screen, and it was said that this "should be taken into account in organizing countermeasures against aircraft carriers."[63]

The precise role which missile-launching submarines should play in Soviet plans appears to be a much debated subject, particularly as regards their contribution to strategic operations against land targets. While generally recognizing that "submarines are the principal striking force of our Navy,"[64] Soviet statements often tend to associate missile-launching submarines with operations against enemy naval forces at sea rather than with strategic operations.[65] Part of the burden of Admiral Alafuzov's criticism of the first Sokolovskii edition in the previously-mentioned review was that the book failed to give sufficient recognition to the strategic role of Soviet missile-launching subs,[66] which would further suggest that this has been an issue in Soviet defense planning.

An indication that this issue may have come closer to being resolved in the 1962–1963 interval between the two Sokolovskii editions was furnished by the second edition, which gave considerably more attention to the strategic role of the missile-launching submarine. In four instances, for example, the 1963 volume spoke of missile-launching submarines as participating elements in strategic operations, along with the strategic missile forces and long-range aviation units.[67] In this connection, it is interesting that the Sokolovskii authors' discussion of missile-launching submarines did not dwell on Soviet capabilities for submerged launching of missiles, such as possessed by Polaris submarines. Other Soviet statements, dating back to Khrushchev's visit to fleet exercises in northern waters in July 1962, have occasionally made claim to a Soviet submerged-launching capability.[68]

In the evolution of Soviet naval roles, one of the more interesting developments of the last year or so has been the increasing attention given in military literature to the question of amphibious landing capabilities. Critics, both foreign and Soviet, have in the past noted the paucity of treatment given this subject in Soviet military doctrine, the more striking because of the doctrinal prescription that Soviet forces would have to be put ashore to occupy the territory of an overseas enemy before victory could be consolidated.[69] Again, the most outspoken Soviet critic on this point is Admiral Alafuzov, who scored the first Sokolovskii edition for failing "to remember that if it is a question of a 'maritime opponent,' his final destruction and the taking of his territory cannot be accomplished without conducting amphibious operations."[70] To drive home his point, Alafuzov said one must not overlook the naval forces,

without which the ground forces would be in a terrible quandary, to say the least, in attempting invasion of enemy territory across the sea.[71]

In their revised volume, the Sokolovskii authors went part way toward rectifying their previous neglect by adding a notation to the effect that:

In developing the navy, one must take into account the mission of combined operations with the ground forces, and above all, make provision for amphibious operations.[72]

Meanwhile, in other Soviet military writing in 1963, the question of amphibious operations began to receive more attention. A particularly notable contribution to the literature on this subject was a serious article by a navy captain in the September 1963 issue of *Morskoi Sbornik*. The author, Captain N. P.

Viunenko, reviewed many of the problems attending amphibious landings in the nuclear age, and while stressing the hazards, came to the conclusion that "it is possible to carry out amphibious landings even under modern conditions."[73] At one place he made the point that a nuclear attack on the defenses prior to a landing would be the most effective way to ensure success[74]—an approach to the problem which apparently has received attention in actual training exercises.[75] Perhaps the most significant observation in Viunenko's analysis was that large-scale landings of a significant strategic order—such as presumably would be involved in operations against a major adversary—could be expected to occur only "when the nuclear capabilities of the belligerents have declined and when the conflict has taken on a more protracted character."[76] One pertinent point not discussed was the resources required to develop amphibious landing capabilities of a significant order.

Chapter XV

STRATEGIC DEFENSE OF THE SOVIET UNION

Heavy reliance on active defense against strategic attack has been a conspicuous feature of Soviet strategic thinking in the nuclear age.[1] This emphasis on active defense has been accompanied by the commitment of very substantial Soviet resources over the past decade or so to the development of a system of air defense against strategic bombers,[2] and there is a strong doctrinal basis at least for attempting a similar active defense effort against missiles.

The Soviet air defense system[3] entered its main period of growth after the Korean War, at a time when U.S. strategic bomber forces were also being greatly strengthened. There has always been an implicit competition for resources and attention between Soviet strategic offensive and defensive forces, resolved more often in favor of the latter, at least until the advent of strategic missiles. In a sense, the Soviet leadership seems to have followed a course of building a deterrent strategic delivery force and pursuing a low war-risk foreign policy on the one hand, while taking out insurance on the other hand in the form of extensive air defenses against the possibility of an unexpected war. To the extent that such defenses might make the success of an air attack on the Soviet Union look uncertain, they would also contribute to deterrence.

How germane such a rationale may remain in the missile era is one of the prime factors bearing on the evolving role of Soviet strategic defense forces, as well as the civil defense effort, which in Soviet eyes is regarded as "one of the essential elements of the over-all defense preparations of the country."[4] The problems which the Soviet Union has faced in preparing itself to cope with bomber attacks are dwarfed by those opened up by the advent of missile delivery systems. These problems involve not only difficult technical and operational questions, as the duel between offense and defense goes on, but also the commitment of very large additional resources. The recent trend of Soviet discourse suggests that many problems in this area remain unresolved, although there has also been an obvious attempt to convey the impression that progress is being achieved.

VIEWS ON ANTIMISSILE DEFENSE PROSPECTS

Since Khrushchev's much-quoted statement in July 1962 that the Soviet Union has an antimissile missile that "can hit a fly in outer space,"[5] public Soviet claims in this field have multiplied rapidly.[6] They became particularly pronounced following the display at the November 7, 1963, military parade in Red Square of a new type of surface-to-air missile, which Soviet commentary placed in the antimissile class.[7] Marshal Biriuzov, Chief of the General Staff, asserted on November 8th, for example, that the Soviet armed forces now possessed antimissile weapons "capable of intercepting any missile in the air. This circumstance," he said, "permits our country to be defended against any enemy attack."[8] A similar emphatic claim was made a few days later by a Soviet artillery general, who said: "These long-range, air-defense missiles are capable of destroying any means of air-space attack."[9] Air Force Marshal V. Sudets, Commander of the National PVO and the man immediately responsible for any actual operations against a missile attack, was just a shade less categorical in January 1964 when he stated:

The combat capabilities of the weapons of these [PVO] forces permit the destruction of practically (*prakticheskii*) all modern means of air-space attack, at maximum range, high and low altitudes, and supersonic speeds.[10]

The treatment of antimissile defense in the revised Sokolov-skii volume was somewhat more restrained than some of the Soviet claims advanced elsewhere, but it too reflected a slightly more optimistic appraisal of the prospects for effective anti-missile defense than the 1962 volume. Several changes in the text illustrate this point. The new text, for example, omitted a passage in the first edition stating that ballistic missiles "are still practically invulnerable to existing means of air defense" and that it will be possible to counter their massive use "only as special instruments of antimissile defense are developed."[11] In another place, discussing the problem of creating an effective antimissile defense, the original text stated:

In principle, a technical solution to this problem has now been found. In the future this form of defense must be perfected.[12]

The revised edition dropped the second sentence, again conveying the inference that some progress had been achieved in the interim.[13] Although the Sokolovskii authors made no categorical assertions that the Soviet Union now possesses a system of effective antimissile defense, the revised volume contained a new statement alluding to the future possibility of such a system in more positive terms than before:

The great effectiveness of modern PVO resources permits a successful solution to the difficult and important task—the complete destruction of all attacking enemy planes and missiles, preventing them from reaching the targets marked for destruction. The crux of the matter lies in making skillful use of the great potential of modern means of antiaircraft and antimissile defense.[14]

Together with the growing Soviet tendency to suggest that a solution to the problem of defending the Soviet Union against missile attack has already been achieved, or is just around the corner, there has been a systematic denigration of Western antimissile defense (ABM). Both Marshal Sudets and General Baryshev, in the articles mentioned above, compared alleged

Soviet success with American failure to solve "the problem of combating ballistic missiles, as admitted by American scientists and military men themselves."[15] Among the arguments used by General Baryshev was that heavier Soviet strategic missile payloads would permit the use of "decoy warheads" to penetrate any antimissile defense the West might devise, and that "maneuverable warheads" foreseen "for the future" would further degrade Western defenses.[16] The effect of decoys and maneuverable warheads on Soviet defenses was not mentioned.

While an occasional Soviet statement has linked antimissile defenses in general terms with other elements of Soviet military strength as a factor helping "to cool down" the imperialists,[17] it is interesting that the more explicit arguments designed to enhance the credibility of the Soviet second-strike posture have not included the subject. Thus, for example, in the Nevsky and Glagolev-Larionov articles previously mentioned as well as in the revised Sokolovskii work, no specific claims were made for antimissile defenses as one of the factors that would make the success of a U.S. counterforce strike problematical and the survival of Soviet retaliatory forces certain. This might indicate that antimissile defenses are being thought of by the Soviet Union in terms of defending cities, or simply that they are not yet taken seriously enough to be introduced into the argument at this stage.

In the Soviet discussion of the ABM question, it is difficult to distinguish propaganda from sober evaluation. As usual, Soviet secrecy makes it difficult to determine where the Soviet Union may actually stand in the development of antimissile defenses. The great difference between boasting of being able to "hit a fly in space" and actually deploying an effective ABM system[18] has been ignored in Soviet discourse. Further, if the Soviet leaders have thought at all of the effect that Soviet ABM claims might have in exerting upward pressure upon both U.S. and Soviet arms expenditures[19]—a pressure they seem currently anxious to deflate—little sign of this has crept into the Soviet commentary.

At the same time, the Soviets do discuss seriously the prospects for active defense against both strategic air and missile attacks. While this suggests that the Soviet Union is proceeding with organizational arrangements as well as developmental programs in the antimissile field,[20] it also seems to indicate that official optimism is tempered by a number of sobering considerations on the relationship of offense to defense in the missile age.

THE OFFENSE-VERSUS-DEFENSE QUESTION

Despite consistent emphasis on the value of active defense, Soviet strategic doctrine also holds that the offense can overpower the defense in nuclear warfare. This judgment, which has implications reaching beyond the immediate question whether missiles can relatively easily stay ahead of antimissiles, is implicit in the Soviet position on the primacy of the strategic missile forces.[21] However, it also has been made explicit. In both editions of the Sokolovskii work, for example, the authors stated:

One must recognize that the present instrumentalities of nuclear attack are undoubtedly superior to the instrumentalities of defense against them.[22]

Both editions of the Sokolovskii work also voiced a closely related view on the offense-versus-defense question which amounted to saying that a good offense is the best defense. Thus, the point was made that the task of protecting the country against nuclear attack "will be achieved primarily by destroying the enemy's nuclear weapons where they are based."[23] Retention of this passage was the more notable in light of the fact that great sensitivity has been shown to any implication that the Soviet Union might contemplate pre-emptive action in order to blunt an enemy attack. It is difficult to argue that the enemy's nuclear forces should be destroyed at their bases without conceding that an attack against them would have to be attempted before they left those same bases.

This is not to imply that Soviet thinking calls for starting a war. In fact, given the balance of forces in the world, it is hard to picture the circumstances in which a war-initiation policy would look attractive to the Soviet Union. Yet there are anomalous areas in the policies of states where political strategy pulls one way and military strategy another. This seems to be the case with regard to Soviet doctrine on the question of offense versus defense. The notion of adopting the strategic defensive at the outset of a modern war, and counting on active and passive defenses to pull the country through until a counteroffensive can be mounted, has no standing in contemporary Soviet military thought.[24] If this was an acceptable principle of early postwar military theory, it has outlived its day since the advent of the nuclear age. The strategic defense forced upon the Soviets in the early period of World War II is now treated in Soviet military literature as a necessary but costly prelude to a counteroffensive. The World War II achievements of Soviet arms in the period of the strategic defense are lauded, and rightly so, together with admission of errors in conducting it, but this all belongs to history.[25] Today the situation is different, as emphasized by Colonel General Shtemenko, Chief of Staff of the Soviet ground forces:

The striking power and range of modern weapons puts the question of strategic defense in a different light than formerly. Our contemporary military doctrine flows from the decisiveness of the goals in a war. The combat potential of modern armed forces manifests itself to the greatest degree in the offense, not in the defense. Therefore, Soviet military doctrine regards the strategic defense as an unacceptable form of strategic operations in a modern war.[26]

Other Soviet military men have expressed in still stronger terms the unacceptability of "orienting oneself on the strategic defense . . . in the initial period of a modern war, which means dooming oneself beforehand to irreparable losses and defeat."[27] While there is a school of Soviet military thought that banks on the prospect of reversing the strategic-economic-morale balance in Soviet favor in the course of a protracted war, as previously discussed, even this school does not deny the critical importance of trying to seize the strategic initiative at the very outset.[28] Thus, Soviet military strategy finds itself in a position where its conception of the need to take the strategic offensive immediately must live, so to speak, in a state of uneasy coexistence with political imperatives against Soviet initiation of nuclear warfare. One may suppose that the latter imperatives will continue to govern so long as the Soviet leaders remain persuaded that neither active defenses nor a Soviet first-strike—nor the two in any feasible combination—offers much hope of preventing unacceptable damage to the Soviet Union in a nuclear war.

There is, understandably, no open Soviet literature on what calculations the Soviet leadership may have made on this score. The literature does concede, however, that some enemy blows could not be prevented, even under conditions which seem to imply a Soviet pre-emptive strike. For example, a passage in the revised Sokolovskii volume stated:

One must assume that our retaliatory nuclear blow will considerably weaken the enemy's nuclear attack forces. However, one cannot exclude the possibility that a certain number of enemy missiles and aircraft will nevertheless be launched to strike our targets.[29]

The critical element in this calculus is, of course, the "certain number" of enemy missiles and aircraft envisaged, and on this point Soviet reticence is not likely to be broken. Neither such data nor detailed studies of the damage the Soviet Union might suffer in a nuclear war are to be found in professional Soviet discussion. However, there is a voluminous literature in circulation in the Soviet Union in connection with the civil defense program, from which the Soviet population can doubtless draw its own conclusions concerning the dislocation that a nuclear world war would bring.

CIVIL DEFENSE

In Soviet thinking, passive measures have been accorded an important place along with a system of active defense as an integral part of the Soviet Union's military posture in the nuclear age. As a prominent Soviet military leader put it early in 1964, "not a single defense measure can be decided under modern conditions without considering civil defense needs."[30] There are many other expressions on record of Soviet interest in civil defense as "an inseparable part of the defensive strength of our Motherland" and "one of the most important factors determining the potential strength and survivability of the state under war conditions."[31] These have been backed up over the past ten or twelve years by a large-scale program of civil defense indoctrination and training of the Soviet population.[32]

Contrary to a general impression abroad of official Soviet indifference to civil defense, this activity continues to absorb the time and energies of a great many people in the Soviet Union. For example, the organization DOSAAF (Voluntary Society for Assistance to the Army, Air Force, and Navy, organized in 1951), with a membership of more than 30 million, is involved in training the population-at-large in civil defense. Compulsory training courses have been in effect since 1955, and at present the fifth course in this series is under way.[33] In the years 1955–1963, more than 120 books and manuals dealing with civil defense were issued in the Soviet Union, and the number of conferences and lectures on the subject was evidently very large. One Soviet account mentions that 2500 lectures were given in Sverdlovsk oblast alone in 1961.[34] Late in 1963 it was announced that the monthly journal *Voennye Znaniia* was to be increased in size and was to "expand considerably the publication of training articles and reporting on the activities of civil defense committees and staff."[35] Military responsibilities in connection with the civil defense program, which have included the furnishing of troops for rescue, rehabilitation, and other civil defense operations,[36] were underscored in the fall of 1963 by Marshal Chuikov. In a discussion of new Garrison and Guard Service Regulations for the armed forces issued in 1963, Chuikov emphasized that garrison commanders were charged with assisting civil defense authorities in their areas in developing civil defense plans and "conducting the required measures."[37]

All this does not mean, to be sure, that the Soviet civil defense program is prepared to cope with the problems of a nuclear war, or even that Soviet officialdom is fully agreed upon the value of civil defense under many of the conditions that a heavy nuclear attack would create. Exhortations to improve the training program and admissions that "the problems of protecting the population are not solved"[38] have been a regular feature of the Soviet literature on civil defense. Evidence of internal debate on the subject appeared in early 1962, when Colonel General Tolstikov, then acting head of the Soviet Civil Defense Service (Grazhdanskaia Oborona), referred to differences of view on civil defense, but noted also that the question has been resolved in favor of continuing with a vigorous program.[39]

Judging from occasional remarks questioning the value of shelters in an era of multi-megaton weapons,[40] one might presume that this was probably one of the questions at issue. The absence of published Soviet information on the scope of shelter construction and availability has made this a matter of wide speculation abroad.[41] Although references to the construction and use of shelters continue to appear in Soviet literature,[42] it remains unclear precisely how far the Soviet Union has gone or intends to go in pursuing a mass shelter program. This becomes a particularly pertinent question in connection with any Soviet intention to deploy antimissile defenses on a large scale, for, as pointed up by discussion of analogous questions in the United

States, the usefulness of active defenses against missiles in reducing population losses would depend to a great extent on the existence of an adequate system of shelter against radioactive fallout.[43] The Soviet leadership thus finds itself having to decide not only whether to commit the very large resources needed to support an antimissile system, but also whether to provide an accompanying population protection program.

It is interesting to note that no "lobby" against civil defense has appeared in the Soviet Union, comparable to those which have exerted pressure against civil defense programs in some Western countries. With the exception of occasional comments on the inadequacy of shelters (made, incidentally, in the context of protection against direct nuclear effects rather than fallout), Soviet spokesmen have presented virtually a united front in endorsing a serious Soviet civil defense effort. In Soviet military circles, all schools of thought have stressed the importance of civil defense in either a short or a protracted war. However, proponents of the view that the Soviet Union must prepare for a protracted war have laid particular emphasis upon the contribution to be made by a large-scale program for protection of population and industry, including shelters, dispersal and hardening of key installations, evacuation from cities, rehabilitation measures, and so on.[44]

Recent Soviet treatment of civil defense matters in the revised Sokolovskii edition and elsewhere has continued to dwell on the need for a broad civil defense program to reduce casualties and help the country to recuperate, but it has also shown certain shifts of emphasis. Greater attention has been given, for example, to the psychological impact which the first "devastating nuclear strikes" might have, not only on the civil population, but even upon well-disciplined military personnel.[45] The consequent need for better psychological preparation is implied by such expressions of concern. Some vacillation concerning the importance, or perhaps the feasibility of pre-attack evacuation of the urban population also has been evident. One of the new air defense manuals issued in late 1962, for example, gave very limited attention to evacuation measures,[46] in contrast with previous extensive treatment of this subject in civil defense literature. The revised Sokolovskii edition also followed this trend by omitting the principle passage in the 1962 edition on the subject of pre-attack evacuation from cities and border zones.[47] Other statements, however, have indicated a continuing place for pre-attack evacuation in civil defense planning. An article in *Voennye Znaniia* in August 1963 said that "during the threat of enemy attack, it may be decided to evacuate the population of some cities to rural areas." The article gave advice on what to do in such a case, which included taking along a three-day food supply.[48] Writing in the same publication in 1964, Marshal Chuikov stated that dispersal and evacuation from cities were the "basic methods of protecting the population," together with use of protective shelter.[49] In contrast with Chuikov's assessment of shelters, the revised Sokolovskii edition took a somewhat negative view in a discussion devoted to criticism of U.S. counterforce strategy, where it was observed that the role of shelters in a future war was "problematical."[50]

Chapter XVI

MILITARY USES OF SPACE

Given the rapid development of space technology, one of the world's newer and potentially more troublesome problems is the uses to which space eventually may be put. So far as any concrete Soviet plans and intentions with regard to military exploitation of space are concerned, we learn little either from Soviet military writing or from the positions the Soviet Union has taken on space questions in various international bodies. Most Soviet military thought, for example, continues to be focused on the problems of war as a terrestrial phenomenon, although in the past few years increasing attention has been given to the prospect that space might become an active dimension in any future war. In international sparring over space policy within and outside the United Nations in recent years, the Soviet Union has sought to picture itself as the champion of peaceful uses of space. Furthermore, its adherence to the United Nations resolution of October 17, 1963, barring weapons of mass destruction from outer space,[1] has suggested a Soviet interest in mutual efforts to discourage an extension of the arms race to the medium of space, at least with regard to systems of orbital bombardment.

At the same time, however, there have been persistent and vocal Soviet allegations that the United States has already embarked upon an ambitious military program for "mastery of outer space," from which the argument has followed that the Soviet Union must give attention to ways of using space for defense purposes and to prevent the "imperialist camp" from gaining "any superiority in this area."[2] This has all the marks of a Soviet rationalization for pursuing a military space program of its own, for which the technological base is already available.[3] Moreover, Soviet leaders have shown no disposition to forgo opportunities to exploit Soviet space achievements for political and propaganda gains, both in the international arena and domestically.[4] The further opportunity that development of a military space program might afford for exerting political and psychological pressure upon the West is thus a factor to be weighed by the Soviet leaders, along with the military pros and cons of such a program, and the effects it might have in stimulating a more intense level of arms competition. All of these considerations tend to leave the question of Soviet attitudes toward the military uses of space open to much speculation,[5] if indeed the Soviet leaders themselves know at this juncture the directions in which it would best suit their interests to move.

SOVIET CHARGES OF U.S. MILITARY EXPLOITATION OF SPACE

Perhaps the most conspicuous feature of the Soviet attitude toward the military uses of space has been the attempt, mentioned above, to demonstrate that American activities in space are aggressively oriented and that therefore the Soviet Union is justified in looking to its own defense. Soviet military writers, space law experts, and international negotiators all have followed this general line. As one American writer has put it, the Soviets have tried "to create a moral dichotomy between American and Soviet space technology,"[6] in order to give the impression that the United States is using its space capabilities to intensify the cold war and pursue aggressive aims, while the Soviet Union uses its space technology in the interest of "peaceful coexistence."

Since the first Soviet sputnik was launched in 1957, prompting the Soviet Union to reverse its traditional position on the question of unlimited national sovereignty over airspace,[7] Soviet theory on space law has been subject to continuous improvisation intended to keep Soviet political interests meshed with the changing perspectives opened up by space technology.[8] Partly as a result of this, the formal Soviet position on the military uses of space has developed in a somewhat uneven fashion. The Soviets have argued that the military use of space should be prohibited, but they have also asserted that space may be used in conformity with Article 51 of the UN Charter for "a retaliatory blow at the aggressor in the course of legitimate self-defense."[9] Arguing that the "peaceful uses" of space should be restricted to "non-military uses," they have dismissed the contention that "non-aggressive military uses are permissible,"[10] which strikes at the U.S. position that the nonweapon character of U.S. military space programs is compatible with the use of space for peaceful purposes.[11] In the controversy over permissible and impermissible uses of space, the Soviet Union has centered much of its fire on reconnaissance satellites, charging the United States with using satellite systems for espionage "in order to organize an attack on the socialist countries,"[12] and holding that reconnaissance satellites should be considered illegal before other prohibitions on military activity in space are settled.[13] At the same time, the Soviet Union has shown some interest in the reconnaissance potentialities of satellites, as will be discussed presently, and when a resolution on legal principles governing activities in outer space was finally adopted by the UN General Assembly in December 1963, the Soviet Union quietly dropped its previous insistence on condemnation of reconnaissance satellites in this document.[14] Finally, while arguing in general for the "demilitarization" of space, Soviet space law writers, such as E. A. Korovin, Chairman of the Space Law Commission of the USSR Academy of Sciences, have also stated that the demilitarization of space cannot be realized until disarmament on earth has been achieved.[15]

The Soviet position on space in the sphere of international law thus seems contrived for blaming the United States for "militarizing" outer space and for inhibiting U.S. developments considered detrimental to Soviet interests. At the same time it leaves the Soviet Union free to take such steps as it may consider necessary to its security. Meanwhile, Soviet military literature shows a somewhat parallel effort, apparently designed to lay the groundwork for whatever military space measures the Soviet leadership may choose to sanction. There is some possibility, at the same time, that a certain amount of special pleading may be involved in military statements on the subject, particularly if the Soviet political leadership should still find itself uncertain at this juncture over how deeply to become committed to a military competition in space.

Among the first statements to present an emphatic case for Soviet military interest in space, on the grounds that the Soviet Union could not afford to ignore U.S. military space preparations, was a series of two articles in March 1962 in *Red Star*. The author was V. Larionov, then a lieutenant colonel, whose contributions to Soviet military literature have grown impressively since that time. In the first article, Larionov argued that the United States had set its sights on a long-term program for the military mastery of space because it could not hope to catch up with the Soviet Union "in the next few years." No mention of Soviet response to this challenge was made in the first article, although in some passages Larionov seemed to be calling the attention of the Soviet leadership to the advantages of military space capabilities. He said, for example, that

the creation and employment of various space systems and apparatus can lead immediately to major strategic results. The working out of efficient means of striking from space and of combat with space weapons in combination with nuclear weapons places in the hands of the strategic leadership a new, powerful means of affecting the military-economic potential and the military might of the enemy.[16]

In the second article several days later, Larionov was more explicit. Here he not only argued that the Soviet Union must counter the United States with military space measures of its own, but also suggested that the status of Soviet space technology gave the Soviet Union a head start in such a competition. After accusing the United States of preparing a large array of military space systems from bombardment satellites to anti-satellite weapons, Larionov said that the Soviet Union

cannot ignore all these preparations of the American imperialists and is forced to adopt corresponding measures in order to safeguard its security against an attack through outer space. It is no secret that the technical basis for the launching of earth satellites and spaceships is the ballistic missile and its guidance system. Such complex, perfected technical equipment, which is many times superior to American technology, is in the possession of the Soviet Union.[17]

The Larionov formula has since been taken up by others. Both editions of the Sokolovskii work, for example, dwelt on American military space plans as the basis for declaring that "the imperialists must be opposed with more effective weapons and methods of using space for defense."[18] Both volumes also made the assertion that: "It would be a mistake to allow the imperialists to gain any superiority in this area."[19] In the 1963 edition, several expanded passages accused the United States of stepping up its program for military exploitation of space, and charged that the U.S. program attaches special significance to using the moon for military purposes:

Research is being conducted to determine the military potential of the moon. Studies are being made of the possibility of using the moon for communications, reconnaissance and as a base for cosmic means of attack.[20]

Another accusation, based on an article in the U.S. periodical press, was that the United States contemplates placing bombardment satellites armed with nuclear weapons in orbits "passing over the Soviet Union."[21] Since the new Sokolovskii volume went to press before the adoption in October 1963 of the United Nations resolution against mass destruction weapons in space, it is not clear whether the Sokolovskii authors would choose to soften this particular accusation if they had it to do over again. However, a similar accusation was repeated later in November 1963 by Major General Baryshev,[22] and in a December 1963 article another Soviet military writer charged that the U.S. Dyna-Soar program "confirmed once again the insidious intentions of the imperialists . . . to turn the cosmos into an arena of war,"[23] notwithstanding prior announcement by the U.S. Department of Defense that the Dyna-Soar program was being canceled.[24]

Along with the theme that U.S. military activities in space justify corresponding measures on the Soviet part, Soviet spokesmen have sounded regularly the companion theme that the Soviet Union would possess the edge in any military space competition that might develop. In January 1963, for example, a Soviet scientist pointed out that "powerful Soviet rockets and heavy satellites can carry out military tasks much better than low-capacity American rockets and satellites."[25] In the same connection, Khrushchev and others have called attention to the military significance of Soviet manned space flights, as when Marshal Malinovskii said after the twin flights of Vostoks III and IV in August 1962: "Let our enemies know what techniques and what soldiers our Soviet power has at its disposal."[26]

SOVIET THINKING ON THE MILITARY SIGNIFICANCE OF SPACE

Since the mid-1950's, occasional Soviet expressions of interest in the military utility of space have found their way into print, and have included reference to the military potential of satellites for both reconnaissance and bombardment purposes.[27] However, the development of a coherent doctrine of space warfare seems to have been inhibited by the necessity to preserve a propaganda image of the Soviet Union as a country interested solely in the exploration of space for peaceful purposes. Only in the past few years, parallel to the increasing attention given to alleged U.S. military ambitions in space, can one find an emerging set of Soviet views on the possible significance of space in Soviet military strategy. Even so, the Soviet literature on the subject remains rather uninformative as to the specific direction which any Soviet military space projects might take.

As noted previously, the first Larionov article in March 1962 called attention to the "major strategic results" which might be attained by space operations, and other Soviet military literature has since reflected the view that outer space must be included as a likely domain of military operations in the future. The revised Sokolovskii edition, for example, in speaking of the spatial dimensions which would characterize a future war, included a new statement:

The concept of the "spatial scope" of a future war must be basically amended, because military operations can also embrace the cosmos.[28]

Apart from acknowledging the significance of space operations in general, the Soviets have focused their interest and concern upon the need to develop antisatellite capabilities. Incentives for such interest are suggested by the intense Soviet political campaign against reconnaissance satellites and Soviet insistence that "the right of a state to destroy a satellite-spy . . . is indisputable."[29] In June 1960, when the U-2 incident was fresh in his mind, Khrushchev told an audience in Bucharest, with apparent reference to possible reconnaissance satellite operations, that "these efforts, too, will be paralyzed and a rebuff administered."[30] Marshal Malinovskii in early 1963 indicated that Soviet air defenses were not only expected to counter aircraft and missile attacks, but also to deal with reconnaissance satellites. The defense forces, he said, were "assigned the extremely important role of combating an aggressor's modern means of nuclear attack and his attempt to reconnoiter our country from the air and from space."[31]

In their revised edition, the Sokolovskii authors introduced some new references to the need for antisatellite as well as anti-missile defenses.[32] They also indicated that antisatellite defenses would be intended for use against not only reconnaissance satellites, but also other types of satellites carrying out "the widest variety of missions," including communications, navigation, and bombardment.[33] It was not made clear by the Sokolovskii authors whether the antisatellite defenses the Soviets have in mind would be ground- or space-based systems, or both. Neither was it made clear what progress has been achieved toward setting up such defenses. One statement in the revised edition said that "under contemporary conditions, an important task is to create a reliable system of antisatellite defense,"[34] from which it might be inferred that the job still lies ahead. Another comment suggested less subtly that solutions to the problem of antisatellite defense are still, figuratively speaking, somewhat up in the air:

It is still too early to predict what direction the solution of this problem will take. However, as means of attack are developed, so will means of defense be created.[35]

In this connection, when discussing antimissile and anti-satellite defense research in the West, the new volume twice alluded to a number of esoteric developments that were not mentioned in the 1962 edition. In addition to high-speed neutrons and electromagnetic flux, cited in the first edition, the new text also mentioned the following developments:

Various systems of radiation, anti-gravity, anti-matter, plasma (ball lightning) etc., are under study as a means of destroying missiles. Particular attention is devoted to lasers (death rays), and it is believed that in the future powerful lasers will be able to destroy any missile or satellite.[36]

The extent of Soviet interest in the development of bombardment satellite systems has been less clearly delineated than in the case of antisatellite weapons, even though Soviet space technology presumably is capable of developing bomb-carrying satellites.[37] On a number of occasions, Soviet spokesmen have drawn attention to the convertibility of Soviet manned space vehicles into bombardment vehicles, as did Khrushchev in December 1961 when he said: "If we could bring the spaceships of Yuri Gagarin and Gherman Titov to land at a prearranged spot, we could of course send up 'other payloads' and 'land' them wherever we wanted."[38] In early 1963, Marshal Biriuzov, then commander of the Soviet strategic missile forces, apparently meant to convey a similar suggestion when he said: "It has now become possible, at a command from the earth, to launch missiles from satellites at any desired time and at any point in the satellite's trajectory."[39] Since adoption of the October 1963 UN resolution against orbiting nuclear weapons in space, Soviet suggestions of this sort have ceased, although as noted above, the United States is still sporadically charged with harboring plans for orbital-bombardment satellites. Whether the Soviet Union might pursue the development of such systems despite the UN resolution, on the grounds that it was merely taking precautionary measures against possible capitalist perfidy, is a question on which opinion may vary, but only time will furnish the answer.

Another direction of potential Soviet interest in space is the development of reconnaissance capabilities, which Soviet literature had canvassed in some detail as early as 1959.[40] Owing perhaps to the Soviet effort to discredit any American development of reconnaissance satellites, there have been no specific expressions of Soviet intent to play this game. However, the capacity to take photographs from satellites has been demonstrated by the Soviet cosmonauts themselves,[41] and detailed discussions of the photographic potentialities of satellites have appeared in Soviet literature at various times.[42] The high premium placed by Soviet military men on the role of reconnaissance under modern conditions would suggest that they have not remained indifferent to the contribution which satellites might make to this requirement. A typical expression of Soviet emphasis on the importance of reconnaissance was given by Colonel General S. Shtemenko in February 1963. He wrote:

The role of reconnaissance in modern war has been increased to an extraordinary degree by the destructive power of nuclear weapons and the great speed and accuracy of their delivery to target. The rapid and accurate selection of targets for nuclear strikes can decide the outcome of battle . . . On the other hand, poorly organized reconnaissance can result in great expenditure of nuclear weapons to no purpose, and in the last analysis, in failure to fulfill combat tasks.[43]

Another comment indicative of Soviet interest in reconnaissance satellites was made by Alexei Adzhubei, editor of *Izvestiia* and Khrushchev's son-in-law, during a visit to Finland in September 1963. In a speech to the Paasikivi Society published in a Finnish newspaper, Adzhubei referred to publication in the West of a photograph of Moscow, allegedly "taken by a satellite at an altitude of 750 kilometers, in which the headquarters of *Izvestiia* can be seen clearly." Adzhubei then went on to say: "We don't publish these kinds of photographs, but I think we could publish a similar picture of New York taken by our satellite."[44] Khrushchev himself later made the point more specific when, in a conversation with former United States Senator William H. Benton in Moscow in May 1964, he reportedly said: "If you wish, I can show you photos of military bases taken from outer space. I will show them to President Johnson if he wishes."[45] Khrushchev's reference to satellite reconnaissance photography by the Soviet Union was made in connection with a suggestion to Mr. Benton that such space photography had eliminated the need for aircraft reconnaissance flights by the United States over Cuba.

Chapter XVII

COALITION ASPECTS
OF SOVIET STRATEGY

Soviet strategic thinking in the postwar period has been pre-occupied largely with problems relating to the confrontation between the United States and its NATO allies on the one hand and the Soviet bloc on the other. Increasingly over the past few years, however, the Soviet Union has been obliged to turn part of its attention inward, as it were, to questions arising from internal military relations within the communist camp. Two phenomena have been largely responsible: one, the gradual emergence of the Warsaw Pact countries toward a status of somewhat greater autonomy within the Soviet camp; the other, the eruption of the bitter and far-reaching dispute between Moscow and Peking. In this chapter, we shall touch upon some of the developments in Soviet strategic thinking and internal bloc military relations which have accompanied each of these phenomena.

DEVELOPMENT OF WARSAW PACT COOPERATION

Looking at the development of the Warsaw Pact over the past nine years, one is struck by the irony that what began primarily as a paper mechanism to counter the entry of West Germany into NATO has become gradually an institution with a meaningful role to play in Soviet coalition strategy. This is not to suggest that the Warsaw Pact countries wield anything comparable to the weight of the European NATO partners in the determination of coalition strategies on the respective sides. Nevertheless, with the passage of time, the military cooperation of the Eastern European countries seems to have become more important to the Soviet Union in both a political and a practical sense.

At its inception in May 1955, as a Soviet-engineered response to ratification of the Paris Agreements on March 26, 1955, the Warsaw Pact[1] apparently was intended as a device to permit Soviet negotiations with NATO, as one observer has put it, "on the basis of two 'equal' European security organizations."[2] The new Warsaw Treaty supplemented an existing series of bilateral mutual assistance treaties,[3] under which the Soviet Union presumably could have pursued any necessary military arrangements with the East European countries had not a collective pact seemed to be a desirable political-propaganda instrument for dealing with the West. Early Soviet propaganda treatment of the Warsaw Pact and the rare meetings of its formal organs, together with apparent failure to flesh out these bodies in the first few years of the Pact's existence, tended to support the view that its symbolic political role initially carried far more weight in Soviet eyes than its cooperative military aspects.[4]

Two major bodies were provided by the Warsaw Treaty to carry out the functions of the Pact. One of these was a Political Consultative Committee, whose meetings have been attended normally by Party First Secretaries or government Premiers, together with their Foreign and Defense Ministers.[5] In addition to its political functions, this organ is said to have "important functions in military matters," which include decisions on "strengthening of the defense capability and organization of the Joint Forces" and "matters of delivery of arms and other materials."[6] The second major organ set up by the Warsaw Treaty was a Joint Command. Its announced function is "to carry out direct coordination of military operations" and "to prepare beforehand for effective defense in the event of armed attack."[7]

The Joint Command has always been headed by a Soviet officer. There have been two commanders-in-chief to date, Marshal I. Konev, and the incumbent, Marshal A. Grechko. The commander-in-chief is assisted by deputies, who are the Ministers of Defense of the Pact countries and who nominally are supposed to retain "command of the armed forces of each member state allocated to the joint forces."[8] It is interesting and perhaps revealing that this concept was contradicted by the description in both Sokolovskii editions of the way Warsaw Pact command arrangements might be expected to work out in wartime. The Sokolovskii formula stated:

Operational units including armed forces of different socialist countries can be created to conduct joint operations in military theaters. The command of these units can be assigned to the Supreme High Command of the Soviet armed forces, with the representation of the supreme high commands of the allied countries.[9]

Only after thus establishing the principle of Soviet control did the Sokolovskii authors add that: "In some military theaters, the operational units of the allied countries will be under their own supreme high command." Militarily, the concept of Soviet control of operations, and presumably of strategic direction of a war as well, doubtless makes sound logic from the Soviet viewpoint, but given the growing strength of nationalist sentiment in most of the Eastern European countries, it may add some political strain to intrabloc relations.

The path to closer military cooperation among the Warsaw Pact countries in the earlier days of the treaty was by no means smooth. The crushing of the Hungarian rebellion in 1956 by the Soviet army certainly dealt a setback to the idea of a socialist military alliance based on common goals, and the apparently narrow margin of decision against applying similar treatment to Gomulka's defiance of the Soviet Union probably did not bolster a sense of common cause. At the same time, however, events in the fall of 1956 did have the effect of prompting the Soviet Union to negotiate a series of "status-of-forces" agreements with various East European countries in the course of the next year, and may also have led the Soviet Union eventually to conclude that closer military relationships under the aegis of the Warsaw Pact was the best way to avoid future Hungarys.

These relationships were already close in some respects, of course, particularly on a bilateral basis, for the Soviet Union had largely equipped and trained the national forces of the new communist regimes in Eastern Europe in the early 1950's. With respect to air defense arrangements, which apparently became more closely integrated with those of the Soviet Union from around 1955 on,[10] there was necessarily a rather high degree of collaboration. The principal outward sign of change in over-all military relationships in the late 1950's and early 1960's was a greater Soviet tendency to stress the joint strength of the socialist countries and their cooperation,[11] culminating finally in a series of well-publicized joint military exercises in 1961 and 1962.

This process of upgrading the Warsaw Pact publicly in terms of common defense of the socialist camp was typified by two statements of Marshal Grechko, uttered two years apart. On May 9, 1960, he said:

The might of the Soviet army is a reliable safeguard of world peace, a reliable guarantee of the security of our Motherland's borders, a guarantee of the security of the fraternal socialist states.[12]

Two years later, he said:

Together with the Soviet armed forces, the fraternal armies of the Warsaw Pact countries are vigilantly standing guard over the peace.[13]

The trend toward emphasis on the joint strength of the Warsaw Pact countries became particularly noticeable as part of the Soviet military reaction to heightened tension over Berlin in the summer of 1961, when the first of several joint Warsaw Pact military exercises was held.[14] The following year, three additional exercises took place, involving Soviet forces in joint maneuvers at one location or another with all of the East

European countries except Bulgaria. In early 1962, a Soviet general wrote that "the joint armed forces of the Warsaw Pact countries have grown qualitatively and have become still stronger during the past year."[15] Another officer, appraising the exercises of the previous year, wrote in 1963: "The joint exercises conducted recently by a number of the armies of the Warsaw Pact countries have proved that the joint armed forces are ready at any moment to deal the aggressor a destructive retaliatory blow."[16] The same officer, Colonel S. Lesnevskii, stated in a long article on the Warsaw Pact later in 1963 that cooperation among the Pact countries had increased their military capabilities and resulted in their "closing ranks in a single military family."[17] Marshal Malinovskii spoke even more dramatically when he declared in 1963 that the "pact was sealed in blood."[18] In line with this frequent recitation of measures that were helping to bring the "socialist armies closer together," the published report of a conference on military doctrine in Moscow in May 1963 noted that one of the items seriously discussed was the necessity of developing "a single military doctrine" for all of the Warsaw Pact countries.[19]

While it might be inferred from this latter comment that military collaboration had not proceeded quite as far as other accounts sought to convey, the fact remains that the Soviet Union has found it useful to stress the close military bonds among the Warsaw Pact countries. To what extent this effort derives from military as distinct from political considerations, it is not easy to say. The two are closely interrelated. Perhaps the principal Soviet motive can be traced to the fact that, in addition to opposing NATO, Soviet forces in Eastern Europe have long had a kind of garrison function to insure that regimes sympathetic to Soviet policy remain in power, as Hungary rather vividly demonstrated. As the countries of Eastern Europe have come gradually to acquire a larger measure of autonomy in the economic, cultural, and even political spheres, the naked garrison aspect of a Soviet military presence in Eastern Europe would become increasingly awkward were it not for the Warsaw Pact, which confers collective sanction on the Soviet presence under the name of defense against the NATO threat. The differing Polish and Soviet interpretations of the Hungarian episode suggest that there is still room for friction and misunderstanding between the East European countries and the Soviet Union as to how far the Warsaw Pact can be stretched to cover Soviet policing actions.[20] Nevertheless, the Pact would certainly seem of greater value to the Soviet Union today for its internal cohesive functions than it probably appeared nine years ago.

In the strictly military sphere, some advantages for the Soviet Union doubtless arise from closer cooperation with other Warsaw Pact armed forces. In peacetime, Soviet access to maneuver areas, transit, logistic support, and the like are probably simplified under the Pact. In the event of local hostilities, involving perhaps West Germany, closer Soviet control of national armed forces might be facilitated by the Pact, although this would not appear to be a central consideration, especially as long as Soviet policy continues to keep nuclear weapons out of the hands of other Pact forces, which appears to have been the case up to now. Should major hostilities occur, there would be obvious advantages in having carried out prior maneuvers, joint planning and staff arrangements, and so on. However, on the key question—the extent to which a growing sense of Soviet military dependence on other Warsaw Pact armed forces may have accounted for upgrading of the Pact in the past few years—there is no ready answer.

Soviet strategic missile strength, particularly in the large medium-range missile forces trained against Western Europe from USSR territory proper, would seem, on the surface, to have reduced somewhat Soviet dependence on the East European countries. Another point—the reliability of the East European armies in Soviet eyes—also is germane. In this connection, it is perhaps significant that the modernist school of Soviet military thought has never brought up the point that existence of large East European armed forces mitigates the requirement for Soviet mass armies on the earlier scale, although this would seem to be a logical argument for the modernists to make. This suggests that the Soviet Union may entertain some doubt as to how much reliance may be placed on other Pact forces, and that Soviet military plans may be based on meeting the requirements of warfare in the European theater essentially from their own resources.

Finally, Soviet emphasis on the collective strength and military unity of the Warsaw Pact countries has run curiously parallel to the worsening of relations with Peking, which suggests that one function of the Warsaw Pact cooperation theme is that of a counter to Chinese charges that the Soviet Union is guilty of splitting the communist camp and of placing its own interests ahead of those of other communist states.

SINO-SOVIET MILITARY RELATIONS

In retrospect, it has come to be felt by many students of Sino-Soviet affairs that military relations between these two largest communist states were never as close as popularly assumed, even before open disclosure of the growing rift between them in 1960.[21] While this is not the place to undertake a full review of earlier Sino-Soviet military relations, it may be useful to note briefly the background against which the post-1960 airing of differences over matters of strategy and military policy has developed.

The seeds of future discord apparently were sown before the Chinese Communists came to power on the mainland in late 1949. Even during the postwar years when the Chinese Communists were fighting the final chapter of the Civil War against the Nationalists, Stalin evidently held a skeptical view of Chinese Communist military prospects, as indicated by his comments in 1948 to Dimitrov and Kardelj.[22] Stalin seemed to be hedging his bets by extending military help and advice sparingly to Mao and by maintaining relations with Chiang's government until the Chinese Communists took over.[23] With the Sino-Soviet Treaty of February 14, 1950, a formal military alliance aimed principally at Japan and the United States came into being. Under this agreement, and presumably its various unpublished protocols, the Soviet Union began to furnish military advisors and equipment to China.

In the fall of 1950, when Soviet expectation of a quick North Korean victory was upset and Chinese "volunteers" had to be committed on a large scale, Moscow and Peking faced perhaps the first real strain on their cooperative military relationship. The Soviets found themselves obliged to rely on the Chinese to salvage a war they themselves had apparently begun,[24] and in turn Moscow had to contemplate the possibility that the war might expand to a nuclear level at a time when the Soviet military posture was far from adequate to deal with a nuclear threat. In any event, however, the threat did not materialize and the Sino-Soviet partners were spared the "agonizing re-appraisal" of their situation which events might have forced upon them. By the time the war was closed out after Stalin's death in 1953, the Chinese had benefited greatly from Soviet aid in building up modern, regular military forces.[25] At the same time, however, Chinese dependence on the Soviet Union had greatly increased. This was particularly true with regard to the future, for if China was to acquire the kind of nuclear military power possessed by the Soviet Union and the United States, and the technical-industrial base to support it, Moscow's help in rather massive doses was necessary.[26]

Apparently, this help was never to become available as freely as the Chinese would have liked, although in the period from 1954 to 1960, the Soviet Union did prove more cooperative in some respects than in Stalin's time. Following the Khrushchev-

Bulganin visit to Peking in late 1954, for example, some of the earlier hard bargains driven by Stalin were relaxed: Port Arthur was turned back to the Chinese in 1955, and the arrangement for exclusive Soviet exploitation of Sinkiang uranium was revoked. Increased help in building up Chinese industry, including an indigenous arms industry, also was forthcoming, and in 1955 a scientific-technical agreement was signed. This was to be followed in October 1957—as the polemics subsequently revealed—by a secret treaty dealing with "new technology for national defense."[27]

Nevertheless, despite Soviet cooperation with Peking from 1955 to 1960, a rather tight rein apparently was kept on Soviet military commitments to the Chinese during this period.[28] This included the somewhat ambiguous Soviet backing of Mao's Taiwan Straits venture of 1958, which took the form of a warning from Khrushchev to President Eisenhower on September 18, 1958, that the Soviets would retaliate with nuclear weapons in the event of a U.S. nuclear attack against China.[29] It also has since become known that during this period Sino-Soviet relations became seriously snarled over the question of nuclear assistance to China, with Peking now charging that on June 20, 1959, the Soviet Union "unilaterally tore up" the new technology agreement of October 15, 1957, and "refused to provide China with a sample of an atomic bomb and technical data concerning its manufacture."[30] In short, the strains which have since become evident in Sino-Soviet military relations were already well advanced before the open rift of mid-1960.

The principal issues of a military nature exposed during the Sino-Soviet polemics since 1960 tend to spill over well beyond the bounds of strictly military considerations. This is certainly the case with regard to the central question of war and peace. The Soviet leadership, sobered by its understanding of the consequences of nuclear warfare and as yet the sole custodian of nuclear capabilities within the communist camp, has perforce been saddled with the responsibility of taking practical steps to avoid the risk of nuclear war. The Chinese, long-inclined to expect greater political dividends from Soviet military power than the Russians themselves,[31] and unencumbered with practical responsibility for the control of weapons they do not possess, have been more assertive in urging pressure upon the West under the umbrella of Soviet missile and space accomplishments. To some extent, the Chinese view may be colored by their own experience in the Korean War and in Southeast Asia, where rather heavy pressures upon the West did not bring a nuclear response.

These differences of attitude have come to a focus in Chinese criticism of the way the Soviet Union has been conducting the policy of peaceful coexistence—what one observer has called Moscow's own "theory of containment" directed against the West. Perhaps Chinese criticism is basically a fear that the tactical device of peaceful coexistence, by which the Soviet leaders hope to regulate pressure on the West so as not to risk a nuclear disaster, may become in the course of time a way of life—a mellowing of earlier militant communism, with gradual divergence between the long-range aims of the world communist movement and the national interests of the Soviet Union.

High on the list of specific issues over which the Soviet Union and China have fallen out is the Chinese determination to break into the "nuclear club," most graphically expressed by the Chinese avowal to go "with or without pants" for this purpose if necessary.[32] While it is not clear how far the Soviets had gone in helping the Chinese toward a nuclear capability before they had second thoughts on the subject, we know now from the polemical exchanges mentioned above that Sino-Soviet relations deteriorated rapidly after the alleged abrogation in June 1959 of Soviet commitments to furnish a sample bomb and weapons production data. Soviet second thoughts on the desirability of furnishing other advanced military items to the Chinese also are evident. In June 1959 Khrushchev told Averell Harriman that the Soviet Union already had sent some missiles to China (he did not specify whether with or without nuclear warheads or Soviet crews) to help defend it against Taiwan.[33] However, somewhere along the line further Soviet largesse ceased, and China has since been denied even aircraft of up-to-date types furnished by the Soviet Union to such non communist countries as Indonesia and Egypt.[34]

Why the Soviet Union decided to withhold nuclear assistance to China is open to speculation. Concern over being drawn by the Chinese into a nuclear confrontation with the United States, particularly after the Taiwan episode of 1958, is one possible motive. This is given some weight by rather frequent Soviet accusations, beginning with Khrushchev's speech of December 12, 1962, on Cuba, that the Chinese hope to provoke a U.S.-Soviet nuclear war, while themselves "sitting it out"—more or less in the role of *tertius gaudens,* waiting to pick up the pieces.[35] A second possibility is that the Soviet leaders may have calculated erroneously that nuclear denial would force the Chinese to modify some other aspect of their behavior not to Soviet liking. Signs that there was internal Chinese division over the question of jeopardizing Soviet military aid or "going it alone" may have encouraged Moscow to believe that this pressure tactic would work.[36] A third Soviet motive which has been professed openly in connection with the test ban dialogue is that, if the Soviet Union were to furnish nuclear weapons to China, the United States would follow suit by giving them to countries like West Germany and Japan, which, in the Soviet view, would only "intensify the arms race" and "complicate the defense of the socialist camp."[37]

Closely related to the issue of withholding nuclear weapons from China as a source of Sino-Soviet friction has been the question of how firmly Soviet deterrent power is committed to the support of Chinese interests. Ultimately, this issue brings the very validity of the Sino-Soviet Treaty itself into question.

Soviet assurances have been given in the course of the polemics that the Soviet nuclear-missile shield extends to China. Indeed, this is part of the Soviet rationale for withholding weapons.[38] At the same time, the Soviets have left no doubt that there are limits to their commitment,[39] and that it can be considered good only so long as the Chinese take their policy cues from Moscow. As Marshal Malinovskii put it in January 1962, Soviet military power always stands ready to defend "those socialist states *friendly* to us."[40] Another Soviet Marshal, Eremenko, put it more picturesquely in October 1963, when he quoted an old Russian proverb to the Chinese: "Do not spit into the well, because you may one day need drinking water."[41]

For their part, the Chinese have visibly chafed at being dependent on Moscow, and have made plain their determination to acquire nuclear weapons by their own efforts, stressing that all of China's problems, including those of "national defense," can be solved without Soviet help.[42]

The question of the policy to be pursued with regard to national-liberation struggles and local wars has been another vexed issue between Moscow and Peking. As our previous discussion in Chapter X has suggested, the Soviets seem to be seeking a more flexible position on the escalation potential of local struggles, partly to reduce their vulnerability to Chinese charges of "capitulationism," which grew more strident after the Cuban crisis of 1962. The Soviet Union has not remained wholly on the defensive, however, with regard to Peking's pretensions to a superior doctrine for winning revolutionary wars. They not only have counterattacked by reminding Peking that both the socialist camp and national-liberation movements live under the protection of Soviet nuclear power. They also have even accused the Chinese of courting war on the basis of Maoist military theories that would pit man power against nuclear weapons. This line of attack was pursued in October 1963 by Major General Kozlov, military correspondent of the Soviet news agency *Novosti*, who baited Mao Tse-tung in the process.

Referring to the "strategy and tactics for the victory of the weak over the strong," developed by Mao in his work, *On Protracted War*, Kozlov said: "The tendency and idea that victory in a war can be won through 'weakness' is naïve, to say the least, if not criminal."[43] Stating that "it is impossible to entertain any hope of success when modern techniques of warfare are ignored," Kozlov charged that the Chinese idea of "reducing everything solely to a numerical superiority over the enemy in the number of troops" would simply "doom small nations to hopelessness." Further, said Kozlov, in trying "to impose their limited experience and corresponding theories as a guide for all, the Chinese leaders . . . distort the Marxist-Leninist theory of war and do great harm to the communist cause."

On the other hand, the Chinese have also made an issue of the man-versus-technology question. As noted earlier in Chapter VIII, several Chinese statements on this subject have seemed to be calculated to exacerbate internal Soviet political-military relations by appealing to sentiment unsympathetic to Khrushchev's military theories within some circles of the Soviet military establishment. In an interview with Japanese correspondents on October 28, 1963, for example, Foreign Minister Chen Yi pointedly observed that in his opinion "the CPSU, the Soviet people, and the Red Army will not readily give up their friendship toward China."[44] A more specific stroke to separate Khrushchev from the Soviet military was delivered in the Chinese statement of November 18, 1963, which attacked Khrushchev for "nuclear fetishism" and for lopsided emphasis on technology over man. Declaring that while the Soviet army remains "a great force safeguarding world peace," the Chinese also said that at the same time:

Khrushchev's whole set of military theories runs completely counter to Marxist-Leninist teachings on war and the army. To follow his erroneous theories will necessarily involve disintegrating the army . . . [45]

Besides the issues which have been publicly aired in the Sino-Soviet polemics by the participants themselves, signs of friction over other matters of military cooperation have come to light from time to time. Edward Crankshaw, the British writer, disclosed in an article in February 1961 that one of the concrete issues which had come up during the behind-the-scenes arguments at the Conference of 81 Communist Parties in Moscow in November–December 1960 concerned a plan for a joint Sino-Soviet naval command in the Pacific.[46] Presumably the Chinese charged that the Soviet Union wished to impose an unacceptable subordinate status on China in this arrangement. Raymond Garthoff, in the *Annals* essay previously cited, speculates that Chinese sensitivity over equality of status may have similarly prevented full integration of air defense systems. Newspaper reports of border clashes in Sinkiang and of the strengthening of garrisons by both sides along their frontiers in Inner Asia,[47] while possibly exaggerated, may also reflect more friction in Sino-Soviet military relations than is supposed to occur among communist states. In this connection, it is interesting that recently released secret Chinese Communist army documents of 1960 and 1961 contained a directive on the need to preserve the security of the Sino-Soviet frontiers of China.[48]

Although the deterioration of bonds between Moscow and Peking has gone much farther than the shrewdest prophet might have foreseen a decade ago, one may rightly hesitate to predict the future of Sino-Soviet military relations. At one extreme, it is not inconceivable that at some future date the two sides may find themselves shooting at each other, although this does not seem likely unless their political relations decline even beyond the point they have reached today. Both sides certainly have great cause to maintain some semblance of unity vis-à-vis the Western alliance, and if the choice presented to the Soviet Union were either to assist China or see the mainland wrested from communist control, one might perhaps expect the Soviet Union to lend a helping hand. Likewise, if the Soviet Union were to become involved in a major war originating outside of the Far East, China's fulfillment of her treaty obligations to the USSR might be expected, although uncertainty as to what form Chinese support might take is likely to be a touchy problem of Soviet strategy.

Short of such extreme situations which make prediction hazardous, the tendency of both powers to define their policy in terms of their own interests seems likely to persist, with the prospect that their military relations will continue to be guarded and somewhat distant. Soviet strategy will probably reach a major crossroads of decision, however, when China becomes a nuclear power in her own right. At that time, the Soviet Union may have to choose between seeking an accommodation of some kind with her populous neighbor in the East, or making other arrangements for Soviet security which could greatly alter the structure of East-West relationships as they exist today.

Chapter XVIII

THE SEARCH FOR
A WAR-WINNING STRATEGY

While the Soviet leadership may be increasingly assailed by grave doubt that a nuclear war would serve any rational policy purposes at all, this sentiment has not yet seeped down into the main body of Soviet military doctrine and strategy. Soviet military literature provides no room for the concept of "no victor" in a future war. In this respect it continues to echo the doctrinaire ideological position that in the event of war, "the true balance of political, economic, and military forces" between the opposing systems "guarantees" victory for the communist camp.[1]

However, when it comes to laying down the military path toward attainment of the "decisive political and military goals" set for the Soviet camp in any future general war with the Western coalition, Soviet military theory seems still beset by conflicting views and uncertainty. It reflects a continuing ambivalence between the concepts of a short, decisive war and a long one, between the radical notion that the shock effect of modern strategic weapons might bring quick victory by paralyzing an enemy's will to resist and the more traditional view that victory is to be secured only by large-scale combined-arms operations, ending with occupation of the enemy's homeland.

The 1963 Sokolovskii edition seemed to be as much at cross-purposes with itself on this question as its predecessor. Key passages expressing both viewpoints were retained. For example, the prospect was still offered that "modern strategic weapons . . . make it possible to achieve decisive results in winning victory in war sometimes even without resort to tactical and field forces,"[2] and that a country subjected to "massive missile blows may find it necessary to surrender even before its armed forces have suffered decisive defeat."[3] On the other hand, the more traditional view was also repeated, with the argument that for final victory

it will be absolutely necessary to smash the enemy's armed forces completely, deprive him of strategic areas of deployment, liquidate his military bases, and occupy his strategically important regions.[4]

In other recent Soviet military discourse, perhaps as part of the traditionalist school's effort to hold its ground against the troop-reduction implications of Khrushchev's December 1963 policy statement, there has been a notable tendency to place renewed emphasis on the combined-arms formula for final victory. The *Red Star* series on the "revolution in military affairs," which began in January 1964 with General N. Lomov's two-part exposition on military doctrine, was particularly weighted in this direction.[5]

CONTINUED DEBATE ON CHOICE OF STRATEGY

Western commentary on the first edition of *Military Strategy* had pointed out that in terms of an over-all strategic design, the work failed "to lay out a promising formula for winning a war against the United States if such a war should have to be fought."[6] The alternative prospects for a Soviet military victory, given the strategies expounded in the book and the existing relationship of forces, appeared to rest either on the hope that U.S. morale would collapse early in the war or that the Soviet Union could outlast its adversary in a protracted struggle— neither of which possibilities offered a very convincing basis for a winning military strategy.

There was no effort at direct rebuttal of this assessment in the revised Sokolovskii edition. On the contrary, the authors seemed to lend further strength to the impression that Soviet military strategy still cannot provide a promising design for victory.

There was, in fact, a new suggestion that considerable internal debate still turns on questions of choice between a European land-war strategy and a strategy for a new kind of war involving a powerful transoceanic enemy. In a section of their book dealing with "Methods for Conducting Modern Warfare," the Sokolovskii authors included a new statement:

A debate continues around all of these questions. In essence, the argument is over the basic ways in which a future war will be conducted. Will it on the one hand be a land war with the employment of nuclear weapons as a means of supporting the operations of ground forces, or will it on the other hand be a fundamentally new kind of war in which the main means of solving strategic tasks will be missiles and nuclear weapons?[7]

It strikes one as somewhat strange to find the issue posed in this fashion, after the enormous outpouring of assertions from all schools of Soviet military thought that a new war would be "fundamentally" different from any past war and that strategic nuclear-missile weapons would be the "decisive means" employed. At the very least, the passage attests to the stubborn vitality of the traditionalist outlook, against which some military leaders still find it necessary to inveigh.[8] However, the question at issue in this case may have been less a matter of selecting one basic strategy versus the other, than of debate over ways in which theater campaigns on the Eurasian continent should be related in scope, character, and timing to global strategic operations. The latter are clearly of the greatest importance to Soviet military theorists seeking a strategy for any general war with the United States, as attested by the bulk of the material in the Sokolovskii book itself.

At the same time, an undercurrent of rivalry for command prestige and pride of place between old line field generals and a new generation of technically oriented, engineer-trained Soviet officers also seems to run through the debate over theater warfare versus strategic operations. This issue came to the surface in one of the January 1964 *Red Star* articles, written by Colonel General S. Shtemenko, Chief of Staff of the ground forces. The article dealt with the question whether the combined-arms commander could still be considered under modern conditions "the basic organizer of combat and operations." Shtemenko argued in the affirmative, but in the course of doing so, he noted that the higher technical qualifications required in modern warfare "gave a few comrades the opinion that a contemporary combined-arms commander must necessarily be an engineer."[9] While Shtemenko spoke only in the context of ground forces personnel, an extension of the field officer-versus-technical specialist issue to wider circles within the Soviet military establishment is implied by the unusual publicity build-up of the special qualities of strategic missile officers, to which we have referred earlier.

AWARENESS OF SHORTCOMINGS IN STRATEGIC DOCTRINE

In the revised Sokolovskii edition of 1963, there were several amendments which tended to show an awareness of logical shortcomings in current strategic doctrine, especially as regards the question of how an essentially continental land power like the Soviet Union can find a realistic strategy against an overseas adversary if it is obliged to follow the doctrine of invading and occupying the enemy's homeland. One such amendment occurred in a discussion of requirements for gaining "complete victory over an enemy." In the original version, it was said that this could be accomplished, after strategic nuclear attack against the enemy state,

only by completely defeating the enemy's armed forces and capturing his territory, *including the regions where strategic weapons are reliably protected.*[10] [Italics added.]

In the revised version, the words italicized above were omitted. The inference to be drawn here is twofold. First, that

228

the authors recognized a certain lack of reality in suggesting that the deep interior of a country like the United States could be readily invaded and captured by Soviet troops. Second, that somewhat greater weight may have been attached to the prospect of the enemy's collapse after nuclear bombardment, in which case occupying his territory would be a different matter from fighting one's way in.

A second amendment in the 1963 Sokolovskii edition concerning amphibious landing capabilities has already been discussed in connection with naval forces in Chapter XIV. This change, recognizing the need "to make provision for amphibious operations,"[11] was paralleled by other Soviet commentary which appeared to concede that, in a war against an overseas opponent, the ground forces cannot be expected to accomplish their mission of final destruction of the enemy and seizure of his territory without naval and amphibious operations.

The display of greater realism appears to take at least partial cognizance of an important lacuna in the doctrine of combined operations customarily expounded in Soviet military literature. It may be meant to suggest no more than that Soviet amphibious capabilities should be improved for operations around the Soviet periphery or in local conflict areas. However, if it is meant to imply the build-up of invasion capabilities on a more ambitious scale, it opens up perhaps larger questions than it answers, particularly as regards the matter of resources that would be required if the Soviet Union were to embark upon development of naval and amphibious capabilities on the scale required for invasion of an overseas opponent like the United States. In light of the pressure already exerted upon Soviet resources by other military and civilian requirements, an ambitious new program of this sort would seem difficult to realize unless the Soviet leaders were prepared to boost their defense budget very substantially—a step for which they apparently have little enthusiasm, as suggested by the trimming of the Soviet military budget for 1964.

Thus, while the advocates of the combined-arms path to victory may have worked some of the kinks out of their theory, they apparently have not sold their case so far as claims on the Soviet budget are concerned. Unless the Soviet political leadership places more confidence in the alternative strategy of a shock-effect first strike than it has manifested to date, this would appear to leave the search for a military path to victory in the category of an unfinished item on the Soviet agenda.

Chapter XIX

SOVIET MILITARY STRATEGY
AND DISARMAMENT

Soviet disarmament policy customarily has been part and parcel of an over-all strategy designed to improve the Soviet Union's military and political position, while strewing restraints in the path of its major adversaries.[1] The prospect that the Soviet military search for a war-winning strategy may prove unrewarding, or that victory in a nuclear war, even if attainable, may come to look increasingly barren, does not mean, of course, that the Soviet leadership will find it necessary or even possible to seek a disarmed world as the only alternative answer to the problem of Soviet security. The intermediate ground between armed peace and a disarmed world is broad and unexplored. How long it may take to cross it, no one can predict. But it seems safe to say that during whatever lengthy passage may lie ahead, the Soviet leaders will continue to regard Soviet military power as an indispensable safeguard of their security and a strong support for their political strategy.

At the same time, one must recognize that the character of the links between political and military power has been changing. In a world where nuclear war may seem no longer a rational course and where the possibilities of altering the political balance by use or threat of military action are otherwise fraught with great danger, Soviet attitudes toward the management of military power in the service of politics may well undergo change. Along with this process could come also some shift in the customary Soviet approach to disarmament. While the political-propaganda exploitation of the disarmament issue has been a central feature of Soviet disarmament policy,[2] we shall be primarily concerned in this chapter with the relationship of disarmament to Soviet military strategy and with Soviet military attitudes toward disarmament.

TIES BETWEEN MILITARY STRATEGY AND DISARMAMENT POLICY

It is hardly surprising that Soviet disarmament proposals have frequently been made with an eye to improving the Soviet strategic position or altering the military balance to Soviet advantage. This pattern is familiar in the history of disarmament negotiations generally, and in the Soviet case—as in pre-Soviet Russia—disarmament initiatives often have coincided rather closely with strategic and military needs.[3] Many of the various Soviet disarmament proposals since World War II have had a rather close connection with the evolving requirements of Soviet military strategy. This is not, however, to suggest that the timing and nature of these proposals were wholly a matter of subordinating other aspects of Soviet disarmament policy to immediate military considerations. It may be useful to recall a few examples of Soviet disarmament positions which have had a fairly obvious link with strategic developments. One of these occurred in the first years after the war in response to the 1946 Baruch Plan for international "control or ownership of all atomic energy activity potentially dangerous to world security."[4] After definitive rejection of the Baruch Plan in early 1947, the Soviet Union countered with demands for a ban on atomic weapons and destruction of all stocks.[5] This was followed by successive Soviet proposals from 1947 to 1949 to reduce all conventional forces by one-third, concurrently with a ban on atomic weapons.[6] The effect of these proposals would have been to deprive the United States of the new weapons in which it was superior to the Soviet Union and to leave the latter with far superior conventional strength in Europe.[7] The fact that the proposals were unlikely to be accepted would permit the Soviet Union in the meantime to pursue its own program to acquire nuclear weapons, unhindered by international constraints, which of course is what happened.

Another example of rather close correlation between Soviet strategic interests and disarmament policy is afforded by the major set of proposals put forward by the Soviet Union in May 1955, not long after Khrushchev forced Malenkov out of the leadership hierarchy. By 1955, the strategic situation had greatly changed. The Korean War was followed by a vigorous build-up of U.S. strategic delivery forces and the extension of a world-wide network of American bases, bringing home more forcefully than ever to the Soviet leadership the potential consequences of a nuclear war. In Europe, the portent of a stronger NATO was raised by the imminent re-arming of West Germany, also posing a troublesome new problem for Soviet strategy. While Soviet military power had not been neglected, and the U.S. nuclear monopoly had by now been broken, the strategic situation from the Soviet viewpoint was nevertheless deteriorating. Precisely at this juncture the Soviet Union put forward its new set of disarmament proposals in May 1955.[8] They called for a two-stage program, beginning with an immediate "freeze" of all forces, to be completed by the end of 1957. Conventional forces would be reduced to levels previously suggested by an Anglo-French plan,[9] and elimination of nuclear weapons would begin when 75 per cent of conventional reductions were completed. Among other significant provisions, liquidation of all military bases on foreign soil would begin in the first stage, and all countries would renounce the use of nuclear weapons. To prevent surprise attack, observers would be stationed at communications junctions, ports, and airfields. When completed, the program would leave the major powers with a fixed level of conventional forces, and with no nuclear weapons or foreign bases.

From the Soviet viewpoint, these proposals, if accepted, would have cleared the board of those aspects of Western military power which gave the Soviet leaders most concern. Soviet conventional superiority in Europe would be retained, German rearmament would be nipped in the bud, NATO and other Western alliances would come apart at the seams when U.S. bases were dismantled, and the Soviet Union would finally have abolished the threat of U.S. nuclear power.

Some of the subsequent Soviet disarmament proposals in the next years after 1955 also showed a continuing link with the changing strategic situation and Khrushchev's emergent military policies. For example, in early 1956, as Soviet nuclear capabilities were growing[10] and Khrushchev's ideas of substituting "firepower for man power" began to take shape, the Soviet Union proposed that nuclear disarmament be shelved for the time being while making a fresh effort to reduce conventional arms.[11] Although these suggestions led to no disarmament agreements, in 1956 the Soviet Union began unilateral troop cuts,[12] suggesting that Khrushchev hoped to obtain some disarmament "mileage" from measures to be taken anyway in connection with his military reforms. Somewhat similar efforts to turn unilateral troop reductions to account in the disarmament market were to be observed in Khrushchev's troop-cut statements in January 1960 and December 1963. Soviet troop reductions have also been cited in the context of the strategic dialogue, as discussed earlier, in Chapter III, to support the argument that the West cannot justify its arms programs on the grounds that the Soviet armed forces are larger than those of the West. Another argument has been that Soviet unilateral reductions have removed the Western pretext for insisting on inspection.[13]

The revival of a Litvinov-style proposal for general and complete disarmament, marked by Khrushchev's speech to the UN General Assembly in September 1959,[14] had quite different implications in a strategic sense than previous postwar Soviet proposals. It was much more tenuously linked with immediate military considerations, and aimed at bigger game. Politically, the sweeping Khrushchev proposal was doubtless meant to put the West on the defensive, with little expectation that it would lead to anything more concrete than prolonged and inconclusive negotiations from which the Soviet Union could hope to extract maximum political-propaganda advantages. On the outside chance that a plan somewhat along the lines of this and subsequent Soviet total disarmament proposals might be adopted,[15] what opportunities might it seem to offer from the Soviet viewpoint?

For one thing, the rather drastic change of relationships in a world abruptly and totally disarmed might seem likely to the Soviet leaders to create a favorable environment for well-organized revolutionary movements to gain the upper hand.[16] During the process of dismantling military machinery, for example, real opportunities could arise to accelerate "national-liberation movements" without fear of effective Western intervention. This seems to have been the sense of Mikoyan's reproach in early 1962 to Chinese critics of Soviet disarmament policy, when he said that disarmament as proposed by the Soviet Union would *not* make the national-liberation struggle more difficult, but rather would strip the imperialists of the means of "resisting the revolutionary actions of the proletariat and the peasantry."[17]

Even well short of a totally disarmed world, the Soviet leaders might feel that partial implementation of such measures as the scrapping of nuclear delivery systems and withdrawal from overseas military bases would bring about the demoralization and collapse of the Western alliance system—a political and strategic prize well worth seeking in itself.

Militarily, adoption of a Soviet-style plan would ultimately leave only national militia forces, equipped with light arms, for the maintenance of internal order. Units of national militia would also be made available to the UN Security Council for international peace-keeping purposes.[18] With the proportionately larger militia which the Soviet Union and its East European auxiliaries would have at their disposal, and protected by the veto in the Security Council, the Soviet leaders might feel that opportunities would arise to intervene in the event of civil uprisings in noncommunist countries of Western Europe.[19] The United States, of course, would have no means for coming to the rescue. The only cloud in this otherwise bright sky might be China, which presumably would possess even larger militia forces than the Soviet Union.

The possible advantages of a total disarmament plan to the Soviets would, of course, include an end to the risk that a nuclear war might destroy Soviet society, and the freeing of resources for nonmilitary purposes. It would also eliminate the problem of holding their own in a stepped-up arms race, although this problem might then be replaced by problems of keeping up in a "peace race" *à outrance*.

But however interested the Soviets might be in a radical replacement of present military arrangements by total disarmament, there are factors which doubtless work in the other direction. One of these is reluctance to trade off a powerful military machine and familiar security arrangements for the unproven benefits of disarmament. Another is a realistic view of the intimate dependence of Soviet political strategy on the authority of military power. Closely related to these considerations in the minds of the Soviet leaders is the conviction that Soviet deterrent power is mainly responsible for preventing war and protecting the political and territorial integrity of the Soviet bloc.

Still another factor is the persistent belief that communist superiority in the political, economic, and military elements of power must be attained before a new communist order can be expected to replace capitalism in the world. The possible future threat posed by China also enters the picture. And, finally, there is the unpalatable invasion of Soviet secrecy and the dilution of the Party's internal monopoly of power which would be implied by acceptance of international authority over the disarmament and peace-keeping processes.

This list, too, could be extended, but the point is evident that the Soviet leaders are not likely to embrace total disarmament all at once. What they might do is to show somewhat less concern for fashioning disarmament proposals so as to yield obviously one-sided military and political advantages for the Soviet Union, and somewhat more concern for measures promising to reduce the danger of war, to lighten the burden of armaments, and to control the character of the arms competition.

The possibility of employing arms control measures to reduce the tempo of the arms race and to channel it in directions which the Soviet Union might find less burdensome would seem to have a particular appeal to the Soviet leadership at a time when converging demands upon Soviet resources are great. If no positive gains for the Soviet military posture were forthcoming, an arms control program which prevented "weapons' gaps" from widening might still look attractive in terms of the relative correlation of forces between the two sides.

This raises again an important but as yet unanswered question bearing on the Soviet approach to disarmament. Does the Soviet leadership still consider that improvement of the Soviet Union's relative power position is an essential objective to be sought in disarmament negotiations, or does it now recognize areas of mutual interest in which both sides might give up something in order to attain a common benefit? The test-ban treaty signed on August 5 and ratified in September 1963, seems to have involved both of these elements. On the one hand, it probably contributed to some easing of international tension and may have marked a step toward slowing down the proliferation of nuclear weapons which both sides professed to find to their mutual interest. On the other hand, the Soviet Union was quick to observe that the treaty foreclosed testing of the kinds of weapons "in which superiority is on the side of the Soviet

Union," while permitting the Soviet Union "to conduct underground tests of nuclear weapons if necessary for the security interests of the Soviet Union and other socialist states."[20] The Soviet leaders themselves may be uncertain as to which of these criteria is the more important. The chances are, however, that even when the criterion of mutual interest enters the picture, as in the test-ban case, the Soviet leaders will continue to base their decisions essentially on self-interest.

SOVIET MILITARY ATTITUDES TOWARD DISARMAMENT

The role played by the Soviet military in the formulation of disarmament policy, and military interest in the technical aspect of a subject which obviously impinges closely upon military affairs, are matters on which very little light is shed by public Soviet discourse. Ritual advocacy of Soviet disarmament proposals is expected of and, as we shall note, obtained from military leaders, but their public interest in the subject seems to stop there. Soviet military literature itself is distinguished by an almost total indifference to disarmament and arms control as a technical problem of serious professional interest to military theorists and planners.

One cannot find—either in Soviet military publications or in the abundant output of political-propaganda organs on the subject of disarmament[21]—anything comparable to Western exploration of arms control techniques to lower risks of accidental war, to tighten command and control arrangements, and to help in the management of crisis situations.[22] Neither does Soviet writing furnish any equivalent to the growing body of Western literature in which various concepts of deterrence, strategic posture, and arms control are viewed as interrelated aspects of the international security problem. At the same time, it is true, as noted previously, that there has been some tendency of late for Soviet writers, especially in media designed mainly

for foreign readers, to employ the technical idiom of this literature even though continuing to attack its concepts.[23] In part, the
relative absence of a technical-analytical literature of disarmament in the Soviet Union can be explained by the fact that such
literature does not carry the emotional force and high moral tone
demanded by the general Soviet disarmament line. Secondly,
the treatment of sophisticated concepts on the interrelation of
arms control and strategy not only calls for spelling out more
details of Soviet military posture and strengths than normal
Soviet practice allows, but such concepts tend to make poor
propaganda for Soviet advocacy of radical and highly oversim-
plified disarmament solutions. Finally, the voluminous Soviet
literature on war itself provides the basic underpinning for the
Soviet disarmament position, which takes the view that arms
control schemes and concepts are attempts to "legalize" nuclear
war and the arms race.

The Soviet military outlook on disarmament customarily finds
expression in the formula that "as long as no agreement has
been reached and no universal disarmament implemented, the
Soviet Union and all other countries of the socialist camp are
maintaining and will continue to maintain their defense might
at the necessary level."[24] One gets the impression that, having
got this off his chest, the average Soviet military man goes
about his business with little further thought about disarmament
as a practical expectation to be reckoned with. The formula is
sometimes carried a bit further, however, to suggest that Soviet
military men are more willing to hang up their uniforms and call
it a day than their Western counterparts. Thus, Marshal A.
Eremenko declared in January 1964 that:

Some people in the West may find it incongruous that Soviet military
circles should join in advocating disarmament and the exclusion of
interstate wars from the life of society. It is well known that Western
military men try hard to prove . . . that a world nuclear war, or at
least a restricted, local one, is quite acceptable and even necessary.[25]

It is interesting that Marshal Eremenko's formula barring "interstate wars" left room for the continuance of what the Soviets define as "national-liberation struggles," even in a disarmed world. A colleague, the somewhat nebulous General Nevsky, offered another point omitted by Eremenko when he said earlier that "Soviet military men are willing to change their uniforms for civvies if the Soviet proposals for general and complete disarmament are carried out," because, said Nevsky: "They have no private interests running counter to the peace policy pursued by the Soviet government."[26]

This general picture of a Soviet military elite which stands ready and eager to dissolve itself is a conventional Soviet fiction which may have some basis in fact, but which hardly amounts to an accurate description of the complicated realities of Soviet life. Disbandment of the armed forces and their absorption into civil society would involve not only social and institutional problems of considerable magnitude, but also a difficult shift of values which the Soviet leadership has sought unremittingly to inculcate in the Soviet fighting man for the past four-and-a-half decades. To make light of these problems would suggest that the possibility of facing them on a large scale has not been taken very seriously.

At the same time, it should be recalled that the Soviet Union has carried out substantial demobilization programs in the postwar period.[27] While not comparable to uprooting the whole military elite and expunging its role in Soviet life, these programs are instructive on at least two counts. First, they *were* carried out, despite the dislocation of personal lives involved and over some opposition apparently from military leaders. Second, there *was* dissatisfaction and lowering of morale, and in at least one case—the January 1960 reduction program—the troop cuts were halted before completion. Military morale was not the only issue involved in this case, however, as we have pointed out earlier, in Chapter II.

Some of the "temporary" dislocations and problems experienced in the 1954–1959 period of demobilizations were rather frankly described in a speech by Marshal Malinovskii in January 1960, on the eve of a new round of cuts.[28] Rumblings of discontent and adjustment difficulties also found their way into print after the 1960 reduction program began, particularly with regard to officers, of whom some 250,000 were to be prematurely retired.[29] Even after suspension of the program in 1961, there were signs that re-employment of demobilized officers had not been solved, such as an appeal to reserve officers in *Red Star* in March 1962 to migrate to the Far East where farm help was needed.[30] A year later, partly as a response to continuing problems of readjustment, an extension of the January 20, 1960, decree providing benefits for discharged military men was announced in *Red Star*.[31]

Other glimpses into the state of the Soviet military mind suggest that the Soviet officer's feeling about his place in Soviet life and his dedication to military values, are somewhat more complicated phenomena than the fiction of the compliant officer would indicate. For example, some disenchantment over civilian unconcern for the hardships of the officer's life has occasionally found expression in the press. Testimony on this point was furnished by N. Makeev, the editor of *Red Star,* writing for a civilian audience in *Izvestiia,* in February 1963. In a bitter comment on the "unconcerned citizen," Makeev wrote: "What does he care that while he sleeps, thousands of officers tirelessly carry on their difficult duties . . . what does the unconcerned citizen care if the ten-times-wounded colonel has changed his place of service twelve times since the war . . ." Makeev concluded by reminding his civilian readers that the contribution of the officer to Soviet life is not less than that of "the farmer, the engineer, the agricultural specialist, or the doctor."[32]

Other Soviet military writers similarly have commented from time to time on civilian "misunderstanding" of military personnel and their contributions to Soviet society.[33] Such comments suggest that the Soviet officer corps nurses a wounded pride that would tend, at the least, to complicate its reassimilation into civilian life.

Sensitivity to undermining of the martial values and heroic deeds upon which the morale of the Soviet fighting man rests has also been displayed by the military leaders. Addressing a group of Soviet writers and artists in February 1964, for example, Marshal Malinovskii was critical of "incorrect tendencies" in portraying the last war, charging that various artistic works contained "pacifist themes and abstract negation of war" and brought "irresolute and petty people" to the center of the stage. Conceding that war was cruel and devastating, Malinovskii said nevertheless: "We reject such a one-sided approach to this important subject."[34] While pacifist values are not condoned in the Soviet Union, and no popular literature of the *Fail Safe* genre is permitted to portray the Soviet soldier as a greater threat to his country's security than the enemy,[35] it is nevertheless interesting that Marshal Malinovskii should display concern over the possible contamination of Soviet youth by antimilitary art.

Such occasional glimpses into the military state of mind in the Soviet Union do not, of course, furnish grounds for concluding that Soviet military men would be either more or less resistant to a general disarmament program than their counterparts in other countries. What they do suggest is that the exaggerated simplicity of the official Soviet view covers many problems that would have to be dealt with by the Soviet leadership no less than by leaders of other societies.

Chapter XX

IMAGE OF THE ADVERSARY

At a time when both the United States and the Soviet Union seem to be seeking ways to clarify the complexities of their strategic relationship in the nuclear-missile age, greater importance than ever before attaches to their perception of each other. In this regard, as noted earlier in this book, the picture of the West that emerges from Soviet discourse of the past year or two has begun in some respects to take on more objective dimensions, notably in treating the United States as a strong but withal somewhat more responsible adversary than was formerly the case. Both editions of the Sokolovskii work were landmarks of a sort in this connection.

The first Sokolovskii volume conveyed an image of the West that in some respects departed notably from familiar Soviet lore on the "imperialist enemy." Though colored, to be sure, by serious distortions of Western motives and intentions, the work contained a relatively straightforward and generally realistic account of U.S.-NATO military strength and strategy. The revised volume largely followed the pattern of the first in this respect, again picturing the United States as a formidable and resourceful opponent. However, its appraisal of Western military strength was tempered by somewhat more stress on internal contradictions and instability of the NATO alliance.

One should caution against assuming that greater realism in looking at the United States is universal among Soviet writers, or that it necessarily connotes a softening of the basic hostility with which the West is viewed. As much of the material which has come under examination in this book indicates, the premises upon which Soviet spokesmen base their interpretation of the adversary remain essentially unchanged. There is a further point to be borne in mind also. Publicly expressed Soviet views of the West more often than not are meant to serve propaganda ends of one sort or another, such as demonstrating aggressive intent in every Western move. The private Soviet assessment, on the other hand, may vary from one case to another. Thus, the image of the West reflected in Soviet public statements does not necessarily correspond in all respects with what Soviet leaders may think privately about the strategies and intentions of their opponents.

SOVIET VIEW OF STRENGTHS AND WEAKNESSES OF WESTERN MILITARY POSTURE

Until quite recently, it was the fashion for Soviet military writers to picture the United States as the devotee of a one-weapon strategy, paying only lip service to the concept of balanced forces. This view has now shifted—to the extent that at least one Soviet military leader, Marshal Chuikov, has intimated that American rejection of "one-sided" theories is an example which the Soviet Union should bear in mind.[1] The general Soviet tendency today is to credit the United States with having changed its strategy and force structure in recognition that victory in a global nuclear war can only be attained by the joint effort of all arms, even though strategic forces still have the central role.[2] This, interestingly enough, is a concept very close to the one that most Soviet strategists have claimed as their own. At the same time that Soviet commentators speak of the general trend of U.S. strategy with a certain amount of oblique approbation, however, they also have been highly critical of a particular development in U.S. strategic thinking—the "counterforce" or "city-sparing" doctrine enunciated by Secretary McNamara in 1962. We shall take up this subject at greater length presently.

The United States was obliged to shift from a once-rigid strategy of "massive retaliation" to that of "flexible response," according to the Soviet view, because of the growth of Soviet retaliatory power, which would make general war unprofitable for the United States.[3] There is an obvious inconsistency, which Soviet writers have conveniently overlooked, between this description of a change in U.S. strategy and the continued assertion that the United States is also preparing to wage a "preventive" general war.[4] As our earlier discussion has suggested, there is probably a certain amount of habit as well as tendentiousness in the Soviet accusation that the United States is planning a preventive war, a danger which the top Soviet leadership itself now appears to regard as somewhat remote.[5] There is, however, no such evident reservation in Soviet views at all levels concerning U.S. interest in and planning for local war operations as part of an effort to strengthen the U.S. position in the underdeveloped world.[6]

With regard to the Soviet assessment of Western military strength, there is explicit recognition in Soviet military writing of the build-up of strategic delivery and conventional forces in the West.[7] The most fully elaborated account of Western forces and programs in the open Soviet literature remains that given in Chapter II of the Sokolovskii work, as revised in the 1963 edition. Though it made no changes of major import in the description of Western military programs and capabilities in the revised edition, it up-dated its account. The new material, reflecting data in open Western sources since publication of the first volume, dealt with both numbers and in some cases qualitative changes in Western weapons systems. For comparison at a glance, some of the figures given in the successive editions for U.S. strategic force strength are summed up on the next page.[8]

The figure given in the second Sokolovskii edition for over-all manpower strength of the U.S. armed forces was increased from 2.5 million at the end of 1961 to 2.8 million in 1962.[9] As in the previous volume, no comparative figures for Soviet and Western forces were offered, preserving the discreet silence with which

	1963		1966	
ICBM	1st Ed.	2nd Ed.	1st Ed.	2nd Ed.
Atlas	132	126	132	132
Titan-1	—	54	108	54
Titan-2	—	—	—	54
Minuteman	—	20	800	950
	132	200	1040	1190
Bombers				
Heavy	600*	630	900	900 to 1000
Medium	1300*	1100		
Missile Subs				
Subs	6	9	41	41
Missiles	96	144	656	656
Space Weapons	—	—	34	34

this subject is invariably treated in Soviet military literature. With regard to ground forces, the combined strength of NATO, SEATO, and CENTO was given as approximately 5 million men, or about 180 divisions, compared with 160 divisions in the previous edition.[10] Of these, NATO was said to have 90 divisions, as before.[11]

On the question of nuclear weapons, the absence in the 1962 edition of any figures for the U.S. stockpile was remedied in the new edition by a reference to "about 40,000," a number cited by Khrushchev on several occasions.[12] The Soviet stockpile was described cryptically in the same passage as being "more than enough." Among additions to the description of U.S. missile capabilities were figures for warhead yield, given as 3 megatons for Atlas-E, 4 megatons for Titan-1, and 600 kilotons for Minuteman.[13]

In a book intended, among other things, to argue the case for Soviet military superiority, the rather candid appraisal of American military power in both editions doubtless presented certain problems for the Sokolovskii authors. If left to stand alone, the picture of a militarily formidable Western opponent would

---

* These figures given for the year 1962.

hardly help to enhance the Soviet image as the dominant weight in the world power balance.[14] Perhaps for this reason, the authors showed a somewhat greater tendency in the revised volume to offset their description of Western military strength by references to internal strains and contradictions in the Western alliance system. These comments, of course, were not without some basis in developments over the past year or so. In expanding on the theme of growing instability within NATO, the new volume ascribed this in part to increasing opposition by the European partners to U.S. leadership in the sphere of "military policy and strategy."[15]

The tendency of the revised edition to discern Western political and morale weaknesses was matched by increased emphasis elsewhere in the book,[16] as in other recent Soviet military literature, on the superior morale and political qualities which the Soviet system is said to engender, both among troops and the population. It may be recalled from our earlier discussion of the short-versus-long war issue in Chapter XI that one school of Soviet thought has particularly stressed this factor. A representative statement of this school put the matter as follows:

The imperialist states will not be able to bear the hardships of modern war . . . in case of war the political-morale potential of the world socialist system will be vastly superior to the morale capabilities of the imperialist aggressor. This will determine to a considerable extent the outcome of the struggle in favor of socialism.[17]

Apart from the political-morale factor, Soviet commentary professes to find several other weak points in the Western posture. One of these is the vulnerability of Europe, both because of the density of its population and industry in the event of nuclear war,[18] and because of its peacetime role as a "hostage," to which Khrushchev is fond of alluding. No less important, in Soviet eyes, is the passing of the day when the United States could consider itself invulnerable. As Khrushchev put it when talking with a group of American businessmen in Moscow in

November 1963: "The time when the United States, being separated from Europe by the vast expanse of the Atlantic Ocean, could feel itself secure and never involved in conflict and war, that time has passed."[19]

While fully aware that the Soviet Union itself can be brought under nuclear attack, the Soviet leaders seem to feel that the vulnerability of the U.S. homeland is the one factor more than any other that represents the Achilles heel of their major adversary. With respect to U.S. overseas bases, the Soviet view is somewhat inconsistent. On the one hand, Soviet spokesmen have argued that these bases are highly vulnerable in the missile age[20] and therefore a liability, while at the same time these very bases have been the target of an intense Soviet diplomatic and propaganda campaign aimed at securing their liquidation. On balance, it would appear that the Soviet Union regards U.S. overseas bases more as an element of Western strength than of weakness.

CRITICISM OF U.S. COUNTERFORCE STRATEGY

In a speech at Ann Arbor on June 16, 1962, Secretary of Defense Robert McNamara gave a definitive outline of a new strategic philosophy that stressed military targets rather than cities and population as the object of attack in a nuclear war. Stating that the West was strong enough to survive a massive surprise attack and still go on "to destroy an enemy society if driven to it," McNamara also emphasized that "we are giving a possible opponent the strongest imaginable incentive to refrain from striking our own cities."[21]

Since McNamara's speech, Soviet commentators have devoted a great deal of attention to criticizing the U.S. "counterforce" or "city-sparing" strategy, terms used more or less interchangeably by Soviet sources with reference to the basic strategy enunciated by McNamara. On several occasions in 1962 Khrushchev and various Soviet military leaders expressed flatly negative views of what they called McNamara's attempt to establish "rules" for nuclear warfare,[22] while some Soviet spokesmen chose to interpret the Ann Arbor speech as the enunciation of a first-strike doctrine and "concrete and practical evidence of preparation for a preventive war."[23] Presumably with these Soviet allegations in mind, U.S. spokesmen sought to make clear that the new U.S. strategy was not tied to a first strike. Later in the year, for example, Secretary McNamara pointed out that the implications of the U.S. strategy were "exactly the opposite," since with "a sure second-strike capability," there would be no pressure whatsoever on the United States to try to strike first.[24]

Subsequent Soviet discussion of U.S. strategy has continued to reflect a concerted effort to discredit the concepts advanced by McNamara at Ann Arbor. However, there have been some interesting shifts in Soviet treatment of the subject, suggesting awareness of the need to present a more persuasive Soviet case. Four points are worth noting in this connection. First, while Soviet strategists have remained unreceptive to the city-sparing aspects of the McNamara doctrine, they themselves have begun to emphasize the second-strike assurance afforded by their own strategic posture.[25] Second, some sensitivity has been displayed, as noted earlier, to the implication that Soviet strategic doctrine is less humane than the counterforce, city-sparing approach.[26] Third, the argument has been introduced that the counterforce doctrine is a further elaboration of the U.S. "flexible response" strategy, representing an attempt to escape from "the crisis of military policy and strategy" in which Western leaders allegedly find themselves.[27] And fourth, there has been more effort to trace the development of the counterforce concept and to demonstrate its untenability from a military standpoint.

These trends became apparent in several Soviet analyses which appeared in 1963, the first of note being the work of General Nevsky, the nebulous military commentator of whom we have spoken before.[28] The points laid out in Nevsky's article were taken up and amplified in the second Sokolovskii edition, which put forward the fullest critique of the U.S. counterforce strategy in Soviet writing to date. This critique is worth observing in some detail, not only as an example of the way the Soviets perceive the process of U.S. strategy formulation, but also for the light it sheds on Soviet thinking about the counterforce doctrine itself.

The first part of the critique covered the development of U.S. counterforce theory, which was said by the Sokolovskii authors to be "the result of prolonged study of the problem of waging nuclear war," aimed at determining the target categories which must be destroyed in order "to bring quick defeat of the enemy."[29] Initially, according to the Sokolovskii authors, differing views were advanced in the United States as to whether it was better to concentrate on destroying the enemy's strategic forces or to attack large population centers. The first alternative presented the greater difficulties, because:

The delivery of nuclear strikes against the enemy's strategic weapons is a more difficult task than striking large cities. In the main, these difficulties are due, first, to the fact that such weapons exist in significant quantities, and second, the majority of them, especially missiles—which under today's conditions are absolute weapons— are emplaced in nearly-invulnerable underground bases, on submarines, etc. Further, the trend toward increasing this invulnerability is growing all the time.[30]

Another factor also affected the choice of which target system to strike, for according to the Sokolovskii authors: "This depends to a considerable extent on the delivery systems available and their numbers." If accuracy of the systems is poor, "they cannot be used against small targets like missile launch pads or airfields." If their numbers are inadequate, they "can only be used against large targets, like cities."[31]

Continuing their description of the process by which the United States arrived at the strategy enunciated by McNamara in June 1962, the Soviet authors said that the U.S. command had conducted war games for several years, using computers "to test various kinds of attacks against the Soviet Union." The findings were that strikes against cities would not "remove the threat of powerful retaliatory strikes," which could wipe out the United States. On the other hand, strikes against the opponent's strategic delivery forces could "significantly reduce his capability to destroy American cities and population."[32]

On the basis of these considerations, the United States "came to the ultimate conclusion that it was necessary to destroy the enemy's armed force, and first of all, his strategic delivery means."[33] Thus, in the Soviet view, evolved the "counterforce" or "city-sparing" strategy which the United States has now offered "as some sort of suggestion to the Soviet Union on 'rules' for the conduct of nuclear war."[34]

The second part of the Sokolovskii critique dealt with problems of carrying out a counterforce strategy. Among obstacles to such a strategy, the Soviet authors enumerated the following: First, how can others be "convinced" of the need to adhere to "new rules" of sparing cities, when "most military targets are located in or near cities?" Second, if these "rules" are to be followed, the United States and its European allies should start to remove all their military installations from cities. However, this is not only unrealistic, but as noted in the Western press, if such a move were carried out, "the USSR would draw the conclusion that the United States was preparing to attack." Finally, counterforce strategy presupposes the need for a large system of population shelters, "whose role and significance in a future war appear quite problematical."[35]

For a counterforce strategy to be "realistic and practical," according to the authors, five basic requirements must be met. These were listed as:[36]

1. Reliable and numerically-adequate reconnaissance means, in order to assure necessary target information.

2. Large numbers of missiles of great accuracy, reliability, and readiness, "since there are considerably more military targets than cities."
3. Reliable systems of command and control, warning and communications.
4. Careful planning to coordinate missile strikes and military operations of the whole coalition, "based on extensive use of computers."
5. Surprise.

With respect to the first item, reconnaissance, the Sokolovskii authors said the United States banks on the use of large numbers of satellites, capable currently of taking photographs "with a resolution of 2 meters." By the 1965–1970 period, they will be capable of "60-centimeter resolution from an altitude of 500 kilometers." However, according to the Soviet authors, prospects for solution of the reconnaissance problem are poor. Citing the American press and Henry Kissinger as authority, they pointed out that Soviet missiles will be increasingly dispersed and hidden in underground silos, and many will be mobile or based at sea, all of which will make reconnaissance more difficult.[37]

With respect to the second requirement, the United States was said to be depending mainly on such solid-fuel missiles as Minuteman and Polaris. While conceding the advantages of Minuteman, the authors pointed out that Polaris is not accurate enough to be employed against any targets other than large cities, which counterforce strategy "is supposed to avoid."[38]

On the third point, the Soviet authors noted that the United States plans to use satellites both to obtain 30-minute warning of missile attacks on the United States, and for invulnerable communications and navigation systems on a global scale. They also mentioned the use of airborne and sea-based command posts. However, they offered no comment on the efficacy of these measures.[39]

As to the coordinated planning problem, the Sokolovskii authors again adverted to the opinion of anonymous U.S. military specialists that the difficulty of obtaining target information on a growing Soviet missile force increasingly complicates the planning and organization of a U.S. missile attack.[40] All these reasons, they said, cast doubt on the effectiveness of a counterforce strategy, which banks on full destruction of the opponent's strategic weapons. Still citing anonymous opinion, the authors then stated that the uncertainty of accomplishing this task means that

the political value of a counterforce strategy may be depreciating even more rapidly than its military value, because it becomes increasingly difficult for the representatives of the military command to convince the political leadership of the absolute reliability of their plans and calculations based on fragmentary intelligence data on enemy targets.[41]

Militarily, the value of a counterforce strategy also will continue to decline during the 1960's, according to the Sokolovskii authors, because: "even if the percentage of the Soviet strategic forces which the United States can destroy remains constant (which itself is a rather optimistic assumption), the absolute number of surviving forces will increase."[42] Finally, turning to the question of surprise attack in relation to counterforce strategy, the authors asserted that such a strategy is in essence aggressive, because it would offer no expectation of victory without preventive war and a surprise attack. "This strategy," they said:

involves first of all the need for a preventive war. A strategy which expects to achieve victory through the destruction of armed forces cannot be based on the idea of a "retaliatory strike"; it is based on preventive action, on the attainment of surprise.[43]

While rounding out their critique of counterforce strategy with the customary allegation that the United States is actively studying ways to achieve "maximum surprise" by means of a first strike, the Sokolovskii authors also added a new note in their 1963 discussion by suggesting that changing conditions may now be reducing U.S. confidence in the feasibility of conducting a surprise attack. On this point they said:

U.S. military experts consider that the possibility of achieving strategic surprise will increasingly decline in the future. This is due to the fact that modern means of detection and warning make it possible to spot ballistic missile launchings, especially strategic missiles, and to send warning information on such launchings to the appropriate command centers.[44]

The above excursus on U.S. counterforce strategy by the Sokolovskii authors, while still polemical in tone and disposed at times to fall back on Marxist-Leninist platitudes about U.S. behavior, nonetheless represents a somewhat more objectively argued analysis than has been customary in Soviet military literature. In this and similar Soviet treatment of the counterforce question, one may discern several factors which presumably help to account for the strenuous Soviet effort to discredit the counterforce, city-sparing concept. First, assuming that Soviet strategic delivery forces are considerably smaller than those of the West, there is an obvious disadvantage in embracing a strategy which, by the Soviets' own account, requires large numbers of delivery vehicles. Second, there would appear to be an incompatibility between the Soviet weapons program, with its recent stress on super-megaton yields, and a strategy calling for precise delivery and measured megatonnage against military targets. To reverse direction of this program would probably entail great practical difficulties, besides depriving the Soviet arsenal of weapons upon which a high political premium evidently is put for their intimidational and deterrent value. Third, the important role played by Soviet secrecy is underscored by the Soviet attitude toward the counterforce strategy. While in Soviet eyes an advantage may lie with their side so far as obtaining target data is concerned, they also appear to feel that their position in this regard may be somewhat shaky, hence the emphasis put on the difficulty of locating targets as a barrier to a counterforce strategy.

On the whole, in terms of the strategic dialogue, the line pursued with regard to the counterforce strategy issue seems intended to lend further support to the Soviet contention that the United States can no longer count on carrying out a successful first strike against the Soviet Union, and that Soviet capability to deliver a retaliatory second-strike is now in any event beyond question.

FUTURE PROSPECTS FOR THE STRATEGIC DISCOURSE

It would be premature in the extreme to suggest that the Soviet image of the West now mirrors reality with reasonable fidelity. Soviet perception of the West is still filtered through ideological and parochial suspicions that produce a woefully distorted picture, particularly of Western motives and intentions. At the same time, it can be said that the successive Sokolovskii editions and some other recent expressions of Soviet strategic thinking have come a little way toward presenting a more objective image of the other side.

This in itself may be a small start toward a more meaningful and mutually instructive dialogue between East and West, particularly between the two great nuclear powers on either side. Some slight change in the mode of discourse—with the discussants talking more directly to each other—is another small start that may be discerned in the present trend of affairs. It generally has seemed that the discussants in the strategic dialogue were speaking from an entirely different conceptual framework, arguing from independent systems of logic—which in fact is not far from the mark. As a result, they have talked past each other more often than not. A change in the mode and quality of discourse—if nothing else, a better mutual grasp of its technical idiom, while unlikely to bridge the conceptual gap, might at least draw the two different systems of logic closer together.

It could be said that there is precious little evidence of improvement in the quality of Soviet discourse in such publications as the two Sokolovskii volumes, the authors' rebuttal addressed to the U.S. editors of their work, the Glagolev-Larionov exigesis on Soviet peace policy and military posture, the Nevsky commentary on problems of strategy, and other recent examples of Soviet strategic thought, not excluding the frequent sallies into this field by policy- and decision-makers like Khrushchev himself. All have more or less in common a penchant for painting the motives of the other side black, the policies of the Soviet Union white, and its superiority unquestionable—a picture which somewhat oversimplifies the situation, to say the least.

And yet, it is perhaps unwarranted to dismiss out of hand the possibility of raising the level of discourse and moving the strategic dialogue onto more productive ground. The expanded discussion of U.S. strategy in the revised Sokolovskii volume is a case in point. One may feel that the treatment of counterforce strategy was prejudiced by being used to support Soviet charges of aggressive U.S. plans and to fortify Soviet claims to an invulnerable retaliatory posture. However, the analysis demonstrated at least that the authors had done some homework and had acquainted themselves with the U.S. literature on the subject. If their rendering of the U.S. process of strategy formulation was imprecise, it showed at least an understanding of some of the factors involved, and in the process revealed some of their own concerns, including the strong dependence of the Soviet military posture on a continuing high level of secrecy. The *Red Star* commentary of the Sokolovskii authors, in itself a forensic development of a rather unusual kind in the strategic dialogue, showed several signs of Soviet desire to clarify foreign understanding of the Soviet military posture, as did the *International*

Affairs article by Glagolev and Larionov and some of the other statements examined in this book.

The question may be raised that an improvement in the quality and level of strategic discourse is not necessarily of any significant moment in itself. No matter how well informed by a common appreciation of the problems and concerns of the parties involved, strategic discourse can never substitute for military force in a world governed by the politics of power. This is no doubt true. Still, the forms and character of the strategic dialogue can influence the policies governing military power. In an age when the destructive potential of military power is so great that its use or misuse is the common concern of all, this would seem to be a sufficient excuse for improving the quality of the dialogue.

One of course should expect no miracles. The strategic dialogue is a form of communication between antagonists, not a means for abolishing hostility or for clearing up a deep-seated clash of purposes. It may help opponents to avoid mistaken impressions about each other's posture. It may, of course, have just the opposite effect, but that is a risk that exists in any event. At best, the strategic dialogue could lead to a useful end if it serves, as Walter Lippmann put it recently when describing President Kennedy's influence on the course of world events: "to convince the Soviet Union that it must perforce and that it can comfortably and honorably live within a balance of power which is decidedly in our favor."[45]

In assessing the prospects for further development of a useful strategic dialogue between the Soviet Union and the United States, the relevance of understandings attained in the field of arms control should not be overlooked. Some improvement in the quality of communication concerning the strategic relationships between the super-powers already has accompanied such steps as the nuclear test-ban treaty, the Moscow-Washington "hot line" agreement, the U.N. resolution against orbiting of nuclear weapons in space, and the joint declaration of intent to cut back the production of fissionable materials. Although the measures do not directly involve disarmament, they can be said to reflect a mutual desire, among other things, to slow the tempo of the arms race, to ease the economic burden of military preparations, and to reduce the danger of war by miscalculation. As such, they tend to complement the strategic dialogue in what might be described as a tentative exploratory effort to "manage" the U.S.-Soviet confrontation so as to keep it within controllable bounds while not sacrificing the political interests of the adversaries. How well this effort may meet the test of time and circumstances remains to be seen.

EPILOGUE: SOVIET STRATEGY
AT THE CROSSROADS

In the opening chapter of this book we noted that the Soviet leaders seem to stand today at a crossroads of decision on many issues of strategy and defense policy. Problems of various kinds, some unique to the Soviet situation and others basically similar to problems with which Western policy-makers and strategists must cope, have converged upon the Soviet leadership at this stage of the twentieth century.

One of the problems of first magnitude, as we have seen, is related to the allocation of resources. Difficulties within the Soviet economy and competing demands upon it evidently have made it more difficult than usual for the Soviet leaders to decide what share of their resources shall be devoted to military purposes.

Another fundamental problem, growing out of the military-technological revolution of the present age, centers upon Soviet awareness of the destructiveness of nuclear war. This has given rise to questions about the feasibility of war as an instrument of policy and the limits of military power in the nuclear-missile era.

The unhealed Sino-Soviet estrangement represents another problem of great magnitude, which, among other things, may have called into question the possibility of future Sino-Soviet military cooperation and some of the basic strategic assumptions upon which Soviet planning probably has been based.

In the immediate area of Soviet military policy and strategy, it would appear that well on to two years after the unsuccessful deployment of Soviet missiles to Cuba, the Soviet leadership is still confronted with a number of unresolved issues in seeking a military posture suitable to Soviet needs in the power contest with the United States. The ongoing military dialogue in the Soviet Union, which we have examined at some length, bears witness to the fact that there are still differing schools of thought on many matters which have been under debate for some time past. To mention a few, these include: (1) the size of the armed forces which should be maintained; (2) the kind of war—short or protracted—for which Soviet forces and the country should be prepared; (3) the prospects of survival under conditions of nuclear warfare; (4) the respective weight of strategic missile forces and combined-arms operations in any future war against a powerful overseas enemy; (5) the question whether the criteria for developing the Soviet armed forces should stress mainly their deterrent and intimidational functions or their war-fighting value; and finally, (6) the problem of finding a winning military strategy for any war that might have to be fought with the United States.

In addition to such questions bearing on practical decisions with regard to defense policy, there has also been continued although inconclusive evidence of a certain amount of underlying strain between Party-political authorities on the one hand and some elements of the professional officer corps on the other.

While it is important to remember that a consensus still binds the various elements of the Soviet leadership together, and that the areas of agreement on purpose and policy are doubtless much broader than the areas of contention, nevertheless, the above brief catalogue of vexatious issues is enough to suggest that Khrushchev and other Soviet leaders have their hands full today in charting the course of Soviet defense policy. Indeed, a convergence of such problems over the past year or two would seem to account in large part for Soviet interest in cultivating a certain measure of détente in U.S.-Soviet relations. It is in this sense that one might say that Soviet strategy is at a crossroads today, as the Soviet leaders play for time, seeking ways to work themselves out of their various difficulties.

In terms of Soviet relations with the United States, a great deal hinges on what direction the Soviet leaders may take should they achieve some substantial measure of success in overcoming the difficulties now before them. Would success signal the end of Soviet interest in détente and resumption of more provocative and risky policies? Or, might the habits of limited cooperation and improved communication continue to grow into some more manageable form of adversary relationship? Obviously, there is no ready answer to these questions. Doubtless, the Soviet leaders themselves remain uncertain as to how the U.S.-Soviet confrontation may develop in the years ahead.

It does seem reasonable to suppose that this confrontation will continue to be the dominant feature of the international scene during at least the next decade or so. At the same time, one must recognize that the U.S.-Soviet conflict will be conducted within a system of world relations that is undergoing some fundamental changes. The familiar bipolar pattern of the past fifteen years, dominated by the two super-powers, is in the process of being transformed into a new and somewhat more diversified structure. Within the two major blocs, each super-power finds itself, in varying degree, increasingly obliged to contend with centrifugal political and economic forces. Each side has its heretics, and each is exposed in some measure to a process of fragmentation. Moreover, an increasing interplay of local and regional relations among states standing apart from the super-power confrontation also seems likely to characterize the emerging international system.

One of the major factors which seemingly has undermined the cohesion of the two great power blocs is the widespread belief that deliberate resort to nuclear war has become rather remote. In effect, member states of both power blocs have been able to afford the luxury of seeking greater autonomy and more independent policies because the danger of direct attack from the opposing side appears to be diminishing. It is sometimes assumed that a world in which some sort of mutual nuclear deterrence operates will tend to be a more stable world. This is not necessarily so. It is perhaps an unpleasant paradox that the very trends which make general nuclear war increasingly improbable as an instrument of policy may also produce a less stable system of international relations. As a larger number of states seek greater freedom of action and pursue more diverse interests under the shield of nuclear deterrence, the potential sources of international conflict may well increase.

The implications of all this for the U.S.-Soviet confrontation are complex. One might suppose that the relationship between these two adversaries would be exposed to accentuated pressures from quite different directions. On the one hand, if new alignments, greater unrest, and erosion of old security arrangements tend to characterize the international scene, the effect could be to lend added urgency to formal or tacit U.S.-Soviet cooperation, in order to stabilize the situation and dampen the risks of escalation to major military conflict. On the other hand, the unstable aspects of the scene might also seem to offer tempting opportunities for political exploitation and advance. The Soviet leaders in particular, pressed by their critics in Peking to show positive results in the world revolutionary struggle, might find it difficult to resist this temptation. Should they succumb, one could hardly expect the U.S.-Soviet confrontation to become less severe.

No one, of course, can predict with confidence what the future will bring. Assuming, however, that man's affairs are not likely to be suddenly transformed by hitherto unknown political and social inventions, it probably can be expected that new international crises of a grave sort will arise from time to time. If the experience of the nuclear age to date is a reliable guide, one might also expect such crises to stimulate further remedial efforts to improve cooperation and communication between the adversary parties, which may serve, hopefully, to keep the East-West conflict under control.

LIST OF ABBREVIATIONS · NOTES · INDEX

LIST OF ABBREVIATIONS

ABM	Antiballistic missile.
ABM System	System of defense against ballistic missiles.
ASM	Air-to-surface missile (launched from aircraft).
ASW	Antisubmarine warfare.
CPSU	Communist Party of the Soviet Union.
DOSAAF	Voluntary Society for Assistance to the Army, Air Force and Navy.
ICBM	Intercontinental ballistic missile.
IRBM	Intermediate range ballistic missile.
MGB	Ministry of State Security.
MRBM	Medium range ballistic missile.
PVO	Air defense (standard Russian abbreviation for air defense forces, from the words *Protivovozdushnaia Oborona*).
R&D	Research and development.

NOTES

1. Communist doctrine has continued to recognize the historical dependence of communism on war, even though the Soviet "revisionist" view holds that revolution is no longer "obligatorily linked with war." An authoritative doctrinal manual, published in 1959 but still cited as valid scripture in the Soviet Union, says for example: "Up to now historical development adds up to the fact that revolutionary overthrow of capitalism has been linked each time with world wars. Both the first and second world wars served as powerful accelerators of revolutionary explosions." *Osnovy Marksizma-Leninizma* (Foundations of Marxism-Leninism), Gospolitizdat, Moscow, 1959, p. 519.

2. *Pravda,* July 14, 1963.

3. Speech to the Sixth Congress of the Socialist Union Party of Germany, *Pravda,* January 17, 1963.

4. The "chemicalization" decisions taken by the December 1963 plenum of the Central Committee indicated, for example, that a seven-year investment of 42 billion rubles in the chemical industry was necessary to increase production of fertilizer and other chemical products. See Khrushchev's report at the CPSU Central Committee plenum, *Pravda,* December 10, 1963.

5. See estimates by the U.S. Central Intelligence Agency, reported in the *New York Times,* January 8, 1964, and report released by Senator Paul H. Douglas, *Annual Economic Indicators for the USSR,* Materials Prepared for the Joint Economic Committee, Congress of the United States, 88:2, February 1964. These studies indicate that the Soviet rate of economic growth declined from an annual rate of 6 to 10 per cent in the last decade to less than 2.5 per cent in 1962–1963. The Douglas report suggests (pp. 93, 98) that the long-term Soviet growth rate for 1960–1970 may average out at around 4.5 to 5 per cent if temporary difficulties, particularly in agriculture, are ironed out. It appears that Soviet sensitivity over the growth-rate issue has prompted a major battle of statistics with U.S. experts. In January, V. N. Starovskii, head of the Soviet Central Statistical Administration, derided the accuracy of the CIA analysis, but at the same time conceded that the growth rate (as calculated in Soviet terms, using the concept of "gross social product") was down from 6 per cent in 1962 to 5 per cent in 1963. *Izvestiia,* Jan-

uary 15, 1964. Omission of certain income statistics in the annual Soviet economic report published in *Pravda*, January 24, 1964, seemed to lend credence to Western analyses of a growth-rate slowdown. See Theodore Shabad, *New York Times*, January 26, 1964. Khrushchev entered the statistical argument in a major speech published in *Pravda*, February 15, 1964; and in *Pravda*, March 14, 1964, Starovskii again attacked the CIA and Douglas reports. Starovskii gave hitherto unpublished figures for gross industrial production, but rather significantly did not furnish figures bearing directly on the over-all growth-rate argument. For another phase of the exchange between U.S. and Soviet experts over Soviet income statistics, see the interesting series of letters to the editor of the *New York Times* by Vladimir Smolyansky, a Soviet economist, and Abraham S. Becker of the Economics Department of The RAND Corporation, February 6, 12, 29, and March 14, 1964. This exchange ended with the Soviet side still apparently reticent to disclose the basis of Soviet national income.

6. See Philip E. Mosely, *The Kremlin and World Politics*, Random House, Inc., New York, 1960, pp. 545, 551, 557.

CHAPTER II. THE INTERNAL SOVIET MILITARY DEBATE

1. *Pravda*, April 26, 1963. For an informative discussion of the relationship between Khrushchev's ascendancy to unquestioned political primacy and the greater room for policy discussion and criticism in the Soviet Union during the past few years, see Zbigniew Brzezinski and Samuel P. Huntington, *Political Power: USA/USSR*, Viking Press, New York, 1964, pp. 280, 299, *passim.*

2. Marshal R. Ia. Malinovskii, *Bditel'no Stoiat Na Strazhe Mira* (Vigilantly Stand Guard Over the Peace), Voenizdat Ministerstva Oborony SSSR, Moscow, 1962, p. 23. (Hereafter this title is given only in translation.)

3. Marshal V. D. Sokolovskii, *et al.*, *Soviet Military Strategy*, with Analytical Introduction and Annotations by H. S. Dinerstein, L. Gouré and T. W. Wolfe of The RAND Corporation, Prentice-Hall, Englewood Cliffs, New Jersey, 1963, p. 513.

4. See U.S. Editors' Analytical Introduction to *Soviet Military Strategy*, pp. 12–41. For other extensive Western analyses of the post-Stalin military debate, see: Herbert S. Dinerstein, *War and the Soviet Union*, revised edition, Frederick A. Praeger, Inc., New York, 1962; Raymond L. Garthoff, *Soviet Strategy in the Nuclear Age*, revised edition, Frederick A. Praeger, Inc., New York, 1962; J. M. Mackintosh, *Strategy and Tactics of Soviet Foreign Policy*, Oxford University Press, London, 1962, especially pp. 88–104.

For a recent Soviet discussion which tends to corroborate the main lines of these Western analyses of postwar changes in Soviet military theory, see: Colonel I. Korotkov, "The Development of Soviet Military Theory in the Post-War Years," *Voenno-Istoricheskii Zhurnal* (Military-Historical Journal), No. 4, April 1964, pp. 39–50.

Korotkov distinguished several stages in the postwar development of Soviet military theory. The first major period was from the end of World War II through 1953, the year of Stalin's death. In this period, "historical truth about the war was trampled upon for Stalin's advantage," and the development of Soviet military theory suffered. Such important new concepts as the importance of the initial period of a modern war and the greatly increased significance of surprise attack with atomic weapons were neglected. Despite the advent of nuclear weapons, according to Korotkov, Soviet military theory also clung to the view that a future war would be "inevitably of a long and protracted character."

The second major period began in 1954 and in its first stage from 1954–1956 a "gradual" change of views occurred, as the impact of nuclear weapons on warfare began to receive attention. While this was a major turning point in Soviet military thought, the employment of new weapons was still conceived "within the framework of previous methods of warfare," and aircraft were the principal delivery means contemplated. Such problems as surprise attack and the initial period now came under study, although the radical changes in war brought about by nuclear weapons were far from being appreciated by everybody, and the new views "only slowly and with difficulty made their way against the old outlook." In particular, according to Korotkov, the idea of a long war persisted, partly explainable by the fact that neither side yet possessed enough modern weapons. When intercontinental ballistic missiles were to become available, the "conditions would be created for a quick, nonprotracted war." The turning point came in 1957 with the appearance of missiles, demanding now a "radical transformation of views on the character of a possible war, methods of warfare, and the roles and significance of all types of armed forces." The years 1960–1961, according to Korotkov, saw the "invigoration of military-theoretical thought," as theoretical discussions were pursued in conferences, military academies and journals, and practical problems were defined and studied. These years also saw the laying down of new principles and concepts of modern war in important speeches by Khrushchev and Malinovskii, and the creation of a new type of forces—the strategic missile forces. Even after these evidences of a "qualitative leap" and "radical" change in the realm of modern war, however, "some comrades" continued to judge the new weapons in terms of the experience of the past war. Bringing his review of the postwar development of Soviet military theory to a close, Korotkov noted that its latter stages have been marked, "after long stagnation," by the output of a series of works on Soviet military strategy, among which he characterized the Sokolovskii book, *Military Strategy,* as one of "the most fundamental" and, "despite some shortcomings . . . a notable phenomenon on the military-theoretical front."

5. *Pravda,* January 15, 1960.

6. An American assessment of Khrushchev's emergence as a military authority, written in 1960, offered a prescient observation about the role he has since played in the military debate. It said: "One of Khrushchev's major achievements in the military sphere, in fact, may prove to be that of wrenching a traditionally conservative Soviet military bureaucracy out of its accustomed groove and forcing it to reorganize in line with the technological facts of life." *Khrushchev's Strategy and Its Meaning for America,* A Study for the Use of the Committee on the Judiciary, United States Senate, U.S. Government Printing Office, Washington, 1960, p. 12.

7. *Pravda,* October 25, 1961.

8. Major General P. Zhilin, "Discussion about a Unified Military Doctrine," *Military-Historical Journal,* No. 5, May 1961, p. 73.

9. *Military-Historical Journal,* No. 4, April 1964, p. 46.

CHAPTER III. THE SOVIET VOICE IN THE EAST-WEST
STRATEGIC DISCOURSE

1. Seldom has the great predicament of the modern world been summed up more simply than in these words from one of the late President Kennedy's last speeches: "The family of man can survive difference of race and religion . . . it can accept differences in ideology, politics, economics. But it cannot survive, in the form in which we know it, a nuclear war." See "Our Obligation to the Family of Man," Remarks by President Kennedy, *The Department of State Bulletin,* November 25, 1963.

2. For a discussion of the U.S.-Soviet strategic dialogue of the past few years, see U.S. Editors' Analytical Introduction to *Soviet Military Strategy,* pp. 24–27. This discussion points out that in mid-1962 the Soviet Union was having some difficulty holding up its side of the strategic dialogue with the United States, and that generally accepted assertions of Western strategic superiority at that time had probably generated pressure on the Soviet leadership to repair the Soviet image in the world power balance. In retrospect, this factor may have had something to do with the Soviet effort to deploy missiles to Cuba, as implied on pp. 32–33, above.

3. Marshal V. D. Sokolovskii, *et al.*, *Voennaia Strategiia* (Military Strategy), second edition, Voenizdat Ministerstva Oborony SSSR, Moscow, 1963, hereafter cited by Russian title to distinguish it from earlier or partial versions in English. A full English translation of the second edition does not yet exist, although a line-by-line comparison of changes is available under the title *Military Strategy: A Comparison of the 1962 and 1963 Editions,* Joint Publications Research Service, U.S. Department of Commerce, Washington, D.C., December 14, 1963.

4. One of the original contributors, Major General N. P. Tsygichko, subsequently died and is listed posthumously in the new volume.

5. Three substantial Soviet commentaries on the book, critical of it in some respects, appeared in early 1963. They were in: *Voennyi Vestnik* (Military Herald), No. 1, January 1963; *Morskoi Sbornik* (Naval Collection), No. 1, January 1963; *Voenno-Istoricheskii Zhurnal* (Military-Historical Journal), No. 5, May 1963.

6. The four Soviet authors were Major Generals: I. Zav'ialov, V. Kolechitskii, M. Cherednichenko, and Colonel V. Larionov. Their article was entitled, "Against Slanders and Falsifications: Concerning the U.S. Editions of the Book 'Military Strategy,' " *Red Star,* November 2, 1963.

7. One of these was *Soviet Military Strategy,* published by Prentice-Hall, to which reference has already been made. The other was *Military Strategy: Soviet Doctrine and Concepts,* Frederick A. Praeger, Inc., New York, 1963, with an Introduction by Raymond L. Garthoff.

8. Most of the *Red Star* criticism was directed in detail at the Introduction to the Prentice-Hall edition, to which the author of this volume was a contributor. It is worth noting that, despite their critical attack upon American interpretations of the Sokolovskii work, the Soviet authors nevertheless found occasion to describe the Prentice-Hall Introduction, written by staff members of The RAND Corporation, as being more "restrained in tone," more "objective" and "professional," and more "scientific-like" in its analysis than earlier "sensational and openly slanderous" press commentaries.

9. L. Glagolev and V. Larionov, "Soviet Defence Might and Peaceful Coexistence," *International Affairs,* No. 11, November 1963, pp. 27–33. *International Affairs,* a monthly political journal circulated both within the Soviet Union and abroad, appears in Russian as *Mezhdunarodnaia Zhizn.* References hereafter to the Glagolev-Larionov article are to the English-language version.

10. Glagolev's title is Director of the Scientific Group for Disarmament of the Institute of World Economics and International

Relations, a body that functions under the auspices of the USSR Academy of Sciences in Moscow. He has visited the United States and has on occasion been able to express his views on the study of disarmament in the American press. See, for example, "A Communication to the Editor of the *Washington Post,*" *Washington Post,* November 27, 1962.

11. *International Affairs,* November 1963, p. 27.

12. General A. Nevsky, "Modern Armaments and Problems of Strategy," *World Marxist Review: Problems of Peace and Socialism,* Vol. 6, No. 3, March 1963, pp. 30–35.

13. Marshal R. Ia. Malinovskii, *Vigilantly Stand Guard Over the Peace,* Voenizdat Ministerstva Oborony SSSR, Moscow, 1962, p. 15.

14. Election speech in Kalinin District, *Pravda,* February 28, 1963.

15. *Pravda,* March 14, 1963.

16. Speech to Construction Workers' Conference, *Pravda,* April 26, 1963.

17. *New York Times,* June 11, 1963.

18. See Colonel S. Baranov and Colonel E. Nikitin, "CPSU Leadership—The Fundamental Basis of Soviet Military Development," *Kommunist Vooruzhennykh Sil* (Communist of the Armed Forces), No. 8, April 1963, p. 22. For a fuller discussion of these developments, see Chap. XII.

19. *Izvestiia,* December 15, 1963; Pravda, December 16, 1963.

20. Soviet statements applauding Soviet virtue in this respect ignored the fact that the Soviet budget reduction announcement trailed by a few days the initiative announced by the new Johnson administration in the United States to close a number of military installations and to lower the U.S. military budget.

21. *New York Times,* January 9, 1964.

22. *Ibid.,* April 21, 1964.

23. *Izvestiia,* December 15, 1963. The single exception among prominent military men was Marshal A. I. Eremenko, who alluded without comment to "the forthcoming cut in the Soviet armed forces" in an article in *Moscow News.* This is an English-language publication distributed abroad rather than to domestic Soviet audiences. See Marshal Andrei Eremenko, "War Must Be Wiped Out," *Moscow News,* No. 2, January 11, 1964.

24. Marshal V. Chuikov, "Modern Ground Forces," *Izvestiia,* December 22, 1963. See Chap. XII for further discussion of the troop reduction issue.

25. See Marshal Pavel Rotmistrov, "The Causes of Modern Wars and Their Characteristics," *Communist of the Armed Forces,* No. 2,

January 1963, p. 31; also, *Soviet Military Strategy*, p. 410; *Voennaia Strategiia*, 2nd ed., p. 383.

26. See Colonel E. Fedulaev, "The Missile-Nuclear Arms Race in the NATO Countries—A Threat to Peace," *Communist of the Armed Forces*, No. 17, August 1963, pp. 84–85.

27. See Khrushchev's concluding speech to the Central Committee Plenum, *Pravda*, December 15, 1963.

28. *International Affairs*, November 1963, p. 30.

CHAPTER IV. GENERAL IMPORT OF THE NEW
SOKOLOVSKII VOLUME

1. For a detailed comparison of the two Sokolovskii editions, see Leon Gouré, *Notes on the Second Edition of Marshal V. D. Sokolovskii's "Military Strategy"*, The RAND Corporation, RM–3972-PR, February 1964.

2. *Voennaia Strategiia*, 2nd ed., p. 85.

3. *Ibid.*, p. 8.

4. *Ibid.*, pp. 218, 221. For the original references to Yugoslavia, see *Soviet Military Strategy*, pp. 273, 276.

5. *Voennaia Strategiia*, 2nd ed., p. 437.

6. For an example of this, see L. Glagolev and V. Larionov, "Soviet Defence Might and Peaceful Coexistence," *International Affairs*, No. 11, November 1963, pp. 27, 29, 30, 32, 33. See also editorial, "The Leninist Course of Our Foreign Policy," *Red Star*, September 24, 1963; Colonel P. Trifonenkov, "The Most Pressing Problem of the Present Day and the Adventurism of the Chinese Dogmatists," *Communist of the Armed Forces*, No. 21, November 1963, pp. 23–29; D. Melnikov, N. Talenskii, A. Iarmonskii, "The Main Problems of the 20th Century," *International Affairs*, No. 9, September 1963, pp. 10–17.

7. The new edition carried neutrality on the question of China to the point of excising an earlier reference that was wholly uncontroversial. It concerned the contributions made to military theory some 2,000 years ago by such Chinese thinkers as Confucius, Sun Tsu, and Su Tsu. See *Soviet Military Strategy*, p. 86, for the passage in question.

8. *Voennaia Strategiia*, 2nd ed., p. 4.

9. *Communist of the Armed Forces*, No. 20, October 1963, p. 94.

10. For a discussion of the internal and external communication functions of the original Sokolovskii volume and their relative weight in the book, see the report of a symposium on Soviet strategy, published under the title *Soviet Nuclear Strategy: A Critical Appraisal*, by the Center for Strategic Studies, Georgetown University, Washington, D. C., November 1963, especially pp. 2–7.

CHAPTER V. THE CREDIBILITY OF THE SOVIET
DETERRENT POSTURE

1. Marshal S. Biriuzov, "Politics and Nuclear Weapons," *Izvestiia,* December 11, 1963.

2. Marshal R. Ia. Malinovskii, "The CPSU Program and Questions of Strengthening the Armed Forces of the USSR," *Kommunist,* No. 7, May 1962, p. 15.

3. *Voennaia Strategiia,* 2nd ed., p. 3.

4. *Ibid.,* p. 4. The pamphlet was *Vigilantly Stand Guard Over the Peace,* p. 25.

5. Concluding speech to 21st Party Congress, *Pravda,* February 6, 1959.

6. See, for example, Marshal K. S. Moskalenko, "The Rocket Troops Are Mounting Guard Over the Motherland's Security," *Red Star,* September 13, 1961; Marshal Malinovskii in *Kommunist,* No. 7, May 1962, p. 14; Marshal N. I. Krylov, "Strategic Missiles," *Izvestiia,* November 17, 1963; Colonel General V. F. Tolubko, "The Main Rocket Strength of the Country," *Red Star,* November 19, 1963; Colonel I. Mareev, "The Indestructible Shield of the Socialist Countries," *Communist of the Armed Forces,* No. 3, February 1964, p. 11; Marshal N. I. Krylov, "Always on the Alert," *Izvestiia,* February 23, 1964.

7. It has now become the customary Soviet formula to claim possession of weapons of "50–100 megatons and more." See Marshal S. Biriuzov, "New Stage in the Development of the Armed Forces and Tasks of Indoctrinating and Training Troops," *Communist of the Armed Forces,* No. 4, February 1964, p. 20.

8. See, for example, Khrushchev's speech to World Peace Congress, *Pravda,* July 11, 1962; Krylov in *Izvestiia,* February 23, 1964.

9. Speech to a session of the Supreme Soviet of the USSR, *Pravda,* January 15, 1960.

10. Marshal R. Ia. Malinovskii, "The Revolution in Military Affairs and the Tasks of the Military Press," *Communist of the Armed Forces,* No. 21, November 1963, p. 8.

11. *Pravda,* November 8, 1963. See also *Red Star,* November 6, *Izvestiia,* November 8, *Pravda,* November 19, 1963.

12. Krylov in *Izvestiia,* November 17, 1963.

13. Tolubko in *Red Star,* November 19, 1963. See further discussion in Chap. VII.

14. Marshal K. A. Vershinin, "The General Line of Soviet Foreign Policy," *Communist of the Armed Forces,* No. 19, October 1963, p. 16.

15. "Ushering in the 46th Anniversary of the Soviet Army and Navy," *Red Star,* February 21, 1964; Krylov in *Izvestiia,* Febru-

ary 23, 1964; Mareev in *Communist of the Armed Forces*, No. 3, February 1964, pp. 12–14.

16. Hearings on Military Posture, U.S. Congress, 88:1, House Committee on Armed Services, January 30, 1963, p. 308; *Bulletin of the Atomic Scientists*, April 1963, p. 38.

17. The previously mentioned Nevsky article contained some of the same points, but they were more fully elaborated by Larionov and Glagolev. See General A. Nevsky, "Modern Armaments and Problems of Strategy," *World Marxist Review*, Vol. 6, No. 3, March 1963, pp. 33–34.

18. L. Glagolev and V. Larionov, "Soviet Defence Might and Peaceful Coexistence," *International Affairs*, No. 11, November 1963, p. 32. The Russian-language version of the journal did not use the expression "talking through their hats." Rather, it said more prosaically that Western views were "groundless."

19. *Ibid.*

20. A similar assertion that Soviet strategic missiles have a very short reaction time was made in November 1963 by Marshal N. Krylov, commander of the strategic missile forces, who said that among the "fine technical properties" of Soviet missiles was the fact that "it takes just a few minutes to prepare them for action," *Izvestiia*, November 17, 1963. See also *Izvestiia*, February 23, 1964.

21. *International Affairs*, November 1963, p. 32.

22. *Ibid.*

23. *Ibid.*, p. 33.

24. It may be useful to clarify what is meant by "pre-emptive" as distinct from "first-strike" forces. The essential distinction is that a first-strike force would be sufficiently powerful to permit a deliberate, premeditated attack on the enemy, with reasonable expectation of not being seriously damaged in return, whereas a pre-emptive force, as customarily defined, would not be capable of assuring such an outcome, but rather would be employed to blunt and disrupt an attack about to be launched by the enemy. A first-strike force—if properly alerted—might be employed in a pre-emptive role, but it would scarcely be rational to use a pre-emptive force, as here defined, in a first-strike role.

25. For a fuller exploration of this question, see Arnold Horelick, *The Cuban Missile Crisis: An Analysis of Soviet Calculations and Behavior*, The RAND Corporation, RM–3779–PR, September 1963. For an abridged version of this paper by the same author and under the same title see *World Politics*, Vol. XVI, No. 3, April 1964, pp. 363–389.

26. Major General I. Zav'ialov, Major General V. Kolechitskii, Major General M. Cherednichenko, and Colonel V. Larionov, "Against Slanders and Falsifications," *Red Star*, November 2, 1963.

27. *Voennaia Strategiia,* 2nd ed., p. 260. For the earlier version, see *Soviet Military Strategy,* pp. 313–314.

28. Colonel General N. Lomov, "Basic Tenets of Soviet Military Doctrine: The Revolution in Military Affairs, Its Significance and Consequences," *Red Star,* January 10, 1964. See also Malinovskii in *Communist of the Armed Forces,* No. 21, November 1963, p. 9; Colonel V. Konoplev, "On Scientific Foresight in Military Affairs," *ibid.,* No. 24, December 1963, p. 31; Mareev in *ibid.,* No. 3, February 1964, p. 15.

29. *International Affairs,* November 1963, p. 32.

30. Colonel General N. A. Lomov, *Sovetskaia Voennaia Doktrina* (Soviet Military Doctrine), Izdatelstvo "ZNANIE," Moscow, May 1963, p. 28.

31. Konoplev in *Communist of the Armed Forces,* No. 24, December 1963, p. 30. Colonel V. Glazov, "Some Features of Conducting Military Operations in Nuclear War," *ibid.,* No. 3, February 1964, p. 43.

CHAPTER VI. THE QUESTION OF WAR AS AN INSTRUMENT
OF POLICY

1. Eugene Rabinowitch, "Scientific Revolution: The End of History," *Bulletin of the Atomic Scientists,* November 1963, p. 9.

2. For a discussion of Malenkov's thesis and his recantation a short time later, see H. S. Dinerstein, *War and the Soviet Union,* revised edition, Frederick A. Praeger, Inc., New York, 1962, pp. 71-77.

3. Khrushchev's speech to 20th Party Congress, *Pravda,* February 15, 1956. See also *Current Soviet Policies II: The Documentary Record of the 20th Party Congress and Its Aftermath,* Leo Gruliow, ed., Frederick A. Praeger, Inc., New York, 1956, p. 37.

4. See, for example, Khrushchev's speech to the USSR Supreme Soviet on the international situation, *Pravda,* December 13, 1962.

5. "Brass Hats: Peking and Clausewitz," *Izvestiia,* September 24, 1963.

6. *Voennaia Strategiia,* 2nd ed., p. 25; *Soviet Military Strategy,* p. 99.

7. *Ibid.,* p. 216.

8. See discussion of Talenskii's sympathy with Khrushchev's outlook in U.S. Editors' Analytical Introduction, *Soviet Military Strategy,* p. 22.

9. N. Talenskii, "The 'Absolute Weapon' and the Problem of Security," *International Affairs,* No. 4, April 1962, p. 24.

10. *Ibid.,* p. 26.

11. Colonel P. Trifonenkov, "War and Politics," *Red Star,* October 30, 1963. It is worth noting that in this article Trifonenkov was

defending the thesis on war as a continuation of politics against Chinese charges that the Soviets had abandoned it.

12. *Ibid.*

13. "Politics and Nuclear Weapons," *Izvestiia,* December 11, 1963.

14. "War and Politics in the 'Nuclear Age,'" *Communist of the Armed Forces,* No. 2, January 1964, p. 21.

15. *Ibid.,* p. 20.

16. *Ibid.,* p. 14.

17. *Ibid.,* p. 16.

18. *Ibid.*

19. *Ibid.,* p. 23.

20. An interesting symptom of this concern was an article by Marshal N. I. Krylov in June 1963, prepared at the request of *Red Star's* editors to set at rest doubts about the present-day role of the military profession. Krylov castigated "those sometimes encountered among us who assume the pose of 'bold free-thinkers'" and talk about the "decline" of the military. Krylov argued that "the military profession is not a thing of the past" and that "Pacifism is a bourgeois ideology alien to us. We must be uncompromising toward it, toward the slightest appearance of it in our ranks." Marshal N. I. Krylov, "An Honorable Profession, Needed by the Nation," *Red Star,* June 9, 1963.

21. That "peaceful coexistence" is permanent is vigorously denied in Soviet interpretations. For example, two Soviet writers affirmed recently that the policy of peaceful coexistence "does not at all signify the 'preservation' of the bourgeois order; it does not recognize the immovability of [this order] which bourgeois ideologists unsuccessfully seek to establish." Sushko and Kondratkov in *Communist of the Armed Forces,* No. 2, January 1964, p. 22. See also G. Starushenko, "The National-Liberation Movement and the Struggle for Peace," *International Affairs,* No. 10, October 1963, pp. 3–4; Colonel N. Voroshilov, "Problems of War and Peace in the Contemporary Epoch," *Communist of the Armed Forces,* No. 6, March 1964, pp. 14–15.

CHAPTER VII. THE DOCTRINE OF MILITARY SUPERIORITY

1. Election speech in Kalinin District, *Pravda,* February 28, 1963.

2. See discussion of this trend in Chap. XVII.

3. Marshal P. A. Rotmistrov, ed., *Istoriia Voennogo Iskusstva* (A History of Military Art), Vol. I, Voenizdat Ministerstva Oborony SSSR, Moscow, 1963, p. 484. See also Raymond L. Garthoff, *Soviet Military Doctrine,* The Free Press, Glencoe, Illinois, 1953, p. 126.

4. Colonel V. Zemskov and Colonel A. Bulatov, "On the Combat Preparedness of Troops in Modern Conditions," *Red Star,* October 5,

1962; speech by Marshal R. Ia. Malinovskii to the All-Army Conference on Ideological Questions, *Red Star*, October 25, 1962; General of the Army I. I. Iakubovskii, "Combat Sharpness," *Red Star*, October 28, 1962. See also Malinovskii, *Vigilantly Stand Guard Over the Peace*, Voenizdat Ministerstva Oborony SSSR, Moscow, 1962, p. 23; Malinovskii, "45 Years on Guard Over the Socialist Fatherland," *Red Star*, February 23, 1963.

5. "The Nation's Exploit," *Izvestiia*, May 9, 1963.

6. "The True Guardian of the Peoples' Security," *Red Star*, May 14, 1963.

7. Colonel I. Sidel'nikov and Colonel V. Smitrenko, "The Present Epoch and the Defense of the Achievements of Socialism," *Red Star*, September 19, 1963.

8. Khrushchev's speech to the USSR Supreme Soviet on the international situation, *Pravda*, December 13, 1962.

9. Speech to a session of the Supreme Soviet, *Pravda*, January 15, 1960; *Pravda*, October 18, 1961.

10. *Pravda*, October 25, 1961.

11. For comment on the treatment of the military superiority theme in the first edition, see U.S. Editors' Analytical Introduction, *Soviet Military Strategy*, pp. 67–69.

12. *Voennaia Strategiia*, 2nd ed., p. 314. See also pp. 297, 303; *Soviet Military Strategy*, pp. 349, 335, 340.

13. *Voennaia Strategiia*, 2nd ed., p. 258.

14. *Ibid.*, p. 297; *Soviet Military Strategy*, p. 335.

15. *Soviet Military Strategy*, p. 409.

16. See U.S. Editors' Analytical Introduction, *Soviet Military Strategy*, p. 23.

17. This point was underscored in a series of articles in January 1964 by Colonel General N. A. Lomov, who is not himself an exponent of the pure traditionalist view, but seems to stand somewhere in between. See "New Weapons and the Nature of War: The Revolution in Military Affairs, Its Significance and Consequences," *Red Star*, January 7, 1964. The second article of the Lomov series, which was largely a condensation of his mid-1963 brochure on military doctrine, appeared in the January 10, 1964 issue of *Red Star*.

18. Marshal Grechko's article in December 1963 voicing support of the December plenum line on heavy investment in the chemical industry concluded with an exhortation to "military-scientific cadres" which seemed to rest on such a rationale. He said that workers in "science and technology, basing their efforts on the latest achievements of our economy, must continue with still greater perseverance to work out military-technical problems—problems of further perfecting the combat capability and organization of the armed forces." "On a Leninist Course," *Red Star*, December 22, 1963.

19. Malinovskii, *Vigilantly Stand Guard Over the Peace,* p. 23.

20. *Ibid.*

21. *Red Star,* February 23, 1963.

22. "The Main Rocket Strength of the Country," *Red Star,* November 19, 1963. See further discussion of missile numbers in Chap. XIII.

23. General Tolubko's superior, Marshal N. I. Krylov, commander of the Soviet strategic missile forces, took a somewhat different line in early 1964 in reference to American statements on the U.S. numerical lead in missiles. Instead of asserting that the USSR could respond with greater numbers, Krylov said: "If the United States has such quantities of missiles, one can draw the legitimate conclusion that U.S. strategy is not based on national defense, but pursues aggressive ends." "Always on the Alert," *Izvestiia,* February 23, 1964.

24. A recent example of this was Khrushchev's statement at the conclusion of the February 1964 Central Committee plenum session on agriculture, when he first said that "The socialist countries have now created armed forces equal to the forces of the capitalist world, as leaders of the imperialist powers have admitted," and then went on to say: "We believe our armed forces are the more powerful." *Pravda,* February 15, 1964. See also *Pravda,* August 8, October 18, 1961; July 11, 1962; January 17, 1963.

25. Commentary on the November 7 parade by A. Leont'ev, Moscow domestic radio, November 12, 1963. See also Lieutenant Colonel A. Leont'ev in *Red Star,* August 30, 1963; editorial, "Shock Front of Communist Construction," *Red Star,* February 18, 1964.

26. *Voennaia Strategiia,* 2nd ed., p. 239. *Soviet Military Strategy,* p. 297.

27. *Voennaia Strategiia,* 2nd ed., p. 317. See also second article in series by Colonel General N. A. Lomov in *Red Star,* January 10, 1964, which asserted that the Soviet Union has managed "to attain superiority over the potential enemy in the decisive means of warfare: rocket-nuclear weapons and, above all, strategic nuclear means."

28. *Voennaia Strategiia,* 2nd ed., p. 230. *Soviet Military Strategy,* p. 285. In this connection, it is noteworthy that, after the December 1963 announcement of a military budget reduction and of a heavy planned investment in the chemical industry, the military press was anxious to make the point that Soviet defenses still needed to be perfected. Thus, an editorial in *Red Star,* December 18, 1963, stated: "In his final address at the plenum, Nikita Khrushchev declared that the planned program for development of the chemical industry will be carried out without detriment to national defense. We are forced to perfect our defenses and take measures to ensure the safety of our friends and allies."

29. *Voennaia Strategiia,* 2nd ed., p. 80. In *Soviet Military Strategy,* the discussion in question occurs on pp. 156–157.

30. The stability of "mutual deterrence" has frequently been questioned in Soviet literature on disarmament. See, for example, V. A. Zorin, ed., *Borba Sovetskogo Soiuza za Razoruzhenie 1946– 1960 gody* (The Soviet Union's Struggle for Disarmament 1946– 1960), Izdatelstvo Instituta Mezhdunarodnykh Otnoshenii, Moscow, 1961, pp. 83–85; D. V. Bogdanov, *Iadernoe Razoruzhenie* (Nuclear Disarmament), Izdatelstvo Instituta Mezhdunarodnykh Otnoshenii, Moscow, 1961, p. 75.

31. *Red Star,* December 22, 1963.

32. *Ibid.*

33. Colonel V. Konoplev, "On Scientific Foresight in Military Affairs," *Communist of the Armed Forces,* No. 24, December 1963, p. 33.

The theme that Stalin was guilty of propounding a pernicious "law" equating peace-loving nations with military unpreparedness has begun to appear more frequently in Soviet military writing. It appears to be a polemical device to counter any tendencies among political leaders to rationalize Soviet strategic inferiority vis-à-vis the West and to settle for a "second-best" position. An example of the argument appeared in a new book on Soviet military science published in late 1963. The author, Colonel Krupnov, asserted that Stalin's proposition that "aggressor nations are bound to be better prepared than peace-loving nations . . . contradicts historical facts and gives an incorrect orientation to military development." Even though everyone knows the Soviet Union is a "peace-loving nation," Krupnov pointed out, nevertheless it must "continue to strengthen its military might . . . as long as the danger of imperialist aggression exists." Colonel S. I. Krupnov, *Dialektika i Voennaia Nauka* (Dialectics and Military Science), Voenizdat Ministerstva Oborony SSSR, Moscow, 1963, p. 40.

34. Colonel I. Mareev, "The Indestructible Shield of the Socialist Countries," *Communist of the Armed Forces,* No. 3, February 1964, pp. 14–15. For a claim that the Soviet system of production creates "favorable possibilities for achieving decisive superiority over capitalism, both in quality of weapons and in training," see Lieutenant General N. A. Sbytov, "The Nature of a World Missile-Nuclear War and the Laws Governing It," *Naval Collection,* No. 3, March 1964, p. 10.

35. Marshal S. Biriuzov, "New Stage in the Development of the Armed Forces and Tasks of Indoctrinating and Training Troops," *Communist of the Armed Forces,* No. 4, February 1964, p. 19.

36. *Ibid.,* p. 18.

CHAPTER VIII. SIGNS OF STRESS IN POLITICAL-MILITARY RELATIONS

1. The literature on the history of Soviet political-military relations is too extensive to cite at length here, but the following are worth particular mention: D. Fedotoff-White, *The Growth of the Red Army*, Princeton University Press, Princeton, New Jersey, 1944, pp. 76–100, 384–407; Merle Fainsod, *How Russia Is Ruled*, Harvard University Press, Cambridge, Mass., 1954, pp. 411–418, 500; John Erickson, *The Soviet High Command*, St. Martin's Press, Inc., New York, 1962, pp. 113–178, 187–191, *passim;* Louis Nemzer, "The Officer Corps as a Political Interest Group," paper read at the 39th Annual Meeting of the American Political Science Association, New York, September 4, 1963, pp. 1–38; Raymond L. Garthoff, *Soviet Strategy in the Nuclear Age*, Frederick A. Praeger, Inc., New York, 1958, pp. 18–40.

2. For a detailed discussion of signs of post-Cuban dissatisfaction with Khrushchev's handling of the crisis, see Roman Kolkowicz, *Conflicts in Soviet Party-Military Relations: 1962–1963*, The RAND Corporation, RM–3760–PR, August 1963, pp. 16–35.

3. Marshal V. I. Chuikov, "The Basic Fundamentals of Military Development," *Red Star*, November 17, 1962.

4. One should be careful in discussions of this sort not to regard "Party" and the "professional military" as two altogether discrete and antipodal groups in more or less constant opposition to each other. Without exception, all responsible military figures in the high command of the Soviet armed forces are also Party members, subject to Party discipline, and so on. At the same time, there are institutionalized interests on both sides which may collide, and which find expression in various forms of bureaucratic in-fighting. It is in this contained area of conflict, so to speak, that tensions in political-military relations arise.

5. Marshal R. Ia. Malinovskii, *Vigilantly Stand Guard Over the Peace*, Voenizdat Ministerstva Oborony SSSR, Moscow, 1962.

6. *Ibid.*, pp. 22–23. This ascription of credit to Khrushchev was in marked contrast to the approach taken in the first edition of the Sokolovskii work, *Voennaia Strategiia* (Military Strategy), whose authors tended to give the military an expanded share of credit for developing the new Soviet military doctrine and by implication staked out a claim for greater military influence on state policy. See *Soviet Military Strategy*, pp. 33ff.

7. In this connection, Khrushchev has admitted a precedent by mentioning in a conversation with former Vice President Richard M. Nixon that he himself had really written a widely publicized article on Soviet military policy which had been attributed to Air Marshal

Vershinin in *Pravda,* September 8, 1957. See article by Earl Mazo on the Nixon trip to the Soviet Union in 1959, *New York Herald Tribune,* September 14, 1960, p. 8.

8. The Main Political Administration has been traditionally an extension of the Party Central Committee's professional staff within the armed forces. A statement on this point in *Communist of the Armed Forces,* No. 6, March 1963, p. 8, went as follows: "Party work in the armed forces is under the leadership of the Central Committee CPSU, through the Main Political Administration . . . which operates with the rights of a section of the Central Committee CPSU." Before donning a uniform to take up his present post, Epishev had been ambassador to Yugoslavia. Earlier in his career, he had been an important secret police official in the MGB.

9. General of the Army A. A. Epishev, "The Growing Role of the CPSU in the Leadership of the Armed Forces," *Voprosy Istorii KPSS* (Problems of the History of the CPSU), No. 2, February 1963, pp. 3ff.

10. Colonel V. Zemskov and Colonel A. Iakimovskii, "Military Strategy," *Military Herald,* No. 1, January 1963, p. 124.

11. A. Golubev, "Some Problems of Military History in the Book 'Military Strategy,'" *Military-Historical Journal,* No. 5, May 1963, p. 90.

12. Reported in an article by Colonel L. Belousov, "Conference on Soviet Military Doctrine," *Military-Historical Journal,* No. 10, October 1963, pp. 121–126.

13. *Ibid.,* p. 122.

14. "On Soviet Military Doctrine," *Communist of the Armed Forces,* No. 10, May 1962, p. 12.

15. *Soviet Military Doctrine,* Izdatelstvo "ZNANIE," Moscow, May, 1963, p. 5.

16. "CPSU Leadership: The Fundamental Basis of Soviet Military Development," *Communist of the Armed Forces,* No. 8, April 1963, p. 17.

17. L. Glagolev and V. Larionov, "Soviet Defence Might and Peaceful Coexistence," *International Affairs,* No. 11, November 1963, p. 27.

18. Major Generals I. Zav'ialov, V. Kolechitskii, M. Cherednichenko, and Colonel V. Larionov, "Against Slanders and Falsifications," *Red Star,* November 2, 1963.

19. *Soviet Military Strategy,* p. 130.

20. *Voennaia Strategiia,* 2nd ed., p. 54.

21. *Soviet Military Strategy,* p. 104.

22. *Voennaia Strategiia,* 2nd ed., p. 30.

23. *Ibid.*

24. See N. M. Kiriaev, "The 22nd Congress of the CPSU on Strengthening of the Armed Forces and Defense Capability of the Soviet Union," *Problems of the History of the CPSU*, No. 1, January 1962, p. 74.

25. Editorials in *Pravda*, November 3, 1957; *Red Star*, November 5, 1957.

26. Moscow broadcast to North America, November 10, 1963.

27. Baranov and Nikitin in *Communist of the Armed Forces*, No. 8, April 1963, p. 19.

28. Report of All-Army Conference of Ideological Workers, *Red Star*, November 1, 1963. Articles in a similar vein turned up around this time in *Communist of the Armed Forces*. See, for example, Colonel A. Tuvlev, "Requirements of the 22nd Party Congress and the Program of the CPSU with Regard to Military Cadres," No. 15, August 1963, pp. 14–45; editorial, "To Strengthen Military Cadres Ideologically," No. 19, October 1963, p. 6.

29. General I. Pliev, "The New Technology and Problems of Strengthening Discipline," *Communist of the Armed Forces*, No. 19, October 1962, pp. 21–28.

30. See *Red Star*, November 18, December 8, 1962; Major General D. Rashetov, "The Highest Level of Marxist-Leninist Training of Officers," *Communist of the Armed Forces*, No. 20, October 1962, pp. 21–23.

31. A. A. Epishev, "Raising Combat Readiness of Troops: The Main Task of Party Work," *Red Star*, December 1, 1962.

32. Colonel General V. Tolubko, "Know Strategic Weapons Perfectly," *Red Star*, January 8, 1963.

33. See, for example, Lieutenant Colonel P. Baranov, "At the Roadside," *Red Star*, March 20, 1963; Colonel General A. L. Getman, "The Sympathetic Commander," *Red Star*, March 29, 1963.

34. Marshal R. Ia. Malinovskii, "Ideological and Organizational Activity of Military Cadres," *Red Star*, March 3, 1964. For article which launched the *Red Star* series, see Colonel General A. Getman, "Unity of Word and Deed: How to Achieve It," *Red Star*, October 10, 1963. Concurrent articles in the periodical military press dealing with the same question included: General of the Army M. Kazakov, "The Command Preparation of Officers: A Daily Consideration," *Communist of the Armed Forces*, No. 23, December 1963, pp. 20–23; Captain First Rank V. Stukalov, "Arm Political Workers with Deep Military-Technical Knowledge," *ibid.*, pp. 24–29. Other evidence that Malinovskii's counsel was still going unheeded in some quarters was provided by exhortations in early 1964 to improve Party indoctrination activities and to make better use of the military press for this purpose. Colonel I. Korotkov, "What the Military Reader Is Waiting For," *Red Star*, January 23, 1964.

35. The "military specialists," comprised of officers with engineering and technical backgrounds, are especially numerous in the missile forces. Marshal N. Krylov, commander of the strategic missile forces, put the proportion of such specialists among officers of his command at "more than 70%" in early 1964. "In the Interests of the Highest Military Preparedness," *Red Star*, January 11, 1964.

36. See Colonel D. Levchenko, "The Commander and the New Technology," *Red Star*, November 10, 1960; Pliev in *Communist of the Armed Forces*, No. 19, October 1963, p. 26.

37. R. Conquest, *Power and Policy in the USSR*, St. Martin's Press, Inc., New York, 1961, pp. 330ff.; Myron Rush, *The Rise of Khrushchev*, Public Affairs Press, Washington, D.C., 1958, pp. 80–81. See also Zbigniew Brzezinski and Samuel P. Huntington, *Political Power: USA/USSR*, The Viking Press, New York, 1964, pp. 252, 339–352.

A study of the June 1957 crisis which takes the view that the military played "a minor but crucial role" is Roger Pethybridge's *A Key to Soviet Politics: The Crisis of the Anti-Party Group*, Frederick A. Praeger, Inc., New York, 1962, especially pages 89–90, 103–106, 128–132.

38. Belousov in *Military-Historical Journal*, No. 10, October 1963, pp. 121–123; Colonel General N. A. Lomov, "Basic Tenets of Soviet Military Doctrine," *Red Star*, January 10, 1964, and same author's *Soviet Military Doctrine*, pp. 5, 18; *Voennaia Strategiia*, 2nd ed., p. 54; Major General S. Kozlov, "Military Doctrine and Military Science," *Communist of the Armed Forces*, No. 5, March 1964, pp. 9–15.

The Kozlov article holds particular interest for its elaboration of the scope and relative influence of military doctrine, military science and military strategy. According to Kozlov, military doctrine is based on "a unified system of state views," and there cannot therefore be "two contradictory doctrines." Once accepted, doctrine changes relatively slowly and should not be subjected to continued question, for rejection of established views on which it is based "causes a serious fissure in the entire military structure." Kozlov does not make clear precisely how changes in doctrine are to be brought about, but implies that change comes only after considerable pressure. Doctrine, he says, "is forced to . . . disregard new phenomena in military affairs until they have gathered force."

On the other hand, military science, according to Kozlov, "does not have the right to decline to analyze new phenomena." Military science looks farther into the future than doctrine, and it may properly include differing propositions and hypotheses, only some of which will be accepted as military doctrine in the course of time.

As for military strategy, according to Kozlov, it represents in a practical sense "the basic instrument of doctrine in working out war plans and preparation of the country and the armed forces for war." Strategic theory also has reciprocal influence on doctrine. In wartime, doctrine is subordinated to strategy, "or more precisely, to the strategic leadership, which directly resolves the problems posed by policy in the concrete situation."

39. Among prominent members of the Stalingrad group are Marshals Malinovskii, Chuikov, Biriuzov, Krylov, Eremenko, and Grechko. For a detailed discussion of the Stalingrad group, see Kolkowicz, *Conflicts*, pp. 37–45.

40. *Voennaia Strategiia*, 2nd ed., p. 4.

41. *Ibid.*, p. 5.

42. *Ibid.*

43. *Ibid.*, p. 30.

44. Lomov, *Soviet Military Doctrine*, p. 19.

45. *Ibid.*, p. 20. See also Colonel V. Konoplev, "On Scientific Foresight in Military Affairs," *Communist of the Armed Forces*, No. 24, December 1963, p. 34.

46. See Colonel V. Siniak and Colonel V. Vare, "Role of Man and Technology in the Command and Control of Troops," *Communist of the Armed Forces*, No. 18, September 1963, p. 50.

47. Chinese criticism of Khrushchev's military theories was most pungently expressed in one of the series of joint *People's Daily-Red Flag* articles on Sino-Soviet relations which appeared November 18, 1963. While Chinese stress on the importance of "man over technology" was undoubtedly related to their own lack of an advanced military technology, including nuclear weapons, it is also likely that their charges against Khrushchev were calculated to exacerbate political-military relations within the Soviet Union, for the Chinese were undoubtedly aware of some Soviet military reluctance to go along fully with Khrushchev's ideas. See further discussion of this question in Chap. XVII.

48. *Red Star*, January 10, 1964.

49. *Voennaia Strategiia*, 2nd ed., p. 477; *Soviet Military Strategy*, p. 496.

50. For an illuminating discussion of the way Soviet historiography on World War II has served as an instrument for arguing the relative weight of military-political roles, see Matthew P. Gallagher, *The Soviet History of World War II*, Frederick A. Praeger, Inc., New York, 1963, especially pp. 169–175.

51. Marshal A. Eremenko in *Pravda*, January 27, 1963; Marshal V. Chuikov in *Pravda*, January 30, 1963; Marshal S. Biriuzov in *Komsomolskaia Pravda*, February 2, 1963.

52. Marshal P. A. Rotmistrov in *Red Star,* January 16, 1963; Marshal N. Voronov in *Pravda,* January 31, 1963; Marshal R. Ia. Malinovskii in *Pravda,* February 2, 1963; Marshal V. Kazakov in *Izvestiia,* February 1, 1963.

53. Malinovskii's grudging attitude in February 1963 toward Khrushchev's Stalingrad role had undergone considerable change little more than a year later, on the occasion of Khrushchev's 70th birthday in April 1964. Among several laudatory articles recognizing Khrushchev's birthday was one by Marshal Malinovskii, in which the Soviet Defense Minister noted that Khrushchev had "encouraged and inspired" the military commanders at Stalingrad. Malinovskii also paid tribute to Khrushchev's postwar role in the development of the Soviet armed forces, crediting Khrushchev, among other things, with having "led and directed . . . the process of adapting the whole of military theory and practice to the demands of modern times." See "In the Leadership of the Party—Our Strength and Invincibility," *Red Star,* April 17, 1964. Even though Malinovskii's article treated Khrushchev favorably, it is interesting that it was somewhat more restrained than a parallel article by another top military leader, Marshal Grechko, commander of the Warsaw Pact forces. Grechko gave more emphasis to Khrushchev's *personal* role, both in executing "radical transformations in the organization of our armed forces" and in "elaboration of our state's modern military doctrine." See "Mighty Guardian of Peace," *Izvestiia,* April 17, 1964. It is probably wise not to read too much into the differing appreciations of Khrushchev's role by these two military leaders. Judging from the two articles in question, however, Malinovskii seemed slightly more concerned than Grechko to suggest that high-level decisions on defense policy were reached after consultation by the Party Presidium with professional military advisors, rather than on the basis of Khrushchev's personal initiative and expertise in military affairs.

54. "Art Triumphs," *Izvestiia,* December 26, 1963.

CHAPTER IX. NATURE AND LIKELIHOOD OF A FUTURE WAR

1. Colonel L. Belousov, "Conference on Soviet Military Doctrine," *Military-Historical Journal,* No. 10, October 1963, p. 121.

2. Speech by Marshal R. Ia. Malinovskii to the All-Army Conference on Ideological Questions, *Red Star,* October 25, 1962. For an elaborate argument on the importance of correct scientific prediction of the nature of a future war in order "to quickly defeat the enemy with minimum losses" and to "avoid mistakes" which could lead to "irreparable consequences," see Colonel V. Konoplev, "On Scientific Foresight in Military Affairs," *Communist of the Armed Forces,*

No. 24, December 1963, pp. 28–29. See also editorial, "Everything Progressive and New in Military Preparation," *ibid.*, No. 2, January 1963, pp. 3–4.

3. *Voennaia Strategiia*, 2nd ed., p. 228; *Soviet Military Strategy*, pp. 282–283. In the Soviet usage, both "imperialist war" and "national liberation war" are customarily in the small war category, the difference being mainly one of political definition, that is, an imperialist war is an "unjust" war waged by an imperialist power against a colonial country, and a "national liberation war" is a "just" war waged the other way around. Current Soviet doctrine admits the slight possibility of wars between "imperialist" powers, but it seems to provide no room for wars between "non-imperialist" countries. See also Khrushchev's speech on 81-Party Moscow Conference, delivered January 6, 1961; *Pravda*, January 25, 1961; Colonel General N. A. Lomov, *Soviet Military Doctrine*, Izdatelstvo "ZNANIE," Moscow, 1963, p. 21.

4. *Voennaia Strategiia*, 2nd ed., p. 233; *Soviet Military Strategy*, p. 287.

5. For treatment by representative Soviet sources of the various general features of a future world war mentioned here, see *Soviet Military Strategy*, pp. 298–315; *Voennaia Strategiia*, 2nd ed., pp. 241–261; Colonel General N. A. Lomov, "New Weapons and the Nature of War," *Red Star*, January 7, 1964; Marshal P. Rotmistrov, "The Causes of Modern Wars and Their Characteristics," *Communist of the Armed Forces*, No. 2, January 1963, pp. 29–32; Colonel General S. Shtemenko, "Scientific-Technical Progress and Its Influence on the Development of Military Affairs," *ibid.*, No. 3, February 1963, pp. 26–28; Konoplev, *ibid.*, No. 24, December 1963, pp. 28–34; Colonel P. Derevianko, "Some Features of the Contemporary Revolutions in Military Affairs," *ibid.*, No. 1, January 1964, pp. 17–25; Major General N. Sushko and Major T. Kondratkov, "War and Politics in the Nuclear Age," *ibid.*, No. 2, January 1964, pp. 15–23; Lieutenant General N. A. Sbytov, "The Nature of a World Missile-Nuclear War and the Laws Governing It," *Naval Collection*, No. 3, March 1964, pp. 9–16.

6. The possibility of accidental war was given somewhat more emphasis in the revised Sokolovskii volume than in the first edition. A new description in the second edition of various technical and command failures which might touch off a war included an allegation that the Commander of SAC, General Thomas Power, without Presidential authority, had ordered his bombers to take off against the Soviet Union in November 1961 on the strength of false radar signals. *Voennaia Strategiia*, 2nd ed., p. 364.

7. *Ibid.*, p. 378.

8. See Colonel S. Lipitskii, "Activity of an Aggressor in the Period When War Threatens," *Military-Historical Journal*, No. 8, August 1963, pp. 11–24. In this discussion, after giving pros and cons of the case for a surprise attack without advance crisis or warning indicators, Lipitskii concluded that one could not be sure of warning, and hence the Soviet armed forces must be in the highest state of readiness for action "not in days or weeks, but in minutes or seconds." He also commented on the need to move warheads to missile sites and air bases in time of crisis, which would suggest a "normal" state of Soviet readiness somewhat less than that needed to respond in "minutes or seconds."

9. The Sokolovskii authors are among those who have tended to tone down their view of Western readiness to launch an attack without warning. In this regard, the second edition of their book omitted a passage in the first edition which had said that, owing to the wide deployment and high combat readiness of their forces, the "imperialists" today were in a much better position to deal a surprise blow against the Soviet Union than Hitler had been. See *Soviet Military Strategy*, p. 397.

10. Rotmistrov in *Communist of the Armed Forces*, No. 2, January 1963, p. 30. See also Malinovskii's speech to 22nd Congress of CPSU, October 21, 1961, *Pravda*, October 25, 1961; *Soviet Military Strategy*, p. 308; *Voennaia Strategiia*, 2nd ed., p. 253.

11. Major D. Kazakov, "The Theoretical and Methodological Basis of Soviet Military Science," *Communist of the Armed Forces*, No. 10, May 1963, p. 11. See also Konoplev in *ibid.*, No. 24, December 1963, p. 28.

12. Khrushchev speech to a session of the Supreme Soviet of the USSR, January 14, 1960, *Pravda*, January 15, 1960. See also Lomov in *Red Star*, January 7, 1964, and Derevianko in *Communist of the Armed Forces*, No. 1, January 1964, p. 20.

13. Shtemenko in *Communist of the Armed Forces*, No. 3, February 1963, p. 27.

14. *Soviet Military Strategy*, pp. 302, 305–306; Major General V. Reznichenko and Colonel A. Sidorenko, "Contemporary Tactics," *Red Star*, February 12, 1964.

15. *Soviet Military Strategy*, pp. 348, 404, 410–414; *Voennaia Strategiia*, 2nd ed., pp. 382–390, 417.

16. *Soviet Military Strategy*, pp. 109, 495; Colonel S. Lesnevskii, "Military Cooperation of the Armed Forces of the Socialist Countries," *Communist of the Armed Forces*, No. 10, May 1963, pp. 71–73.

17. *Soviet Military Strategy*, p. 410; *Voennaia Strategiia*, 2nd ed., pp. 382–383; Lomov, *Soviet Military Doctrine*, p. 26.

18. See discussion of this question in Chap. XI.

19. There had been a perceptible increase of Soviet propaganda on the growing danger of war, dating from the time the new Party Program was promulgated in the summer of 1961 and continuing down to the emergence of the détente spirit in 1963. See *Soviet Military Strategy*, pp. 42, 286, 312.

20. *Soviet Military Strategy*, p. 286.

21. *Voennaia Strategiia*, 2nd ed., p. 232.

22. *Ibid.*, p. 230.

23. See Stewart Alsop, "Kennedy's Grand Strategy," *Saturday Evening Post*, March 31, 1962, pp. 11, 13.

24. *Voennaia Strategiia*, 2nd ed., p. 351. See also L. Glagolev and V. Larionov, "Soviet Defence Might and Peaceful Coexistence," *International Affairs*, No. 11, November 1963, p. 30.

25. See, for example, Lomov, *Soviet Military Doctrine*, p. 29; Marshal R. Ia. Malinovskii, *Vigilantly Stand Guard Over the Peace*, Voenizdat Ministerstva Oborony SSSR, Moscow, 1962, pp. 13–14; Colonel N. Voroshilov, "Problems of War and Peace in the Contemporary Epoch," *Communist of the Armed Forces*, No. 6, March 1964, pp. 11–12.

26. Remarks by Khrushchev in Maritsa, Bulgaria, on May 15, 1962, broadcast on that date by the Sofia domestic radio, but not circulated in the Soviet Union. See U. S. Editors' Analytical Introduction, *Soviet Military Strategy*, p. 43.

27. From the time of the Soviet Union's emergence as a nuclear power, Khrushchev has shown an increasing tendency to emphasize the growing deterrent effect of Soviet military power, and to de-emphasize the likelihood of a premeditated Western attack against the Soviet Union. This suggests that in Khrushchev's private view decisions leading to war have remained largely in Soviet hands, apart from the danger of war arising through irrational or accidental causes. See A. L. Horelick, *"Deterrence"* and *Surprise Attack in Soviet Strategic Thought*, The RAND Corporation, RM-2618, July 1960. For earlier expressions of confidence by Khrushchev that Soviet arms gave assurance against a premeditated attack on the Soviet Union, see *Pravda*, October 15, 1958; January 28, June 1, July 30, 1959; January 15, 1960.

CHAPTER X. LIMITED WAR

1. See *Soviet Military Strategy*, pp. 44, 299.

2. Both Bulganin and Khrushchev were early exponents of the view that limited wars would prove impossible in the nuclear era. See Bulganin's letter to President Eisenhower in *Pravda*, December 12, 1957; Khrushchev's letter to the British Labour Party in the

New York Times, October 16, 1957, and his article "Toward New Victories of the World Communist Movement," *Kommunist,* No. 1, January 1961, p. 18. Among military writers, Major General N. Talenskii was an early and consistent advocate of the view that limited war in the nuclear age was a "utopian idea." See his articles in *Mezhdunarodnaia Zhizn* (International Affairs), No. 10, October 1960, p. 36, and No. 4, April 1962, p. 23. For a review of other Soviet literature on the subject, see *Soviet Military Strategy,* pp. 289–293.

3. *Pravda,* January 4, 1964.

4. "Modern Armaments and Problems of Strategy," *World Marxist Review,* Vol. 6, No. 3, March 1963, pp. 34–35.

5. *Voennaia Strategiia,* 2nd ed., pp. 94–95.

6. *Ibid.,* p. 96. See also p. 61, where a new statement asserts that U.S. limited war theories are an attempt to convince the American people that "war is not so terrible" and that even wars involving nuclear weapons can be "normalized."

7. *Ibid.,* pp. 94–95.

8. *Ibid.,* p. 232; *Soviet Military Strategy,* pp. 286–287.

9. It should be pointed out that occasional statements in Soviet military literature on the need for attention to the problems of local war antedated the first Sokolovskii edition of 1962. See, for example, *Marksizm-Leninizm o Voine i Armii* (Marxism-Leninism on War and the Army), Voenizdat Ministerstva Oborony SSSR, Moscow, 1956, p. 145; Colonel I. S. Baz', "Soviet Military Science on the Character of Modern War," *Military Herald,* No. 6, June 1958, p. 24; Colonel S. Kozlov, "The Creative Character of Soviet Military Science," *Communist of the Armed Forces,* No. 11, June 1961, p. 55.

10. *Voennaia Strategiia,* 2nd ed., p. 234; see also p. 319; *Soviet Military Strategy,* pp. 288, 356. Other Soviet military discussion in the period between the two Sokolovskii editions also adverted in the same fashion to the need for Soviet military doctrine and strategy to concern itself with local war. An example was the raising of this question at the conference on military doctrine in Moscow in May 1963, where it was noted that "the possibility of waging local and limited wars is not to be rejected." See Colonel L. Belousov, "Conference on Soviet Military Doctrine," *Military-Historical Journal,* No. 10, October 1963, p. 123. Recognition that "insufficient attention had been given to study of limited (local) wars" in the past by Soviet military theory was explicitly made in a notable article by Colonel I. Korotkov in April 1964. Korotkov stated that "this deficiency began to be corrected only recently." See "The Development of Soviet Military Theory in the Post-War Years," *Military-Historical Journal,* No. 4, April 1964, p. 48.

11. "The Theoretical and Methodological Basis of Soviet Military Science," *Communist of the Armed Forces*, No. 10, May 1963, pp. 11–12.

12. *Voennaia Strategiia*, 2nd ed., p. 374.

13. *Ibid.*, pp. 374–375.

14. *Ibid.*

15. Colonel General N. A. Lomov, *Soviet Military Doctrine*, Izdatelstvo "ZNANIE," Moscow, 1963, p. 15.

16. "Historic Victory," *Moscow News*, May 11, 1963.

17. Major General I. Anureev, "Physics and New Weapons," *Red Star*, November 21, 1963. General Anureev stated further in this article that the Soviet Union "disposes at the moment of a great assortment of nuclear weapons beginning with low-yield warheads and ending with bombs of more than 50 megatons."

18. Marshal R. Ia. Malinovskii, *Vigilantly Stand Guard Over the Peace*, Voenizdat Ministerstva Oborony SSSR, Moscow, 1962, p. 39.

19. This passage appears on p. 299 of *Soviet Military Strategy*. The U.S. editors' quotation and comment are on p. 44.

20. Incidentally, the word "inevitably" remains in the same passage in the second Sokolovskii edition. See *Voennaia Strategiia*, 2nd ed., p. 242.

21. See N. S. Khrushchev in *Kommunist*, No. 1, January 1961, p. 20.

22. Signs of doctrinal difficulty in discriminating between local and national-liberation wars on a proper Marxist-Leninist basis appeared in General Lomov's mid-1963 brochure on Soviet military doctrine. He wrote on this point: "local wars must not be evaluated on the basis that they can be waged within local territorial limits. If one takes this position, then one must also place in this category wars of national-liberation and civil wars—that is, just wars which also are waged within territorial limits. The only correct criterion for defining the character of wars is their socio-political content." *Soviet Military Doctrine*, p. 21.

23. As Khrushchev put it in 1961, national-liberation wars "must not be identified with wars between states, with local wars." *Kommunist*, No. 1, January 1961, p. 20.

24. Another factor which may be involved in the greater attention being given to national-liberation wars was suggested by the Sushko-Kondratkov article in February 1964 on the question of war as an instrument of politics. As noted previously in Chapter VI, this article took the position that national-liberation wars were "not only permissible, but inevitable," and it ignored the danger of escalation by asserting that the question of using nuclear weapons would not arise in such wars. This may suggest a Soviet military interest in giving

more active backing to national-liberation wars in order to offset the tendency to regard all wars in the nuclear age as too dangerous to serve political purposes. See Major General N. Sushko and Major T. Kondratkov, "War and Politics in the 'Nuclear Age,'" *Communist of the Armed Forces*, No. 2, January 1964, p. 23.

25. *Pravda*, December 22, 1963.

26. See, for example, D. Vol'skii and V. Kudriavtsev, "Practical Reality and the Fantasies of the Splitters," *Red Star*, October 10, 1963; editorials in *Red Star*, October 22, 1963, and December 18, 24, 1963; *Pravda*, January 19, 1964; "Marxism-Leninism—the Basis for 'the Unity of the Communist Movement,'" *Kommunist*, No. 15, October 1963, p. 17, in which Soviet "armed support" of the national-liberation struggle in Indonesia, Yemen, and Iraq was mentioned.

27. *Soviet Military Strategy*, p. 283.

28. *Voennaia Strategiia*, 2nd ed., p. 229.

29. Marshal S. Biriuzov, "Politics and Nuclear Weapons," *Izvestiia*, December 11, 1963.

30. Colonel M. Vasiliev's commentary, Moscow broadcast to Germany, December 6, 1957; Colonel V. Mochalov and Major V. Dashichev, "The Smoke Screen of American Imperialists," *Red Star*, December 17, 1957.

31. *Pravda*, January 4, 1964.

32. The statement in question by the U.S. editors occurred in a discussion (*Soviet Military Strategy*, p. 43) of Soviet views on how a war might start. The statement said that these views included: "escalation from local war, 'accidental' outbreak, and retaliation by the Soviet Union for an attack on another Bloc member. The latter would imply a Soviet first strike against the United States, but despite the crucial implications of this question for Soviet strategy, it receives no explicit attention in the work." The Soviet position on numerous occasions has been that an "attack on any of the socialist countries will be viewed as an attack on the USSR." Lieutenant General S. Krasilnikov, "On the Character of Contemporary War," *Red Star*, November 18, 1960. See also Major General A. Prokhorov, "The Possibility of Averting War and the Danger of War Arising," *Red Star*, December 26, 1962. What Soviet response actually would be to such an attack remains, of course, a major unanswered question. However, in the case of Berlin and more specifically the case of Cuba, Khrushchev has threatened on various occasions that, if military force were used by the United States, the Soviet Union would be prepared to respond with "all means at its disposal," which seems to imply a willingness to be the first to resort to strategic nuclear attacks. See Soviet-Cuban communiqué, *Izvestiia*, January

24, 1964. See also *Tass* communiqué, *Pravda*, September 12, 1962; Marshal R. Ia. Malinovskii in *Pravda*, February 23, 1963; Khrushchev at Secret Cuban Friendship Meeting, *Pravda*, May 24, 1963; CPSU open letter of July 14, 1963, *Pravda*, July 14, 1963; Khrushchev's speech in Kalinin, *Pravda*, January 18, 1964. It should be noted, at the same time, that while Khrushchev has threatened that "an invasion of Cuba would confront mankind with destructive rocket-thermonuclear war" and has strongly implied that Soviet strategic missiles would be launched against the United States in retaliation for such an invasion, he has carefully steered clear of an explicit statement that the Soviet Union would strike the first missile blow.

33. Major Generals I. Zav'ialov, V. Kolechitskii, M. Cherednichenko, and Colonel V. Larionov, "Against Slanders and Falsifications," *Red Star*, November 2, 1963.

34. 1964 New Year's Message to Heads of State, *Pravda*, January 4, 1964.

35. *Voennaia Strategiia*, 2nd ed., p. 362; A. Prokhorov in *Red Star*, December 26, 1962.

CHAPTER XI. THE SHORT-VERSUS-LONG WAR ISSUE

1. *Voennaia Strategiia*, 2nd ed., p. 261; *Soviet Military Strategy*, p. 314; Colonel V. Konoplev, "On Scientific Foresight in Military Affairs," *Communist of the Armed Forces*, No. 24, December 1963, p. 28.

2. Election speech in Kalinin District, *Pravda*, February 28, 1963.

3. Colonel S. Baranov and Colonel E. Nikitin, "CPSU Leadership —The Fundamental Basis of Soviet Military Development," *Communist of the Armed Forces*, No. 8, April 1963, p. 22.

4. Major D. Kazakov, "The Theoretical and Methodological Basis of Soviet Military Science," *Communist of the Armed Forces*, No. 10, May 1963, pp. 10–12.

5. Leont'ev commentary on Moscow radio, November 12, 1963.

6. Marshal R. Ia. Malinovskii, *Vigilantly Stand Guard Over the Peace*, Voenizdat Ministerstva Oborony SSSR, Moscow, 1962, p. 26. See also Malinovskii's emphasis on the decisive results of the initial period in *Red Star*, October 25, 1962.

7. *Vigilantly Stand Guard Over the Peace*, p. 26.

8. "The Revolution in Military Affairs and the Tasks of the Military Press," *Communist of the Armed Forces*, No. 21, November 1963, p. 9.

9. "Scientific-Technical Progress and Its Influence on the Development of Military Affairs," *Communist of the Armed Forces*, No. 3, February 1963, p. 27. An exceptionally forceful statement of the

short-war view was made in March 1964 by a Soviet Air Force general, who said that modern weapons have not only brought "a sharp increase in the role of the initial period of a war," but also "a shortening of its duration." The same writer stressed that under modern conditions the "most important and chief mission" of the Soviet armed forces is to be constantly ready "for wrecking the aggressive plans of the imperialists and defeating their military machines within a short period of time." Lieutenant General N. A. Sbytov, "The Nature of a World Missile-Nuclear War and the Laws Governing It," *Naval Collection*, No. 3, March 1964, pp. 13, 14.

10. "The Causes of Modern Wars and Their Characteristics," *Communist of the Armed Forces*, No. 2, January 1963, pp. 29–30.

11. Colonel P. I. Trifonenkov, *Ob Osnovikh Zakonakh Khoda i Izkhoda Sovremmenoi Voiny*, Voenizdat Ministerstva Oborony SSSR, Moscow, 1962, especially pp. 48, 53–54; Colonel G. A. Fedorov, Major General N. I. Sushko, *et al.*, *Marksizm-Leninizm o Voine i Armii*, Voenizdat Ministerstva Oborony SSSR, Moscow, 1963, especially pp. 187*ff.* An editorial preface to the Trifonenkov book pointed out, incidentally, that some of the author's propositions were of a "polemical nature" and not necessarily agreed to by the reviewing authorities. It was not indicated, however, whether or not this applied to the propositions on protracted war.

12. *Voennaia Strategiia*, 2nd ed., p. 260; *Soviet Military Strategy*, p. 314.

13. *Voennaia Strategiia*, 2nd ed., p. 261. An extended criticism of the first Sokolovskii edition by A. Golubev found fault with it for neglecting the possibility that a future war could be, in Frunze's words, "protracted war" involving "a strategy of attrition." "Some Problems of Military History in the Book 'Military Strategy,' " *Military-Historical Journal*, No. 5, May 1963, p. 99.

14. Colonel General N. Lomov, "On Military Doctrine," *Communist of the Armed Forces*, No. 10, May 1962, p. 15.

15. *Soviet Military Doctrine*, p. 25.

16. *Ibid.*, p. 26.

17. "Basic Tenets of Soviet Military Doctrine," *Red Star*, January 10, 1964.

18. "New Weapons and the Nature of War," *Red Star*, January 7, 1964.

19. See discussion of this question in U.S. Editors' Analytical Introduction, *Soviet Military Strategy*, pp. 36–38.

20. Such an assumption is of course made in Soviet military theory. See *Soviet Military Strategy*, pp. 433–439; *Voennaia Strategiia*, 2nd ed., pp. 291, 410–417.

21. *Voennaia Strategiia*, 2nd ed., p. 500. For a separate discussion by one of the Sokolovskii authors of the changes wrought in the conduct of war by modern strategic weapons, including the importance of making "effective use of the maximum might of the state at the very beginning of armed conflict," see Colonel V. Larionov, "New Means of Combat and Strategy," *Red Star*, April 8, 1964. This article is one of the series begun in *Red Star* in early 1964 under the general title of "The Revolution in Military Affairs: Its Significance and Consequences."

22. Speech to All-Army Conference on Ideological Questions, *Red Star*, October 25, 1962.

23. *Soviet Military Strategy*, pp. 338, 437–438; *Voennaia Strategiia*, 2nd ed., pp. 300, 412.

24. See Khrushchev's letter to President Kennedy, *Izvestiia*, February 24, 1962.

25. In the second Sokolovskii edition, discussion of this subject furnished a new differentiation between peacetime recruitment for "regular formations," which "are recruited on a extraterritorial basis," and mobilization under nuclear war conditions in which "a system of territorial buildup of troops during mobilization is considered the most acceptable." *Voennaia Strategiia*, 2nd ed., p. 412.

26. *Soviet Military Strategy*, p. 439; *Voennaia Strategiia*, 2nd ed., p. 417. This passage concluded with the suggestion that the side which first exploited nuclear attacks by penetrating the other's territory could win a major advantage, particularly in the European Theater.

27. *Voennaia Strategiia*, 2nd ed., p. 21. See also Lomov in *Red Star*, January 10, 1964.

28. *Voennaia Strategiia*, 2nd ed., p. 276. See also Lomov in *Red Star*, January 10, 1964.

CHAPTER XII. DEBATE OVER THE SIZE OF THE ARMED FORCES

1. See previous discussion of these developments in Chap. II.

2. See Khrushchev's speech to graduates of Soviet military academies on July 8, 1961, in *Pravda*, July 9, 1961, and his television address of August 7, 1961, in *Izvestiia*, August 9, 1961.

3. Report to CPSU Central Committee Plenum, *Izvestiia*, December 15, 1963; *Pravda*, December 16, 1963.

4. Major General V. Kruchinin, "Why Massive Armies?" *Red Star*, January 11, 1963.

5. See review by General of the Army P. Kurochkin, *Red Star*, September 22, 1962. See also *Soviet Military Strategy*, pp. 34–39, 523–529.

6. General Kruchinin's January 11th *Red Star* article, in response to a "reader's query," was followed by others that stressed the vital role of ground forces and "multimillion man" armies in a future war. See *Red Star*, February 12, 15, 1963. See also Colonel M. Skirdo, "The Role of the Popular Masses and the Individual in Contemporary War," *Communist of the Armed Forces*, No. 5, March 1963, p. 10.

7. Marshal R. Ia. Malinovskii, *Vigilantly Stand Guard Over the Peace*, Voenizdat Ministerstva Oborony SSSR, Moscow, 1962, p. 43.

8. *Red Star*, February 23, 1963.

9. See U.S. Editors' Analytical Introduction, *Soviet Military Strategy*, footnote on p. 13.

10. Marshal P. Rotmistrov, "The Causes of Modern Wars and Their Characteristics," *Communist of the Armed Forces*, No. 2, January 1963, pp. 29, 30–31.

11. "Leninist Principles of the Construction of the Soviet Armed Forces," *Communist of the Armed Forces*, No. 7, April 1963, p. 14. It is worth noting that the appeal to Lenin's views on a regular standing army has been paralleled in Soviet military writing by frequent reference to the soundness of decisions taken by the 8th Party Congress in 1919, which authorized establishment of regular armed forces in preference to a territorial militia system. This old issue was given new currency by Khrushchev's statement on January 14, 1960, that consideration was being given to the establishment of a territorial militia system in place of some regular armed forces. By adverting to the 8th Congress decisions, military writers seem to be challenging Khrushchev's idea of reviving the territorial militia conception, which may strike the military as being archaic in a highly technical era. For a discussion of this question and its relationship to the present Party Program, see Nikolai Galay, "Soviet Armed Forces and the Programme," in *The USSR and the Future*, Leonard Schapiro, ed., Frederick A. Praeger, Inc., New York, 1963, pp. 222–231. See also Walter C. Clemens, Jr., "Soviet Disarmament Proposals and the Cadre-Territorial Army," *Orbis*, Vol. 7, No. 4, Winter 1964, pp. 778–799.

12. General of the Army A. A. Epishev, "The Growing Role of the CPSU in the Leadership of the Armed Forces," *Problems of the History of the CPSU*, No. 2, February 1963, p. 10.

13. Election speech in Kalinin District, *Pravda*, February 28, 1963.

14. Letter to President Kennedy, *Izvestiia*, February 24, 1962. See also similar views by Khrushchev reported by W. E. Knox, "Close-Up of Khrushchev During a Crisis," *New York Times Magazine*, November 18, 1962, p. 129.

15. See previous discussion of the Soviet military budget debate at this juncture in Chap. III.

16. See discussion in Chap. III.

17. "The Theoretical and Methodological Basis of Soviet Military Science," *Communist of the Armed Forces*, No. 10, May 1963, p. 10.

18. *Ibid.*

19. Colonel L. Belousov, "Conference on Soviet Military Doctrine," *Military-Historical Journal*, No. 10, October 1963, pp. 121*ff*.

20. *Soviet Military Strategy*, p. 338.

21. *Voennaia Strategiia*, 2nd ed., p. 300.

22. See Marshal R. Ia. Malinovskii, "The Defense of the Socialist Fatherland Is Our Sacred Duty," *Pravda*, September 14, 1961; Marshal S. Biriuzov, "Soldiers of Peace Are on the Alert," *Sovetskaia Rossiia*, October 3, 1961; Marshal A. A. Grechko, "The Patriotic and International Duty of the USSR Armed Forces," *Red Star*, October 6, 1961.

23. P. N. Pospelov, *et al.*, *Istoriia Velikoi Otachestvennoi Voiny Sovetskogo Soiuza, 1941–1945* (The History of the Great Fatherland War of the Soviet Union, 1941–1945), Voenizdat Ministerstva Oborony SSSR, Moscow, 1960–1963, 6 volumes (one not yet published). See especially Vol. I, pp. 414–475.

24. One of the contentions of the "modernist" school which has tended to support Khrushchev's approach is that the Central Committee's "wise decisions" with respect to technical development and force structure have enabled the Soviet Union not only "to surpass the imperialists" in the most modern weapons and techniques, but "at the same time have resulted in reducing state expenditures on obsolete military objects and types of arms which have no future." Colonel V. Konoplev, "On Scientific Foresight in Military Affairs," *Communist of the Armed Forces*, No. 24, December 1963, p. 33.

25. *Voennaia Strategiia*, 2nd ed., p. 410. See also pp. 291, 300.

26. *Ibid.*, p. 287.

27. Some Soviet military theorists not identified with the protracted war thesis have also argued that one should not judge the enemy's strength only as it exists before a war starts, but also from the viewpoint of "future changes in the balance of forces and capabilities brought about by combat operations." See Konoplev in *Communist of the Armed Forces*, No. 24, December 1963, p. 33.

28. *Voennaia Strategiia*, 2nd ed., p. 275.

29. *Ibid.*, p. 291.

30. *Izvestiia*, December 15, 1963. Khrushchev's proposal was repeated in much the same language in his interview with UPI correspondent Henry Shapiro, *Red Star*, December 31, 1963.

31. *Pravda*, December 16, 1963. The announced reduction was

from 13.9 billion rubles in 1963 to 13.3 billion for 1964, or about 5 per cent. The actual impact of the announced reduction on Soviet defense programs is difficult to determine, since internal shifts in the budget may have had a compensating effect, such as an increase for scientific research in about the same amount as the defense cut. In any event, it seems unlikely that the new budget could have satisfied advocates of any large expansion of the Soviet defense effort.

32. As pointed out in Chap. III, Marshal Eremenko was the exception, being the only ranking military man to mention the troop-cut proposal in more than a month after Khrushchev's statement. Eremenko's mention of "the forthcoming cut in the Soviet armed forces," which offered neither approval nor disapproval, was made in the English-language newspaper, *Moscow News*, No. 2, January 11, 1964.

33. For example, Marshal A. Grechko, "On a Leninist Course," *Red Star*, December 22, 1963; Marshal V. Chuikov, "Modern Ground Forces," *Izvestiia*, December 22, 1963; Marshal S. Biriuzov, "Guarding the Great Achievements," *Red Star*, January 8, 1964.

34. Editorial, "A Mighty Step," *Red Star*, December 21, 1963.

35. Editorial, "Work Still More Selflessly," *Red Star*, December 25, 1963.

36. Editorial in *Pravda*, December 18, 1963; report of 20th Congress of the Swedish Communist Party, *Pravda*, January 8, 1964.

37. *Izvestiia*, December 22, 1963.

38. Major V. Kozlov, "The Soldier and the Nuclear Bomb," *Red Star*, December 28, 1963; Colonel B. Aleksandrov, "On Land, on Sea and in the Air," *Red Star*, December 29, 1963.

39. "Basic Tenets of Soviet Military Doctrine," *Red Star*, January 10, 1964.

40. Speech at the CPSU Central Committee Plenum, February 14, 1964, *Pravda*, February 15, 1964.

41. *Pravda*, February 28, 1963.

42. *Pravda*, February 15, 1964.

43. See Major General N. Sushko and Major T. Kondratkov, "War and Politics in the 'Nuclear Age,' " *Communist of the Armed Forces*, No. 2, January 1964, p. 23; Army General Pavel Kurochkin, "War Must Be Outlawed," *Moscow News*, February 22, 1964.

CHAPTER XIII. THE PRIMACY OF STRATEGIC FORCES AND OPERATIONS

1. See *Khrushchev's Strategy and Its Meaning for America*, A Study for the Use of the Committee on the Judiciary, United States Senate, U.S. Government Printing Office, Washington, D.C., 1960, pp. 10–12.

2. See Herbert S. Dinerstein, *War and the Soviet Union,* revised edition, Frederick A. Praeger, Inc., New York, 1962, pp. 180–212; Raymond L. Garthoff, *Soviet Strategy in the Nuclear Age,* revised edition, Frederick A. Praeger, Inc., New York, 1962, pp. 61–81.

3. "Learn to Vanquish a Strong and Technically Equipped Enemy," *Red Star,* September 25, 1954.

4. "Atomic Weapons and Antiatomic Defense," *Red Star,* August 3, 1954.

5. "Weapons in a Modern Army," in *Marxism-Leninism on War and the Army,* Voenizdat Ministerstva Oborony SSSR, Moscow, 1955, p. 168.

6. "Basic Tenets of Soviet Military Doctrine," *Red Star,* January 10, 1964.

7. Colonel General N. A. Lomov, *Soviet Military Doctrine,* Izdatelstvo "ZNANIE," Moscow 1963, p. 24.

8. Report by Colonel L. Belousov, "Conference on Soviet Military Doctrine," *Military-Historical Journal,* No. 10, October 1963, p. 125.

9. Captain First Rank Ia. V. Kolesnikov, "Some Categories of Naval Tactics," *Naval Collection,* No. 11, November 1963, p. 19.

10. Marshal P. Rotmistrov, "The Causes of Modern Wars and Their Characteristics," *Communist of the Armed Forces,* No. 2, January 1963, p. 31.

11. Exponents of the modernist view are likely to put the emphasis somewhat differently. For example, Major D. Kazakov, one of the writers who took part in the revival of Khrushchev's strategic views in mid-1963, noted in his May 1963 article that "the combined efforts of all troops" would help gain victory. However, he then added: "But Marxism-Leninism teaches that in this combined effort one must select the main, decisive element. That element at present is nuclear weapons and missiles in the missile forces." "The Theoretical and Methodological Basis of Soviet Military Science," *Communist of the Armed Forces,* No. 10, May 1963, p. 12. For similar stress on strategic missile operation as the "main link," see Colonel V. Konoplev, "On Scientific Foresight in Military Affairs," *ibid.,* No. 24, December 1963, p. 31.

12. For a forthright Soviet description of these phases in the development of Soviet military doctrine and theory, see Colonel I. Korotkov, "The Development of Soviet Military Theory in the Post-War Years," *Military-Historical Journal,* No. 4, April 1964, especially pages 43–45. This account, which cites the work of numerous Soviet military theorists, does not place immoderate emphasis on Khrushchev's personal contributions to Soviet military theory, although it does not neglect his role either. In point of fact, Khrushchev alone was not the source of innovation and reform in Soviet military affairs.

Certainly, the technical basis for the changes he has fostered was laid down by decisions taken in Stalin's time to embark on research and development programs in nuclear energy, jet aircraft, missiles, and other fields. In a sense, this was the military parallel to the process by which many of the political antecedents of Khrushchev's policy carried over from changes already at work in Stalin's day. For a perceptive discussion of this subject, see Marshall D. Shulman, *Stalin's Foreign Policy Reappraised,* Harvard University Press, Cambridge, Mass., 1963, especially pp. 104–138, 255–271.

13. Havana Domestic Radio and Television Networks, June 5, 1963.

14. *Communist of the Armed Forces,* No. 10, May 1963, p. 12. An account by Colonel I. Mareev in the same journal in early 1964 spoke with unusual frankness of the "bold and revolutionary" character of the Central Committee's decision to undertake the missile program, and of the great diversion of resources and skilled personnel that this involved, as well as the "many complex theoretical and technical problems" encountered. This discussion mentioned no open opposition to the program, but the recital of obstacles suggests that it did not enjoy smooth sailing. See "The Indestructible Shield of the Socialist Countries," *ibid.,* No. 3, February 1963, pp. 10–11.

15. *Military-Historical Journal,* No. 4, April 1964, p. 47.

16. *Soviet Military Strategy,* p. 401.

17. *Voennaia Strategiia,* 2nd ed., p. 368.

18. *Soviet Military Strategy,* p. 94. It should be borne in mind that the first Sokolovskii edition took an ambivalent stance on this question, elsewhere adhering to the doctrine that victory can be secured only through combined-arms operations. The second edition was similarly ambivalent. These matters are taken up more fully in Chap. XVII.

19. *Voennaia Strategiia,* 2nd ed., p. 21.

20. *Ibid.,* p. 377. The same point has come up in Soviet discussion elsewhere, particularly on command and control problems arising in modern war. Colonel General S. Shtemenko, for example, wrote in February 1963 that despite the great importance of strategic missiles, one would need the combined action of all arms "under a single central plan and leadership to win the war." Whether this is an argument to counter a trend in Soviet planning toward greater autonomy of the strategic forces is not clear. "Scientific Technical Progress and Its Influence on the Development of Military Affairs," *Communist of the Armed Forces,* No. 3, February 1963, p. 28.

21. *Voennaia Strategiia,* 2nd ed., p. 378.

22. *Ibid.*

23. *Ibid.*

24. *Ibid.*, p. 250; Colonel General V. F. Tolubko, "The Main Rocket Strength of the Country," *Red Star*, November 19, 1963; Lomov in *Red Star*, January 10, 1964. Major General N. Sushko and Major T. Kondratkov, "War and Politics in the 'Nuclear Age,'" *Communist of the Armed Forces*, No. 2, January 1964, p. 21.

25. *Soviet Military Strategy*, pp. 298, 400, 408–410; *Voennaia Strategiia*, 2nd ed., pp. 241, 366, 380–382.

26. Marshal S. Biriuzov, "New Stage in the Development of the Armed Forces and Tasks of Indoctrinating and Training Troops," *Communist of the Armed Forces*, No. 4, February 1964, p. 19.

27. *Soviet Military Strategy*, pp. 399–400; *Voennaia Strategiia*, 2nd ed., p. 366.

28. Historically speaking, a doctrine which regards the enemy's armed forces as the main object of destruction in war has long continuity in Soviet military thought. In a sense, therefore, extension of the doctrine to strategic counterforce operations made possible by modern weapons involves no basic conceptual wrench.

29. *Voennaia Strategiia*, 2nd ed., p. 250; *Soviet Military Strategy*, p. 305.

30. *Voennaia Strategiia*, 2nd ed., p. 241; *Soviet Military Strategy*, p. 298. See also *ibid.*, footnote 26, p. 24, which discusses an ambiguous reference on January 19, 1963, by Khrushchev to the figure of "80 to 120" long-range missiles as the possible size of the Soviet ICBM force. Perhaps the only other actual figures mentioned by a Soviet leader in connection with Soviet missile forces were those cited by Marshal Malinovskii in October 1961, at the 22nd Congress of the CPSU, when he said that "at the present time the missile forces include about 1800 excellent [military] units." This figure, unrelated to numbers or types of missiles, was relatively meaningless. *Pravda*, October 25, 1961.

31. A rather rare statement claiming sufficient Soviet nuclear weapons to "turn to ashes the aggressor's bases, launching sites and military centers" was made by a Soviet general in early 1964, without mention of attack against civilian targets. This apparent "counterforce" targeting statement, in a publication meant for circulation outside the Soviet Union, may have reflected sensitivity to charges that the USSR has adopted a "city-killing" strategy. See Army General Pavel Kurochkin, "War Must Be Outlawed," *Moscow News*, February 22, 1964, p. 3.

32. Lieutenant General N. Sbytov, "The Revolution in Military Affairs and Its Results," *Red Star*, February 15, 1963.

33. "Always on the Alert," *Izvestiia*, February 23, 1964.

34. See U.S. Editors' Analytical Introduction, *Soviet Military Strategy*, pp. 59–60.

35. Radio and television address on the German question, *Pravda,* August 8, 1961. For similar statements by Khrushchev, see also *Pravda,* November 29, 1957; January 15, 1960; July 11, 1962.

36. Marshal V. D. Sokolovskii, "A Suicidal Strategy," *Red Star,* July 19, 1962. General A. Nevsky, "Modern Armaments and Problems of Strategy," *World Marxist Review,* Vol. 6, No. 3, March 1963, p. 33; *Voennaia Strategiia,* 2nd ed., p. 85; Moscow Radio commentary on "Military Objectives," July 13, 1962.

37. L. Glagolev and V. Larionov, "Soviet Defence Might and Peaceful Coexistence," *International Affairs,* No. 11, November 1963, p. 31.

38. Colonel V. Morozov, "Joseph Alsop's 'Boiled Dog,' " *Red Star,* March 21, 1963.

39. *Red Star,* November 19, 1963. A quite contradictory statement on this point appeared in a subsequent *Red Star* article which cited the commander of a Soviet missile unit to the effect that there "were some men among his subordinates who had weak nerves. Expressing a false sense of fear, they requested transfers." Lieutenant Colonel A. Sgibnev and Major A. Shichalin, "Missile Prose," *Red Star,* January 8, 1964.

40. Report to the 22nd Congress of the CPSU, *Pravda,* October 25, 1961. Khrushchev first suggested that separate missile forces had been established in his January 1960 Supreme Soviet speech, but Malinovskii's announcement made it explicit. The literal rendering of the Soviet term for the strategic missile forces is "Rocket Troops of Strategic Designation."

41. See Arnold L. Horelick and Myron Rush, *The Political Use of Soviet Strategic Power,* The RAND Corporation, RM-2831-PR, January 1962.

42. "A Powerful Force," *Izvestiia,* November 8, 1963; "Strategic Missiles are Always in Readiness," *Red Star,* February 21, 1964.

43. Tolubko in *Red Star,* November 19, 1963; Marshal V. Chuikov, "The Defense of the Population Is the Main Task of Civil Defense," *Voennye Znaniia* (Military Knowledge), No. 1, January 1964, p. 3; Mareev in *Communist of the Armed Forces,* No. 3, February 1964, pp. 9–16.

44. Marshal R. Ia. Malinovskii, *Vigilantly Stand Guard Over the Peace,* Voenizdat Ministerstva Oborony, SSSR, Moscow, 1962, p. 43; editorial, "Rocketeers and Artillery Men Are on Guard Over the Fatherland," *Sovetskii Patriot,* November 18, 1962; Major General D. Vorobev, "The Fatherland's Fire Shield, *Sovetskii Patriot,* November 17, 1963; Malinovskii in *Red Star,* February 23, 1963; Biriuzov in *Communist of the Armed Forces,* No. 4, February 1964, p. 19.

45. Glagolev and Larionov in *International Affairs,* November 1963, p. 29.

46. Speech in Kalinin on January 17, 1964, *Pravda,* January 18, 1964.

47. Lieutenant Colonel A. Sgibnev, "Attention: Strategic Rocketeers—An Account of Life in One of the Units of the Rocket Forces," *Red Star,* November 6, 1963.

48. See *Soviet Military Strategy,* pp. 13, 17, 39.

49. See Marshal P. Rotmistrov, "Modern Tanks and Nuclear Weapons," *Izvestiia,* October 20, 1962. An interesting exposition of Rotmistrov's views on the relationship between modern weapons trends and traditional values and methods in military affairs is to be found in his Foreword to *A History of Military Art,* a major two-volume work, of which he was the editor, published by Voenizdat Ministerstva Oborony SSSR, Moscow, 1963. Here, Rotmistrov emphasized the importance of historical study of the military art as an aid to understanding and solving contemporary military problems. He chided unnamed colleagues who "think that studying the experience of past wars . . . has no great meaning at the present time, because a future war will be conducted under completely different circumstances." While "worship of this past experience would be a great mistake," in Rotmistrov's view, still, "whatever from the experience of past wars . . . has preserved its relevance should be used, and whatever has become antiquated should be rejected." Further, Rotmistrov argued, the Soviet Union now has a new generation of officers who "did not go through the bitter school of war and who have no personal combat experience. Studying the history of military art," he said, "helps to make up to a considerable extent for this lack of personal combat experience."

50. The two articles were: "Military Science and the Academies," *Red Star,* April 26, 1964, and "Methodical Experiments or the Pursuit of Sensations," *Red Star,* May 20, 1964.

51. *Red Star,* April 26, 1964. In the second article of May 20, 1964, Rotmistrov dealt not with current problems of military theory but with teaching methods. The article was a critique of "programmed training"—a cybernetics method of teaching favored by modernists and advanced schools of thought among military pedagogues. In early 1964, *Red Star* and other media published articles urging improved training methods and adoption of "programmed training." These originated mainly with modernists and missile commanders, including Colonel General V. E. Tolubko, deputy commander of the strategic missile forces. See his article, "Missiles and Methodologies," *Red Star,* April 11, 1964. Rotmistrov did not deny

that "programmed training" had promise. However, he asserted that it could not replace more conventional methods either, and he charged that it sometimes led to pursuit of sensational but harmful results. In this connection, he singled out for criticism the staff of the Kiev Higher Engineering Radiotechnical School, for using "all sorts of dreamed-up teaching contraptions." This school has pioneered in cybernetics research and theory, including the use of various kinds of teaching machines. In general, Rotmistrov's article seemed to be intended to support his argument against throwing traditional values and methods overboard, which he apparently regards as a vice of the modernist school.

52. Colonel S. I. Krupnov, *Dialektika i Voennaia Nauka* (Dialectics and Military Science), Major General S. N. Kozlov, ed., Voenizdat Ministerstva Oborony SSSR, Moscow, 1963, pp. 109–110.

53. Major General V. Bolotnikov, "Man, Altitude, Speed," *Red Star*, April 25, 1964. This article was one of the lengthy series originating in *Red Star* in January 1964 under the general title of "The Revolution in Military Affairs: Its Significance and Consequences."

CHAPTER XIV. EVOLVING ROLES OF THE TRADITIONAL FORCES

1. "Modern Ground Forces," *Izvestiia*, December 22, 1963; *Voennaia Strategiia*, 2nd ed., p. 246.

2. This dominance was expressed in Lomov's doctrinal exposition of January 1964 in the following words: "In the initial period the operations of the strategic missile forces and the PVO (antiair defense) will be of particularly great significance, since basically it will be precisely these forces which, having been the first to join combat, will solve the main tasks." Colonel General N. Lomov, "Basic Tenets of Soviet Military Doctrine," *Red Star*, January 10, 1964.

3. *Voennaia Strategiia*, 2nd ed., p. 372.

4. *Ibid.*, p. 374.

5. *Ibid.*, p. 377.

6. Chuikov in *Izvestiia*, December 22, 1963; Marshal P. Rotmistrov, "The Causes of Modern Wars and Their Characteristics," *Communist of the Armed Forces*, No. 2, January 1963, p. 31; *Soviet Military Strategy*, pp. 342, 344; Marshal R. Ia. Malinovskii, "45 Years on Guard Over the Socialist Fatherland," *Red Star*, February 23, 1963; Lomov in *Red Star*, January 10, 1964.

7. *Voennaia Strategiia*, 2nd ed., p. 307.

8. *Ibid.*

9. Lieutenant General V. Margelov, "The Precepts of a Paratrooper," *Red Star,* January 31, 1963.

10. *Soviet Military Strategy,* p. 341; *Voennaia Strategiia,* 2nd ed., p. 246; Lieutenant General N. Sbytov, "The Revolution in Military Affairs and Its Consequences," *Red Star,* February 15, 1963; Malinovskii in *Red Star,* February 23, 1963.

11. In Soviet usage, "strategic missiles" include missiles of intercontinental (ICBM), intermediate (IRBM), and medium range (MRBM). These are under the control of the strategic missile forces, directly subordinated to the Soviet High Command. Other missiles of lesser range, designated as "operational-tactical missiles" in Soviet usage, are to be found in the armament of the ground, air, and naval forces. As used above, "tactical missiles" refers to the Soviet category of "operational-tactical missiles." See explanation in *Soviet Military Strategy,* pp. 51, 521.

12. Marshal S. Varentsov, "Rockets: Formidable Weapon of the Ground Forces," *Izvestiia,* December 2, 1962.

13. *Soviet Military Strategy,* p. 341; *Voennaia Strategiia,* 2nd ed., p. 304.

14. *Soviet Military Strategy,* p. 341.

15. *Voennaia Strategiia,* 2nd ed., p. 304.

16. "Scientific-Technical Progress and Its Influence on the Development of Military Affairs," *Communist of the Armed Forces,* No. 3, February 1963, p. 22.

17. "Physics and New Weapons," *Red Star,* November 21, 1963.

18. See Colonel L. Belousov, "Conference on Soviet Military Doctrine," *Military-Historical Journal,* No. 10, October 1963, p. 123; Major D. Kazakov, "The Theoretical and Methodological Basis of Soviet Military Science," *Communist of the Armed Forces,* No. 10, May 1963, pp. 11–12; *Voennaia Strategiia,* 2nd ed., p. 234, 319; *Soviet Military Strategy,* pp. 288, 338, 356.

19. *Soviet Military Strategy,* p. 338; *Voennaia Strategiia,* 2nd ed., p. 299. See also Marshal P. Rotmistrov, "Historic Victory," *Moscow News,* May 11, 1963.

20. See Chap. X.

21. See Robert A. Kilmarx, *A History of Soviet Air Power,* Frederick A. Praeger, Inc., New York, 1962, p. 225.

22. *Soviet Military Strategy,* p. 346.

23. In his message of January 21, 1964, to the Geneva disarmament conference, President Johnson urged that the United States and the Soviet Union agree to explore a verified freeze of the number and characteristics of strategic nuclear offensive and defensive vehicles. *New York Times,* January 22, 1964. The Soviet Union

countered this by proposing the destruction of all bomber aircraft without waiting for an agreement on general and complete disarmament. *New York Times,* January 29, 1964.

24. *New York Times,* June 11, 1963.

25. Sbytov in *Red Star,* February 15, 1963; Malinovskii in *Red Star,* February 23, 1963.

26. *Voennaia Strategiia,* 2nd ed., p. 310; *Soviet Military Strategy,* p. 346.

27. *Voennaia Strategiia,* 2nd ed., p. 310; *Soviet Military Strategy,* p. 346.

28. *Voennaia Strategiia,* 2nd ed., p. 311. In the second edition, examples were given of air-to-surface missiles of "400–600 kilometer range and greater" in the Soviet case, compared with Hound Dog and Blue Streak missiles of "800 and 600–1000 kilometers," respectively, in the Western case.

29. *Ibid.,* p. 310. It may be recalled from the discussion in Chap. V that modern detection capabilities have been emphasized by the Soviets as one of the factors reducing the prospect of a successful U.S. first strike against the Soviet Union, as in the Glagolev-Larionov article in *International Affairs.*

30. *Voennaia Strategiia,* 2nd ed., p. 312; *Soviet Military Strategy,* p. 347.

31. *Voennaia Strategiia,* 2nd ed., pp. 375, 381, 382; *Soviet Military Strategy,* pp. 406, 408, 410.

32. *Voennaia Strategiia,* 2nd ed., p. 312.

33. See *Washington Post,* March 17, 19, and *New York Times,* June 5, 1963.

34. *Voennaia Strategiia,* 2nd ed., p. 400.

35. Service-oriented viewpoints certainly exist in the Soviet Union and are undoubtedly a factor in the internal military policy debate. It is difficult, however, to find a close correspondence between any particular service viewpoint and the modernist-traditionalist schools of thought, except perhaps that the traditionalist outlook may be more widely found in the ground forces merely on strength of numbers. In the air force case, the bent of many officers may be naturally in the modernist direction, but their interests often lie closer to those of the traditionalists. For example, the missile forces, which have become the darling of the Party and where the modernist view flourishes, are esssentially competitors for favor and resources against long-range aviation advocates within the air forces. At the same time, tactical aviation elements in the air forces find their natural allies in the shaping of doctrine and channeling of resources among the staunch traditionalists who want to preserve large combined-arms theater forces.

36. *Red Star*, February 23, 1963.

37. *Red Star*, January 10, 1964.

38. A. Tupolev, "The Missile-Aircraft Carrier," *Aviatsiia i Kozmonavtika* (Aviation and Cosmonautics), No. 6, June 1962, p. 4.

39. *Communist of the Armed Forces*, No. 3, February 1963, p. 24.

40. *Voennaia Strategiia*, 2nd ed., p. 311. This revived emphasis on tactical aircraft for battlefield support is of particular interest in connection with the possible downgrading of tactical missile contributions mentioned earlier.

41. *Ibid.*, pp. 309, 311.

42. *Ibid.*

43. *Ibid.*, p. 399.

44. *Ibid.*, p. 312. See also Marshal K. A. Vershinin, "The Might of the Air Force Is Growing," *Red Star*, February 1, 1964; Margelov in *Red Star*, January 31, 1963; Malinovskii in *Red Star*, February 23, 1963.

45. Marshal P. A. Rotmistrov, "Military Science and the Academies," *Red Star*, April 26, 1964.

46. Major General V. Bolotnikov, "Man, Altitude, Speed," *Red Star*, April 25, 1964.

47. In 1955 Admiral N. G. Kuznetsov, head of the navy, was dismissed for favoring a large surface navy, which may also have been opposed by Marshal Zhukov, then Minister of Defense. See Raymond L. Garthoff, *Soviet Strategy in the Nuclear Age*, revised edition, Frederick A. Praeger, Inc., New York, 1962, pp. 37–38. Khrushchev himself has sometimes been credited as the "father of the submarine fleet," who allegedly overruled Zhukov on the need for submarines. Zhukov has been somewhat tendentiously pictured as the opponent of not only surface vessels but also submarines. See Val. Goltsev, "Atomic Submarine on a Cruise," *Izvestiia*, October 11, 1961.

48. *New York Times*, June 11, 1963.

49. For American commentary on this point, see U.S. Editors' Analytical Introduction, *Soviet Military Strategy*, p. 55. A Soviet critic was Admiral V. A. Alafuzov, writing in a Soviet naval journal in January 1963. Alafuzov found in the first Sokolovskii edition a tendency to take too much for granted the vulnerability of Polaris-type submarines, and found shortcomings in its treatment of other naval problems as well. "On Publication of the Work 'Military Strategy,'" *Naval Collection*, No. 1, January 1963, p. 94.

50. *Voennaia Strategiia*, 2nd ed., p. 398.

51. *Ibid.*, p. 399; *Soviet Military Strategy*, p. 422.

52. *Voennaia Strategiia*, 2nd ed., p. 381.

53. *Ibid.*, p. 399.

54. *Ibid.*, p. 398. Some Soviet naval writers have also continued to assert that Polaris submarines are vulnerable on various grounds, including the "noise" they are alleged to generate when running submerged. Admiral A. Chabanenko, "Nuclear Scouts of the Pentagon," *Izvestiia*, December 1, 1963. See also Captain First Rank Y. Mamaev, "Targets in the Ocean," *Red Star*, April 4, 1963; Captain First Rank V. P. Rogov, "U.S. Imperialists Form a 'Polaris' High Command," *Naval Collection*, No. 5, May 1963, pp. 77–85.

55. *Voennaia Strategiia*, 2nd ed., p. 399.

56. "The Great Tasks of the Soviet Navy," *Red Star*, February 5, 1963.

57. Rear Admiral F. Maslov, "Suddenly and Secretly," *Red Star*, October 12, 1963.

58. Captain Second Rank N. Belous, "Masters of the Deep," *Communist of the Armed Forces*, No. 13, July 1963, p. 51. It should be noted that in this account the submarine ultimately succeeded, despite difficulties, in forcing the ASW barrier.

59. *Naval Collection*, January 1963, p. 95.

60. *Voennaia Strategiia*, 2nd ed., p. 398.

61. *Ibid.; Soviet Military Strategy*, p. 421.

62. *Voennaia Strategiia*, 2nd ed., p. 398.

63. *Ibid.*, p. 397.

64. Editorial, "Principal Striking Force of the Navy," *Red Star*, October 31, 1962.

65. *Ibid.* This editorial, and other material in the same issue of *Red Star*, including an interview with Admiral Gorshkov, appeared in the wake of the Cuban crisis. The emphasis throughout was on the defensive mission of the submarine force, rather than upon a strategic offensive role, which might have been expected to receive emphasis in light of the setback to Soviet offensive strike capabilities implicit in withdrawal of land-based medium-range missiles from Cuba.

66. *Naval Collection*, January 1963, pp. 94, 95.

67. *Voennaia Strategiia*, 2nd ed., pp. 369, 372, 406; *Soviet Military Strategy*, pp. 402, 404, 427.

68. *Red Star*, July 21, 1962; Admiral S. G. Gorshkov, "Great Tasks of the Soviet Fleet," *Red Star*, February 5, 1963. An account in *Izvestiia*, November 8, 1962, identified naval missiles shown in the Red Square parade as types that could be "launched from any position—on the surface or submerged."

69. See U.S. Editors' Analytical Introduction, *Soviet Military Strategy*, pp. 71, 75.

70. *Naval Collection*, January 1963, p. 95.

71. *Ibid.*, p. 92.

72. *Voennaia Strategiia,* 2nd ed., p. 313.

73. Captain First Rank N. P. Viunenko, "Modern Amphibious Landings," *Naval Collection,* No. 9, September 1963, p. 21.

74. *Ibid.,* p. 26. For another discussion of amphibious landing problems which drew the conclusion that nuclear suppression of defenses should be supplemented by conventional firepower from aircraft and surface ships, see Captains First Rank A. G. Svetlov and L. A. Shimkevich, "Features of Amphibious Landings Under Modern Conditions," *Naval Collection,* No. 3, March 1964, pp. 22–27.

75. An article by Lieutenant Colonel B. Burkanov describing a training exercise in which a landing took place after neutralizing "enemy" shore defenses by a simulated nuclear strike appeared in *Red Star,* October 11, 1962.

76. *Naval Collection,* September 1963, p. 27.

CHAPTER XV. STRATEGIC DEFENSE OF THE SOVIET UNION

1. See U.S. Editors' Analytical Introduction, *Soviet Military Strategy,* pp. 55–57.

2. See Robert A. Kilmarx, *A History of Soviet Air Power,* Frederick A. Praeger, Inc., New York, 1962, pp. 265–267.

3. Known as the National PVO, from the formal Soviet designation, *Protivovozdushnaia Oborona Strany,* or Antiair Defense of the Country.

4. Address to the Fifth All-Union Congress of DOSAAF by Marshal V. I. Chuikov, *Sovetskii Patriot,* May 26, 1962.

5. Statement to a group of visiting U.S. newspaper editors, *New York Times,* July 17, 1962.

6. The first specific Soviet claim of success in this field was made by Marshal Malinovskii at the 22nd Party Congress in October 1961, when he said: "I must report in particular that the problem of destroying missiles in flight also has been successfully solved." *Pravda,* October 25, 1961. See also *Pravda,* February 23, 1963. Early public indications that the Soviet Union was interested in the possibility of antimissile defense go back to the mid-fifties, at which time a Soviet officer wrote that "technically, creation of a potent defense system against ballistic missiles is fully feasible." Major F. Kriksanov, "The Problems of the Interception of Intercontinental Ballistic Missiles," *Military Knowledge,* No. 7, July 1957, pp. 15–16. See also Peter Kapitsa, "The Task of All Progressive Mankind," *Novoe Vremia* (New Times), No. 39, 1956, p. 10.

7. Leont'ev commentary on Moscow radio, November 12, 1963; Major General P. Radchenko, "Pilotless Interceptors Are Launched," *Red Star,* November 16, 1963; *New York Times,* November 8, 1963.

8. "A Powerful Force," *Izvestiia*, November 8, 1963.

9. Major General I. Baryshev, "Nuclear Weapons and PVO," *Red Star*, November 13, 1963.

10. "A Reliable Shield," *Izvestiia*, January 5, 1964. The word *prakticheskii* lends itself to ambiguity, for it can be translated as "in a practical sense" or "in practice," which conveys quite a different meaning in English than "practically." However, a *Tass* version of the Sudets article, broadcast in *English* on January 4, 1964, used the expression "practically all modern means" as in the above translation. In a subsequent major article on Soviet air defenses in March 1964, Marshal Sudets claimed without qualification that the Soviet Union had "successfully solved the problem of creating a reliable defense, not only against aircraft, but also against missiles." See "The National PVO at the Present Stage," *Red Star*, March 28, 1964.

11. *Voennaia Strategiia*, 2nd ed., p. 241; *Soviet Military Strategy*, p. 298.

12. *Soviet Military Strategy*, p. 345.

13. *Voennaia Strategiia*, 2nd ed., p. 309. See also p. 393, where a similar implication was conveyed by amending a statement on the possibility of "creating" an antimissile defense so that it now reads: "the task of repelling an enemy's missile strikes becomes a realistic possibility."

14. *Ibid.*, p. 395.

15. *Izvestiia*, January 4, 1964. It may be observed that Soviet commentary has made no mention of the fact that the United States also has intercepted ballistic missiles in flight in connection with developmental programs, as presumably occurred in the Soviet case. See *New York Times*, November 10, 1963.

16. *Red Star*, November 13, 1963.

17. *Ibid.*

18. See, for example, Hearings on Military Posture and H.R. 9637, Statement of Secretary of Defense Robert S. McNamara Before the House Armed Services Committee on the Fiscal Year 1965–1969 Defense Program and 1965 Defense Budget, released by the House Armed Services Committee, 88:2, January 27, 1964, pp. 7010–7011, 7015–7018; Press Conference statement by President Kennedy, August 1, 1963, *New York Times*, August 2, 1963; Richard Witkin, "Air Force Presses for Way to Pierce Missile Defense," *New York Times*, November 9, 1963; Jack Raymond, "Soviet 'Missile Defense' Is Minimized by the U.S.," *New York Times*, November 10, 1963.

19. See comment on this point in Thomas C. Schelling, "Managing the Arms Race," in *National Security: Political, Military, and Eco-*

nomic Strategies in the Decade Ahead, David M. Abshire and Richard V. Allen, eds., Frederick A. Praeger, Inc., New York, 1963, p. 607.

20. On the question of organizational arrangements, Soviet military literature has mentioned on several occasions in the past two years the formal inclusion of antimissile defense in the over-all "anti-air defense" system. See, for example, *Soviet Military Strategy,* pp. 344, 417–418; Malinovskii in *Pravda,* February 23, 1963; Baryshev in *Red Star,* November 13, 1963. Baryshev's account indicated that "the process of developing the PVO proceeded even more intensively after the 22nd Party Congress," from which time new organizational planning may stem. The extent to which antimissile organization is still on paper as distinct from deployment of actual facilities in the field is, of course, a matter on which Soviet discussion is unrevealing. The Western press has furnished some comment on this question, such as the statement in *New York Times,* November 10, 1963, that the Russians are "reported to have built one antimissile missile battery in the vicinity of Leningrad."

21. To some extent, the Soviet argument that air defenses have the upper hand over bombers is also at odds with the obverse contention that missile-launching bombers can foil the defense by staying out of its reach. Occasional tacit acknowledgments to this effect have found their way into the Soviet military press, such as the description of an air defense exercise in which the situation "quickly changed" to the disadvantage of the defense when one of the "attacker's" bombers "launched a missile at a great distance." Major M. Makarov, "Strike Against Missile Carriers," *Red Star,* September 10, 1963.

22. *Soviet Military Strategy,* p. 307; *Voennaia Strategiia,* 2nd ed., p. 252.

23. *Soviet Military Strategy,* p. 417; *Voennaia Strategiia,* 2nd ed., p. 391.

24. The offensive-defensive relationship in Soviet thinking was summed up in 1963 by one writer who said: " . . . it is indisputable that today the offenses must be developed at maximum speed from the very first hours of the war"; he added that to protect "one's country against possible enemy strikes," offense must be combined with "modern air and missile defenses . . . without which it is impossible to win a war." A. Golubev, "Some Problems of Military History in the Book 'Military Strategy,'" *Military-Historical Journal,* No. 5, May 1963, p. 94.

25. See discussion of this subject in *Soviet Military Strategy,* pp. 246–258; *Voennaia Strategiia,* 2nd ed., pp. 186–200; Golubev

in *Military-Historical Journal,* No. 5, May 1963, pp. 100–101. See also Matthew P. Gallagher, *The Soviet History of World War II,* Frederick A. Praeger, Inc., New York, 1963, pp. 128–135.

26. "Scientific-Technical Progress and Its Influence on the Development of Military Affairs," *Communist of the Armed Forces,* No. 3, February 1963, pp. 27–28.

27. Major D. Kazakov, "The Theoretical and Methodological Basis of Soviet Military Science," *Communist of the Armed Forces,* No. 10, May 1963, pp. 10–11; Colonel V. Konoplev, "On Scientific Foresight in Military Affairs," *ibid.,* No. 24, December 1963, p. 28.

28. See *Marxism-Leninism on War and the Army,* Voenizdat Ministerstva Oborony SSSR, Moscow, 1962, pp. 255–256; Colonel P. I. Trifonenkov, *On the Fundamental Laws of the Course and Outcome of Modern War,* Voenizdat Ministerstva Oborony SSSR, Moscow, 1962, p. 29.

29. *Voennaia Strategiia,* 2nd ed., p. 394. One may note here the incongruity of a Soviet "retaliatory strike" which is expected to hit many enemy forces before they can be launched. This would seem to be more aptly a description of a pre-emptive Soviet strike.

30. Marshal V. I. Chuikov, "The Defense of the Population Is the Main Task of Civil Defense," *Military Knowledge,* No. 1, January 1964, p. 3.

31. Colonel General O. Tolstikov, "An Undertaking of Great Importance to the State," *Military Knowledge,* No. 2, February 1962, p. 22. See also address by Marshal Chuikov in *Sovetskii Patriot,* May 26, 1962; Lieutenant General L. Vinogradov, "The 30th Anniversary of Civil Defense," *Sovetskii Patriot,* October 7, 1962.

32. See Leon Gouré, *Civil Defense in the Soviet Union,* University of California Press, Berkeley and Los Angeles, 1962, especially pp. 38–61. Soviet sources date the beginning of civil defense effort back to 1932, but its reorganization and orientation around problems of nuclear-age civil defense occurred in the early 1950's. See Vinogradov in *Sovetskii Patriot,* October 7, 1962.

33. *Sovetskii Patriot,* September 18, 1963. The present 19-hour civil defense training course, announced in *Sovetskii Patriot* on September 30, 1962, evidently began in the summer of 1962.

34. *Sovetskii Patriot,* April 12, 1961.

35. *Sovetskii Patriot,* October 9, 1963.

36. *Soviet Military Strategy,* pp. 462–463; Gouré, *Civil Defense in the Soviet Union,* p. 32.

37. Marshal V. I. Chuikov, "The New Regulations of the Garrison and Guard Services," *Red Star,* October 8, 1963.

38. Tolstikov in *Military Knowledge,* No. 2, February 1962, p. 22; Tolstikov, "Improve the Training of the Population in Every Way,"

ibid., No. 4, April 1963, p. 33. In this connection, two basic civil defense training manuals were severely criticized in *Military Knowledge*, No. 7, July 1963, p. 39, for inadequate "discussion of the destructive effects of nuclear weapons" and other shortcomings. The manuals in question were: N. N. Ivanov, *et al.*, *Grazhdanskaia Oborona* (Civil Defense), Uchpedgiz, Moscow, 1962; P. T. Egorov *et al.*, *Grazhdanskaia Oborona* (Civil Defense), Gosudarstvennoe Izdatelstvo "Vysshaia Shkola," Moscow, 1963.

39. *Military Knowledge*, No. 2, February 1962, p. 22. See also Leon Gouré, *The Resolution of the Soviet Controversy Over Civil Defense*, The RAND Corporation, RM–3223–PR, June 1962.

40. Statements depreciating the value of shelters have been made by Anastas Mikoyan, Mrs. Khrushchev, and Marshal Malinovskii, among others. See *Bulletin of the Atomic Scientists*, May 1959, p. 191; *New York Times*, October 7, 1961; *Pravda*, January 24, 1962.

41. See Gouré, *Civil Defense in the Soviet Union*, pp. 106–110.

42. *Ibid.*, pp. 79–110; Major L. Gorshkov, "Collective Means of Defense," *Military Knowledge*, No. 4, April 1963, pp. 36–37; *Soviet Military Strategy*, p. 529; *Voennaia Strategiia*, 2nd ed., p. 438; Egorov *et al.*, *Civil Defense*, pp. 159–169; Chuikov in *Military Knowledge*, No. 1, January 1964, p. 3.

43. Hearings on Military Posture and H.R. 9637, Statement of Secretary of Defense Robert S. McNamara Before the House Armed Services Committee, 88:2, January 27, 1964, pp. 7017–7018.

44. See Trifonenkov, *Fundamental Laws*, pp. 15, 31, 48, 53, 54; *Marxism-Leninism on War and the Army*, 1962, pp. 187, 255–256, 283, 323; *Soviet Military Strategy*, pp. 451–452, 454–458, 461–463; A. Lagovskii, *Strategiia i Ekonomika* (Strategy and the Economy), Voenizdat Ministerstva Oborony SSSR, Moscow, 1962, p. 32; Colonel I. S. Baz', "Soviet Military Science on the Character of Modern War," *Military Herald*, No. 6, June 1958, pp. 24–25; Colonel I. Sidel'nikov, "On Soviet Military Doctrine," *Red Star*, May 11, 1962; V. Siniagin, "The Creation of the Material-Technological Base of Communism and Strengthening of the Defense Capacity of the USSR," *Communist of the Armed Forces*, No. 14, July 1962, p. 14.

45. *Voennaia Strategiia*, 2nd ed., p. 47. For other expressions of the growing importance of morale-political preparations, see Marshal V. I. Kazakov, "Field Training of Rocketeers," *Red Star*, September 28, 1963; Colonel L. Belousov, "Conference on Soviet Military Doctrine," *Military-Historical Journal*, No. 10, October 1963, p. 125; Major General N. Sushko, "The Laws Determining the Course and Outcome of Wars," *Red Star*, February 7, 1964; Lieutenant General Iu. Votintsev, "Fortitude: How It Is Taught," *Red Star*, February 8, 1964.

46. Egorov *et al., Civil Defense*, pp. 133–134. See also V. Pechorkin, "About 'Acceptable' War," *International Affairs*, No. 3, March 1963, p. 23.

47. The omitted passage, *Soviet Military Strategy*, p. 460, read as follows: "Great importance is now attached to the prior and thoroughly planned evacuation of the population from large cities and border zones during the period when war threatens or during the first days of the war."

48. Colonel V. Moskalev, "Act Skillfully During Civil Defense Alerts," *Military Knowledge*, No. 8, August 1963, pp. 31–32.

49. *Military Knowledge*, No. 1, January 1964, p. 3. Instruction in evacuation procedures and use of shelters was described in an article in the same journal in February 1964, dealing with the carrying out of the 19-hour civil defense training program. See N. Olovianishnikov, "Depending on Conditions," *ibid.*, No. 2, February 1964, p. 20.

50. *Voennaia Strategiia*, 2nd ed., p. 85.

CHAPTER XVI. MILITARY USES OF SPACE

1. See *New York Times*, October 18, 1963.

2. *Soviet Military Strategy*, p. 427.

3. See *Soviet Space Programs*, Staff Report, Senate Committee on Aeronautical and Space Sciences, May 31, 1962, Washington, D.C., pp. 99–150.

4. See Arnold L. Horelick, "The Soviet Union and the Political Uses of Outer Space," in *Outer Space in World Politics*, Joseph M. Goldsen, ed., Frederick A. Praeger, Inc., New York, 1963, pp. 43–70; see also Joseph M. Goldsen in *ibid.*, pp. 15–20.

5. See Alton Frye, "Our Gamble in Space: The Military Danger," *The Atlantic Monthly*, August 1963, pp. 47–49. See also *Soviet Space Programs*, p. 47.

6. Robert D. Crane, "The Beginnings of Marxist Space Jurisprudence?" *The American Journal of International Law*, Vol. 57, No. 3, July 1963, p. 622. See also *Soviet Space Programs*, pp. 207–208.

7. G. P. Zadorozhnii, "The Artificial Satellite and International Law," *Sovetskaia Rosiia* (Soviet Russia), October 17, 1957.

8. See *Soviet Space Programs*, p. 203. See also Robert D. Crane, "Soviet Attitude Toward International Space Law," *The American Journal of International Law*, Vol. 56, No. 3, July 1962, pp. 694–704.

9. G. P. Zhukov, "Problems of Space Law at the Present Stage," Memorandum of the Soviet Association of International Law at the Brussels Conference of the International Law Association, August 1962, pp. 30, 35–36, cited in Crane, *The American Journal of Inter-*

national Law, July 1963, p. 620; G. Zhukov, "Practical Problems of Space Law," *International Affairs,* No. 5, May 1963, p. 29.

10. Zhukov in *International Affairs,* May 1963, p. 28; E. A. Korovin, "Outer Space Must Become a Zone of Real Peace," *International Affairs,* No. 9, September 1963, p. 92.

11. See Frye in *The Atlantic Monthly,* August 1963, p. 47.

12. B. Teplinskii, "The Strategic Concepts of U.S. Aggressive Policy," *International Affairs,* No. 12, December 1960, p. 39; G. P. Zhukov, "Space Espionage Plans and International Law," *ibid.,* No. 10, October 1960, pp. 53–57.

13. N. Kovalev and I. I. Cheprov, *Na Puti k Kosmicheskomu Pravu* (On the Road to Space Law), Institut Mezhdunarodnykh Otnoshenii, Moscow, 1962, p. 123; E. A. Korovin, "Peaceful Cooperation in Space," *International Affairs,* No. 3, March 1962, p. 61.

14. See *Declaration of Legal Principles Governing the Activities of States in the Exploration and Use of Outer Space,* A/RES/1962 (XVIII), 24 December 1963.

15. *International Affairs,* September 1963, p. 93; see also G. P. Zadorozhnii, "Basic Problems of the Science of Space Law," in *Kosmos i Mezhdunarodnoe Pravo* (Space and International Law), Institut Mezhdunarodnykh Otnoshenii, Moscow, 1962, p. 38.

16. "Missiles and Strategy," *Red Star,* March 18, 1962.

17. "Outer Space and Strategy," *Red Star,* March 21, 1962.

18. *Soviet Military Strategy,* p. 427; *Voennaia Strategiia,* 2nd ed., pp. 405–406.

19. *Ibid.*

20. *Voennaia Strategiia,* 2nd ed., p. 404. Soviet charges that "American militarists" are planning to occupy the moon were made as early as 1960. See P. S. Romashkin, "Technical Progress and Soviet Law," *Sovetskoe Gosudarstvo i Pravo* (Soviet State and Law), No. 1, January 1960, p. 21.

21. *Voennaia Strategiia,* 2nd ed., p. 404.

22. "Nuclear Weapons and PVO," *Red Star,* November 13, 1963. Marshal Sudets in January 1964 also charged that the United States was continuing to "use space for military purposes," including "the development of orbital space systems." "A Reliable Shield," *Izvestiia,* January 5, 1964. In the spring of 1964, the Soviet military press continued to charge that U.S. space activities were oriented in a military direction. One writer asserted that "U.S. policy for conquering space . . . bears a pronounced military and, more specifically, aggressive nature." Colonel G. Terentiev, "Mercury-Gemini-Apollo: American Plans for Conquest of Space," *Red Star,* March 26, 1964. Another writer charged that despite the UN resolution the United States was still conducting "a program for creating offensive space

weapons by 1970, including . . . orbital missiles." Colonel B. Trofimov, "Missiles in Orbit," *Red Star*, April 15, 1964.

23. Lieutenant Colonel N. Vasil'ev, "From Airplane to Rocketplane," *Sovetskii Patriot*, December 22, 1963.

24. *New York Times*, December 11, 1963.

25. N. A. Varvarov, Moscow Radio broadcast, January 21, 1963.

26. Telegram to Nikolaev and Popovich, *Red Star*, August 16, 1962. See also Major General I. Baryshev, "What Is Anti-Space Defense?" *Red Star*, September 2, 1962.

27. See Raymond L. Garthoff, "Red War Sputniks in the Works?," *Missiles and Rockets*, Vol. 3, May 1958, pp. 134–136; *Soviet Space Programs*, pp. 56–59.

28. *Voennaia Strategiia*, 2nd ed., p. 254. Another Soviet writer in late 1963 stated: "The present development of military affairs gives one the basis for assuming that space will be used in the future for military ends." Colonel V. Konoplev, "On Scientific Foresight in Military Affairs," *Communist of the Armed Forces*, No. 24, December 1963, p. 32. See also Colonel P. Derevianko, "Some Features of the Contemporary Revolution in Military Affairs," *ibid.*, No. 1, January 1964, p. 20.

29. Zadorozhnii in *Space and International Law*, p. 53.

30. *Pravda*, June 22, 1960. See also G. Zhukov in *International Affairs*, October 1960, p. 55.

31. "45 Years on Guard Over the Socialist Fatherland," *Pravda*, February 23, 1963. See also Baryshev in *Red Star*, September 2, 1962.

32. *Voennaia Strategiia*, 2nd ed., pp. 394, 405, 407.

33. *Ibid.*, pp. 309, 394.

34. *Ibid.*, p. 394.

35. *Ibid.*, p. 309.

36. *Ibid.*, p. 394; *Soviet Military Strategy*, p. 419.

37. See Statement of Secretary of Defense Robert S. McNamara to the House Armed Services Committee, the Fiscal Year 1964–1968 Defense Program and 1964 Defense Budget, January 31, 1963, p. 321, where he said: "The Soviet Union may now have, or soon achieve a capability to place in orbit bomb-carrying satellites . . . "

38. Speech at 5th World Congress of Trade Unions, *Pravda*, December 10, 1961. Khrushchev had earlier linked the Titov flight with an implied Soviet military capability to deliver large-yield nuclear weapons "to any point on the globe," although his statement was ambiguous enough to leave it unclear whether he was speaking of orbital delivery or ordinary missile delivery. *New York Times*, September 8, 1961.

39. Moscow Domestic Service, February 21, 1963.

40. See G. V. Petrovich, "The First Artificial Satellite of the Sun," *Vestnik Akademii Nauk SSSR* (Journal of the USSR Academy of Sciences), No. 3, March 1959, pp. 8–14.

41. See published photos taken on the Nikolaev and Popovich flights in the magazine *USSR*, November 1962, pp. 45–47.

42. See N. Varvarov, "Cosmic Land Surveyors," *Ekonomicheskaia Gazeta* (Economic Gazette), January 8, 1961; *Voennaia Strategiia*, 2nd ed., p. 86.

43. "Scientific-Technical Progress and Its Influence on the Development of Military Affairs," *Communist of the Armed Forces*, No. 3, February 1963, p. 30.

44. *Helsingin Sanomat*, September 3, 1963.

45. See *New York Times*, May 30, 1964.

CHAPTER XVII. COALITION ASPECTS OF SOVIET STRATEGY

1. For a Soviet description of the Warsaw Treaty on Friendship, Cooperation and Mutual Assistance, see G. P. Zhukov, *Varshavskii Dogovor i Voprosy Mezhdunarodnoi Bezopasnosti* (The Warsaw Treaty and Questions of International Security), Sotsialno-Ekonomicheskoe Gosudarstvennoe Izdatelstvo, Moscow, 1961.

2. J. M. Mackintosh, *Strategy and Tactics of Soviet Foreign Policy*, Oxford University Press, London, 1962, p. 103. For some of the basic material in this portion of Chap. XVII, the author has drawn on an unpublished paper by Sol Polansky, "The Development of the Warsaw Pact," January 14, 1964. The interpretations offered are, however, the sole responsibility of the author of this volume.

3. V. Berezhkov, "At the Warsaw Conference," *Novoe Vremia* (New Times), No. 20, October 1955, p. 9; Ludwik Gelbert, *Uklad Warozawski* (Warsaw Pact), Warsaw, 1957, p. 64, cited by Polansky, p. 2.

4. Polansky, pp. 3–5. For comment by a knowledgeable ex-Polish officer on the largely symbolic character of the Warsaw Pact military staff in the 1955–58 period, see Pawel Monat, with John Dille, *Spy in the U.S.*, Harper and Row, New York, 1962, pp. 188–189.

5. Two subsidiary organs of the Political Consultative Committee, a Permanent Commission to deal with foreign policy questions and a Joint Secretariat, were provided by the Treaty, but there has been no reported activity by these bodies. Polansky, p. 3.

6. Gelbert, *Warsaw Pact*, pp. 113–114, cited by Polansky, p. 3.

7. Zhukov, *Warsaw Treaty*, p. 21.

8. V. K. Sobakin, *Kollektivnaia Bezopasnost'—Garantiia Mirnogo Sosuchestvovaniia* (Collective Security: The Guarantee for Peaceful Coexistence), Izdatelstvo IMO, Moscow, 1962, p. 385. The only

other element of the Warsaw Pact command structure that has been mentioned publicly is the Staff of the Joint Armed Forces, composed of representatives of national general staffs and situated in Moscow. Until his death in 1962, this staff was headed by General A. I. Antonov, a close wartime associate of Stalin. Another Soviet officer, General of the Army P. I. Batov, is the incumbent chief of staff. See Colonel S. Lesnevskii, "Military Cooperation of the Armed Forces of the Socialist Countries," *Communist of the Armed Forces*, No. 10, May 1963, p. 72.

9. *Soviet Military Strategy*, p. 495; *Voennaia Strategiia*, 2nd ed., p. 475.

10. Robert A. Kilmarx, *A History of Soviet Air Power*, Frederick A. Praeger, Inc., New York, 1962, p. 267.

11. For example, in 1958 Colonel General G. I. Khetagurov, commander of Soviet forces in Poland, said: "Our combat cooperation with the Polish forces is constantly growing. Units of our fraternal countries exchange visits." "The High International Duty of the Soviet Soldiers," *Red Star*, November 21, 1958. In 1959, Marshal I. S. Konev, the first commander of the Warsaw Pact forces, said: "We no longer stand alone guarding the achievements of socialism. Shoulder to shoulder with us stand our brothers-in-arms." "Preserve the Constructive Labor of the Soviet People Reliably and Watchfully," *Red Star*, May 9, 1959.

12. "A Great Victory," *Pravda*, May 9, 1960.

13. "Mighty Shield of Soviet Power," *Izvestiia*, May 9, 1962.

14. See Marshal A. Grechko, "The Patriotic and International Duty of the USSR Armed Forces," *Red Star*, October 6, 1961.

15. Lieutenant General K. Filiashin, "Guarding Peace and Security," *Military Herald*, No. 5, May 1962, p. 12.

16. Colonel S. Lesnevskii, "Combat Alliance of Fraternal Armies," *Military Knowledge*, No. 5, May 1963, pp. 12–13.

17. Colonel S. Lesnevskii in *Communist of the Armed Forces*, No. 10, May 1963, p. 73. See also Marshal A. Grechko, "The Nation's Exploit," *Izvestiia*, May 9, 1963; Colonel A. Ratnikov, "A Reliable Guard of the Security of People," *Red Star*, May 14, 1963.

18. "45 Years on Guard Over the Socialist Fatherland," *Pravda*, February 23, 1963.

19. Colonel L. Belousov, "Conference on Soviet Military Doctrine," *Military-Historical Journal*, No. 10, October 1963, p. 126. In this connection, an article in the fall of 1963, written with the obvious intention of stressing Warsaw Pact "military fellowship" in contrast to Chinese aloofness, pointed out the need to work out joint actions now because it would be too late for a socialist country "to call for aid" after the bombs start to fall. Colonels I. Sidel'nikov

and V. Zmitrenko, "The Present Epoch and the Defense of the Achievements of Socialism," *Red Star*, September 19, 1963.

20. In this connection, the Polish view has consistently been that "the Warsaw Pact cannot be used as the legal basis for the actions of Soviet troops during the tragic events which took place in Hungary." W. Morawiecki, "On the Warsaw Pact," *Sprawy Miezynarodowz* (International Affairs), No. 5, 1958, p. 29, cited by Polansky, p. 16. The Soviet Union, on the other hand, has continued to dispute Polish statements that Soviet troops could not put down the Hungarian revolt under the legal mantle of the Warsaw Pact. The Soviet view, as recently as May 1963, was that "the operative strength of this cooperation [i.e., the Warsaw Pact] was convincingly demonstrated in the days of the counter-revolutionary putsch in Hungary in the autumn of 1956." Lesnevskii in *Communist of the Armed Forces*, No. 10, May 1963, p. 73.

21. For a persuasive exposition of this view, see Raymond L. Garthoff, "Sino-Soviet Military Relations," *Annals of the American Academy of Political and Social Science*, Vol. 349, September 1963, pp. 81–93.

22. Vladimir Dedijer, *Tito*, Simon and Schuster, New York, 1953, p. 322.

23. See A. Doak Barnett, *Communist China and Asia*, Random House, New York, 1961, pp. 340–344; see also Mark Mancall, "Russia and China: Perennial Conflict," *Problems of Communism*, Vol. 12, No. 2, March-April 1963, p. 65.

24. See Allen S. Whiting, *China Crosses the Yalu*, The MacMillan Company, New York, 1960, pp. iv-v, 124–126; Garthoff in *Annals of the American Academy of Political and Social Science*, September 1963, p. 84.

25. See Harold Hinton, "Communist China's Military Posture," *Current History*, September 1962, p. 151.

26. See Alice Langley Hsieh, *Communist China's Strategy in the Nuclear Era*, Prentice-Hall, Inc., Englewood Cliffs, New Jersey, 1962, pp. 72–75.

27. Statement by the Spokesman of the Chinese Government, September 1, 1963—A Comment on the Soviet Government's Statement of August 21, *People's Daily*, September 1, 1963, Peking, New China News Agency broadcast, August 31, 1963.

28. Garthoff in *Annals of the American Academy of Political and Social Science*, September 1963, pp. 82, 86ff.

29. The extent of Soviet backing is still ambiguous, for the Chinese have subsequently charged that Khrushchev claimed a false victory because his warning came after the danger of nuclear confrontation in the Taiwan crisis had passed. See Chinese Statement,

September 1, 1963, and Soviet Government Statement, September 20, 1963, *Pravda*, September 21, 1963, which reproaches Peking for ingratitude.

30. Chinese Statement of September 1, 1963 and Statement by the Spokesman of the Chinese Government, August 15, 1963—A Comment on the Soviet Government's Statement of August 3, 1963, *People's Daily*, August 15, 1963, Peking, New China News Agency broadcast, August 14, 1963. The Soviet Union has tacitly acknowledged a breach of faith with regard to the October 1957 agreement by criticizing the Chinese for disclosing secret defense information in this connection. Soviet Government Statement, August 21, 1963, *Pravda*, August 21, 1963.

31. See Donald S. Zagoria, *The Sino-Soviet Conflict: 1956–1961*, Princeton University Press, Princeton, New Jersey, 1962, pp. 154–172; Hsieh, *Communist China's Strategy*, pp. 83–99, 169.

32. Chen Yi interview by Japanese newsmen, Tokyo, Kyodo broadcast, October 28, 1963.

33. Hsieh, *Communist China's Strategy*, p. 164.

34. See Garthoff in *Annals of the American Academy of Political and Social Science*, September 1963, p. 92.

35. Khrushchev speech to the USSR Supreme Soviet on the international situation, *Pravda*, December 13, 1962. For other Soviet accusations along the same line, see Marshal A. Eremenko, "A 'Paper' Tiger or a Thermonuclear Tiger?," article written for the Bulgarian paper *Rabotnichesko Delo*, October 10, 1963; editorial, "For the General Line of the World Communist Movement Against Opportunism, Nationalism, and Adventurism," *Kommunist*, No. 14, September 1963, pp. 19, 22.

36. For discussion of internal Chinese schools of thought on defense policy and the question of attitudes toward Soviet aid, see Hsieh, *Communist China's Strategy*, pp. 34–75; Zagoria, *Sino-Soviet Conflict*, pp. 190–194; David A. Charles, "The Dismissal of Marshal P'eng Teh-huai," *China Quarterly*, No. 8, October-December 1961, pp. 63*ff*.

37. Soviet Government Statement, September 20, 1963, *Pravda*, September 21, 1963; Colonel P. Trifonenkov, "The Most Pressing Problem of the Present Day and the Adventurism of the Chinese Dogmatists," *Communist of the Armed Forces*, No. 21, November 1963, p. 28.

38. Soviet Government Statement, September 20, 1963, *Pravda*, September 21, 1963; editorial, "The Leninist Course of Our Foreign Policy," *Red Star*, September 24, 1963; Trifonenkov in *Communist of the Armed Forces*, No. 21, November 1963, p. 28.

39. Curiously, the Western world seems to have taken the strength of this commitment more seriously than the Chinese, ascribing a

rather high "credibility rating" to the Soviet deterrent in the service of China. See discussion of this point in Thomas C. Schelling, "Deterrence: Military Diplomacy in the Nuclear Age," *Virginia Quarterly Review,* Vol. 39, No. 4, 1963, pp. 545–547.

40. *Pravda,* January 24, 1962. See also Zagoria, *Sino-Soviet Conflict,* pp. 335–336.

41. Eremenko in *Rabotnichesko Delo,* October 19, 1963.

42. Chen Yi at scientists' banquet, Peking, New China News Agency broadcast, January 5, 1962; Chen Yi, *Red Flag,* August 16, 1960; see also Hsieh, *Communist China's Strategy,* p. 112.

43. Major General S. Kozlov, "Against Dogmatism and the Distortion of Marxist-Leninist Teaching About War," *Narodna Armiya* (People's Army), broadcast on Sofia radio, October 8, 1963.

44. Tokyo, Kyodo broadcast, October 28, 1963.

45. "Two Different Lines on the Question of War and Peace," comment on the Open Letter issued by the Central Committee of the CPSU, *People's Daily-Red Flag,* November 19, 1963. Peking, New China News Agency broadcast, November 18, 1963.

46. Edward Crankshaw, "Sino-Soviet Rift Held Very Deep," *Washington Post,* February 12, 1961. Chinese charges in a joint *People's Daily-Red Flag* article of September 6, 1963, that the Soviet Union in 1958 had tried "to bring China under Soviet military control" were apparently related to the naval command issue, as indicated by a speech made in Japan by a visiting Chinese official, Chao An-po, reported in the *Japan Times,* February 23, 1964.

47. See "Peking Spars with Soviets Over Wilds of Central Asia," *Christian Science Monitor,* October 2, 1963; Farnsworth Fowle, "Soviet Tightens Watch on China," *New York Times,* November 17, 1963. The question of frontier violations was brought up by both the Soviet and Chinese sides in the spring of 1964. In his speech of February 14, 1964, to the CPSU Central Committee Plenum, which was published on April 3, 1964, M. A. Suslov noted that "violations of the Soviet frontier during 1962–1963 became a constant phenomenon, sometimes taking the form of crude provocations." The Chinese in turn charged in a letter of February 29, 1964, to the CPSU that "the Soviet side has made frequent breaches of the status quo on the border, occupied Chinese territory . . . provoked border incidents . . . flagrantly carried out large-scale subversive activities in Chinese frontier areas." Neither side was able to offer the other a satisfactory procedure for settlement of the Sino-Soviet border question. See "On the CPSU Struggle for Solidarity of the International Communist Movement," Report of Comrade M. A. Suslov to the Plenum of the Central Committee, CPSU, February 14, 1964, *Pravda,* April 3, 1964; letters exchanged between the Chinese and Soviet Parties since November 1963, as released by the Central

Committee of the Chinese Communist Party, Peking, New China News Agency broadcast, May 8, 1964.

48. For further comment on these documents, see Alice Langley Hsieh, *Communist China's Military Doctrine and Strategy*, The RAND Corporation, RM–3833–PR (abridged), October 1963.

CHAPTER XVIII. THE SEARCH FOR A WAR-WINNING STRATEGY

1. *Soviet Military Strategy*, p. 313; *Voennaia Strategiia*, 2nd ed., p. 258. See also N. Talenskii, "The 'Absolute Weapon' and the Problem of Security," *International Affairs*, No. 4, April 1962, p. 26. Major General N. Sushko and Major T. Kondratkov, "War and Politics in the "Nuclear Age,'" *Communist of the Armed Forces*, No. 2, January 1964, p. 20.

2. *Voennaia Strategiia*, 2nd ed., p. 20; *Soviet Military Strategy*, p. 94. See also Colonel V. Konoplev, "On Scientific Foresight in Military Affairs," *Communist of the Armed Forces*, No. 24, December 1963, p. 31.

3. *Voennaia Strategiia*, 2nd ed., p. 32; *Soviet Military Strategy*, p. 105. See also Colonel P. Derevianko, "Some Features of the Contemporary Revolution in Military Affairs," *Communist of the Armed Forces*, No. 1, January 1964, p. 20.

4. *Voennaia Strategiia*, 2nd ed., p. 246; *Soviet Military Strategy*, p. 302. An afterthought was added to this formula in the revised edition, to emphasize the combined-arms aspect of the situation. Where the original text observed that "all these and other tasks can only be accomplished by ground forces," the new text added: " . . . in combined operations with other branches of the armed forces."

5. See *Red Star*, January 7, 10, 1964; Colonel General S. M. Shtemenko, "The New Requirements Posed for the Combined-Arms Commander," *Red Star*, January 16, 1964; Major General N. Sushko, "The Laws Determining the Course and Outcome of Wars," *Red Star*, February 7, 1964.

6. See U.S. Editors' Analytical Introduction, *Soviet Military Strategy*, p. 75.

7. *Voennaia Strategiia*, 2nd ed., p. 367.

8. See, for example, Marshal R. Ia. Malinovskii's exhortation to a group of military editors in November 1963, where he said, among other things: "We must boldly smash and throw out everything that interferes with the creative development of progressive military thinking and . . . be prepared for active, decisive operations to the point of daring under conditions of the employment of missiles and nuclear weapons by both sides." "The Revolution in Military Affairs and the Tasks of the Military Press," *Communist of the Armed Forces*, No. 21, November 1963, pp. 9–10. See also General of the

Army P. Batitskii, "The Main Thing Is Constant Combat Readiness," *ibid.*, No. 18, September 1963, p. 24; Major General I. Y. Krupchenko, "On Teaching History of Military Art in the Higher Service Schools," *Military-Historical Journal*, No. 9, September 1963, pp. 40–41; Konoplev in *Communist of the Armed Forces*, No. 24, December 1963, p. 32; Marshal S. Biriuzov, "New Stage in the Development of the Armed Forces and Tasks of Indoctrinating and Training Troops," *ibid.*, No. 4, February 1964, pp. 19–20. The latter, while criticizing officers who cling to outmoded views, said caustically (p. 19): "There is no place in the missile forces for those who measure the new means of warfare with an old yardstick."

9. *Red Star*, January 16, 1964. See also Chap. VIII for discussion of another aspect of this question, that of the tension between the new "military specialists" and the Party apparatus in the armed forces.

10. *Voennaia Strategiia*, 2nd ed., p. 263; *Soviet Military Strategy*, p. 377.

11. *Voennaia Strategiia*, 2nd ed., p. 313.

CHAPTER XIX. SOVIET MILITARY STRATEGY AND DISARMAMENT

1. See Malcolm Mackintosh and Harry Willetts, "Arms Control and the Soviet National Interest," in *Arms Control Issues for the Public*, Louis Henkin, ed., Prentice-Hall, Inc., Englewood Cliffs, New Jersey, 1961, pp. 141–173; Richard J. Barnett, "The Soviet Attitude on Disarmament," *Problems of Communism*, May–June 1961, pp. 32–37. See also, by the author of this volume, "Khrushchev's Disarmament Strategy," *Orbis*, Vol. 4, No. 1, Spring 1960, pp. 13–27.

2. In this connection, a recent major work on Soviet foreign policy notes that, although no agreements resulted from the Soviet Union's postwar disarmament campaign, the Soviet effort did serve "to expose the enemies of disarmament and to mobilize world public opinion for the struggle against the danger of war." M. Baturin and S. Tarov, *Vneshnaia Politika Sovetskogo Soiuza Na Sovremennom Etape* (The Foreign Policy of the Soviet Union at the Contemporary Stage), Izdatelstvo Instituta Mezhdunarodnykh Otneshenii, Moscow, 1962, p. 67.

3. For example, the Litvinov proposal to the League of Nations Preparatory Commission at Geneva on November 30, 1927, for "Immediate, Complete and General Disarmament" came at a time when the Red Army was undergoing major reform and reorganization and the first Five Year Plan for industrialization was about to begin, placing the Soviet Union in a position which made a check upon the armament efforts of the other powers a strategic necessity.

An earlier pre-Soviet Russian proposal which led to the Hague Conference of 1899 came similarly at a time when Russia needed to modernize her forces and was concerned by Austrian and German military strength in the West and the growing power of Japan in the East. See Count Witte's confidences to his advisor, Dr. E. J. Dillon, in E. J. Dillon, *The Eclipse of Russia,* George H. Doran Co., New York, 1918, pp. 44–46. See also Michael I. Florinsky, *Russia,* Vol. II, The Macmillan Company, New York, 1958, pp. 1260–1261.

4. *Documents on Disarmament, 1945–1959,* Vol. I, Department of State, Washington, D.C., 1960, pp. 7–16.

5. *Ibid.,* pp. 17–19, 66–82.

6. *Ibid.,* pp. 84, 176, 187, 188, 191, 193.

7. See Mackintosh and Willetts in *Arms Control Issues,* p. 145.

8. *Documents on Disarmament,* Vol. I, pp. 456–466.

9. The force levels adopted from the Anglo-French plan of June 1954 were 1.5 million men for the Soviet Union, United States, and China, respectively, and 650,000 for Britain and France.

10. See Mackintosh and Willetts in *Arms Control Issues,* p. 152.

11. *Documents on Disarmament,* Vol. I, pp. 603–607.

12. *Ibid.,* Vol. I, pp. 630–639; Vol. II, p. 780.

13. For examples of these arguments, see V. A. Zorin, ed., *The Soviet Union's Struggle for Disarmament, 1946–1960,* Izdatelstvo Instituta Mezhdunarodnykh Otnoshenii, Moscow, 1961, pp. 83, 212, 302. The same work also argues, pp. 73*ff.*, that Western arms control proposals are intended to serve the West's strategic objectives, to gather intelligence, lull public opinion, and so on, rather than to stop the arms race.

14. *New York Times,* September 19, 1959.

15. For copies of the original 1959 proposal and subsequent versions offered by the Soviet Union up to 1962, see *The Soviet Stand on Disarmament,* Crosscurrents Press, Inc., New York, 1962, pp. 9, 25, 53, 80.

16. See Thomas W. Wolfe, *Some Factors Bearing on Soviet Attitudes Toward Disarmament,* The RAND Corporation, P-2766, July 1963, p. 9.

17. Election speech in Yerevan, *Pravda,* March 15, 1962.

18. While traditional Soviet opposition to an international police force for peace-keeping purposes was unexpectedly softened in mid-1964, the Soviet position still appears inhospitable to the idea of an international armed force independent of a Soviet veto. A Soviet memorandum of July 7, 1964, proposed a UN force organized on the "troika" principle, with Western, neutral, and communist countries represented. The proposal did not make clear whether this would be a standing force or one to be assembled when need arose. It did

make clear that troops from the major powers would be barred from the force and that decisions on its use would be subject to big-power veto in the Security Council. *New York Times,* July 8, 1964.

19. See Mackintosh and Willetts, in *Arms Control Issues,* p. 156.

20. Editorial, "To Strengthen Our Country's Might," *Red Star,* September 21, 1963. See also Leont'ev in *Red Star,* August 30, 1963; editorial, "In the Interests of All Mankind," *Pravda,* September 26, 1963.

21. In addition to Soviet publications on disarmament already cited, some of the more representative recent works on the subject are V. M. Khaitsman, *SSSR i Problema Razoruzheniia* (The USSR and the Problem of Disarmament), Izdatelstvo Akademii Nauk SSSR, Moscow, 1959, a monograph on the history of Soviet disarmament policy; E. K. Fedorov, *Prekrashchenie Iadernykh Ispytanii* (Cessation of Nuclear Testing), Izdatelstvo Akademii Nauk SSSR, Moscow, 1961, an account by a Soviet scientist of the test-ban issue; O. V. Bogdanov, *Iadernoe Razoruzhenie* (Nuclear Disarmament), Izdatelstvo Instituta Mezhdunarodnykh Otnoshenii, Moscow, 1961, a description of Soviet policy on the subject and criticism of Western views; I. S. Glagolev, ed., *Ekonomicheskie Voprosy Razoruzheniia* (Economic Problems of Disarmament), Izdatelstvo Akademii Nauk SSSR, Moscow, 1961, a collection of articles following the Marxist-Leninist view of this subject.

22. For a convenient listing and critical discussion of some of the voluminous U.S. arms control and disarmament literature, see James E. Dougherty, "The Disarmament Debate: A Review of Current Literature," in two parts, *Orbis,* Vol. 5, No. 3, Fall 1961, pp. 342–359, and Vol. 5, No. 4, Winter 1962, pp. 489–511.

23. Among examples of this trend in Soviet writing are V. Pechorkin, "About 'Acceptable' War," *International Affairs,* No. 3, March 1963, pp. 22–25, an attack on strategic concepts of Herman Kahn and Raymond Aron; Boris Dimitriev, *Pentagon i Vneshnaia Politika SShA* (The Pentagon and the Foreign Policy of the USA), Izdatelstvo Instituta Mezhdunarodnykh Otnoshenii, Moscow, 1961, a somewhat dated propaganda attack on military influence in the United States, with portions devoted to concepts of "massive retaliation" and "mutual deterrence"; N. Talenskii, "Sincere?—Yes. Realistic?—No," *International Affairs,* No. 3, March 1963, pp. 98–100, a criticism of zonal disarmament and inspection proposals advanced by Louis B. Sohn (an accompanying "guest" article by Prof. Jay Orear of Columbia University, defending the zonal concept, appeared in the same issue); A. A. Blagonravov, "Destruction of Means of Nuclear Delivery," *Novoe Vremia* (New Times), No. 52, 1960, p. 10, an earlier discussion by a Soviet scientist which went into

problems of detecting missile launchings. In addition, this category includes the previously mentioned articles by General Nevsky in the *World Marxist Review*, March 1963, the Glagolev-Larionov article in *International Affairs*, November 1963, and portions of the 1963 revised Sokolovskii edition of *Voennaia Strategiia* (Military Strategy). See also "guest" article by Yuri Shemin, "A Soviet Scientist Looks at Disarmament," *Bulletin of the Atomic Scientists*, January 1964, pp. 19–22, in which the Soviet author argues that the American concept of "arms control" cannot provide an adequate substitute for the "non-trivial" approach of "complete and universal disarmament."

24. Colonel A. M. Iovlev, "New Technology and Mass Armies," *Red Star*, April 5, 1961. See also editorial, "The Strength and Pride of the People," *Pravda*, February 23, 1964.

25. "War Must Be Wiped Out," *Moscow News*, No. 2, January 11, 1964.

26. A. Nevsky, "Modern Armament and Problems of Strategy," *World Marxist Review*, No. 3, March 1963, p. 30. The argument that Western military men are more opposed to hanging up their uniforms than Soviet soldiers is paralleled by the argument that "monopoly-dominated" Western economies have a vested interest in the arms race, whereas the controlled Soviet economy is held to be free of such interests. See V. Onushkin, *"Atomnyi Biznes" Amerikanskykh Monopolii* (The "Atomic Business" of American Monopolies), Setsekgiz, Moscow, 1960, pp. 4–140. At the same time, the customary Soviet line that the U.S. economy could not shift from arms production to disarmament has been altered recently in some Soviet writing to concede that the transition could be made without big problems. See Zorin, *The Soviet Union's Struggle*, p. 293.

27. In his January 14, 1960 Supreme Soviet speech, Khrushchev retroactively stated that Soviet forces stood at 2.8 million men by the end of 1948, were brought back up to 5.7 million by 1955, and subsequently reduced to 3.6 million by January 1960. There is some uncertainty as to whether all of these figures can be taken at face value, but nevertheless a sizeable reduction appears to have taken place. See *Pravda*, January 15, 1960.

28. Report to the meeting of the commissioned officers' *aktiv* of the Moscow garrison, *Red Star*, January 20, 1960.

29. See "Care and Attention," *Red Star*, July 9, 1960; A. Isaev, "And the Haunting of Thresholds Began," *Red Star*, December 14, 1960.

30. Retired Major A. Liashov, "The Far East Country Is Rich," *Red Star*, March 16, 1962.

31. *Red Star*, March 29, 1963. A certain amount of chronic readjustment difficulty associated with the "normal" return of discharged

draftees to civilian life also is reflected in the Soviet press from time to time. See Colonel A. Mitiashin, "A Soldier Comes Home," *Izvestiia*, January 30, 1964.

32. "The Honor of a Soviet Officer," *Izvestiia*, February 12, 1963. The problem of the Soviet military's place in the national life is an old one. In the mid-1920's, for example, this was one of the questions addressed by M. V. Frunze, who played a central role in reform of the armed forces after Trotsky's ouster. Frunze argued on the basis of Lenin's prediction that the Soviet Union would one day be involved in "frightful bloody clashes" with Western "imperialism," that the Soviet military must be imbued with a sense of purpose and "should not be isolated from the political life of the country." M. V. Frunze, *Izbrannie Proizvedeniia* (Selected Works), Vol. II, Voenizdat Ministerstva Oborony SSSR, Moscow, 1957, pp. 219, 274, *passim*.

33. See Colonel M. Makoveev, "Our Officer," *Red Star*, February 18, 1964.

34. *Red Star*, February 9, 1964. For similar military criticism of artistic works which failed to provide proper "heroic" inspiration, see Captain Second Rank A. Chernomys and Lieutenant Colonel V. Fedorov, "Wherein Lies the Beauty of an Heroic Deed," *Red Star*, January 29, 1964; Marshal I. Bagramian, "Mighty Means of Patriotic Education," *Sovetskii Patriot*, January 29, 1964. See also Marshal Krylov's comments on pacifism, "An Honorable Profession, Needed by the Nation," *Red Star*, June 9, 1963.

35. See Sidney Hook, *The Fail-Safe Fallacy*, Stein and Day, New York, 1963, pp. 19–23.

CHAPTER XX. IMAGE OF THE ADVERSARY

1. "Modern Ground Forces," *Izvestiia*, December 22, 1963. See discussion of Chuikov's special pleading on this point in Chap. XII.

2. *Soviet Military Strategy*, pp. 168–170; *Voennaia Strategiia*, 2nd ed., pp. 83–86.

3. *Soviet Military Strategy*, pp. 157–159; *Voennaia Strategiia*, 2nd ed., pp. 75–77; General A. Nevsky, "Modern Armaments and Problems of Strategy," *World Marxist Review*, No. 3, March 1963, pp. 32–33; B. Teplinskii, "U.S. Grand Strategy," *International Affairs*, No. 2, February 1964, pp. 24–25.

4. *Soviet Military Strategy*, p. 160.

5. See earlier discussion of Soviet views on likelihood of war in Chap. IX.

6. Colonel E. Dolgopolov, "Cecil Rhodes and the Present," *Red Star*, November 27, 1963; *Soviet Military Strategy*, pp. 158–159; Teplinskii in *International Affairs*, February 1964, pp. 25–27, 29.

See also our previous discussion in Chap. X of the increased attention given to U.S. limited war theory in the second Sokolovskii volume.

7. See, for example, Marshal A. Grechko, "On a Leninist Course," *Red Star*, December 22, 1963; Marshal V. Chuikov in *Izvestiia*, December 22, 1963.

8. *Voennaia Strategiia*, 2nd ed., pp. 103, 109; *Soviet Military Strategy*, pp. 173, 177.

9. *Voennaia Strategiia*, 2nd ed., p. 257; *Soviet Military Strategy*, p. 311.

10. *Voennaia Strategiia*, 2nd ed., p. 114; *Soviet Military Strategy*, p. 182.

11. *Voennaia Strategiia*, 2nd ed., p. 114; *Soviet Military Strategy*, p. 183.

12. *Voennaia Strategiia*, 2nd ed., p. 244.

13. *Ibid.*, p. 103.

14. At the same time, it should be recalled that from the viewpoint of the Soviet military, the picture of a Western military threat of great magnitude is not without certain self-serving aspects, since it would tend to fortify the case of those urging further strengthening of the Soviet military posture. See discussion in Chap. XII.

15. *Voennaia Strategiia*, 2nd ed., p. 35; see also pp. 97, 206. For a Soviet analysis of internal NATO difficulties, in which an attempt was made to demonstrate that despite growing disunity the threat of NATO aggression has not diminished, see F. Fyodorov, "NATO and the Demand of the Times," *International Affairs*, No. 2, February 1964, pp. 38–41.

16. *Voennaia Strategiia*, 2nd ed., pp. 47, 50, 491, 495.

17. Colonel P. I. Trifonenkov, *On the Fundamental Laws of the Course and Outcome of Modern War*, Voenizdat Ministerstva Oborony SSSR, Moscow, 1962, p. 48.

18. *Soviet Military Strategy*, pp. 409–410; *Voennaia Strategiia*, 2nd ed., pp. 340–341.

19. Time-Life News Service, Transcript of Interview with Chairman Khrushchev and American Businessmen in the Kremlin, November 6, 1963, p. 8. See *Pravda*, February 6, 1959, for one of Khrushchev's earlier comments on the same theme; see also Teplinskii in *International Affairs*, February 1964, p. 24.

20. Marshal R. Ia. Malinovskii, "15th Anniversary of the Victory Over Fascist Germany," *Pravda*, May 10, 1960; Marshal A. Eremenko, "The Strategic and Political Value of Military Bases," *International Affairs*, No. 11, November 1960, pp. 59–60; Khrushchev interview in *Pravda*, September 10, 1961; Colonel I. Mareev, "The Indestructible Shield of the Socialist Countries," *Communist of the Armed Forces*, No. 3, February 1964, p. 13; Marshal A. Eremenko,

"Modern Strategy and Border Conflicts," *International Affairs*, No. 3, March 1964, p. 8.

21. *Vital Speeches of the Day*, August 1, 1962, pp. 626–629.

22. Khrushchev speech to World Peace Congress, *Pravda*, July 11, 1962. See also Major General M. Mil'shtein, "Certain Strategic Military Concepts of the American Imperialists," *Mirovaia Ekonomika i Mezhdunarodnie Otnosheniia* (World Economics and International Relations), No. 8, August 1962; Major General N. Talenskii, "Preventive War—Nuclear Suicide," *International Affairs*, No. 9, September 1962, pp. 10–16; Colonel General A. Rytov, "USSR Air Force Day," *Communist of the Armed Forces*, No. 15, August 1962, p. 14.

23. Marshal V. D. Sokolovskii, "A Suicidal Strategy," *Red Star*, July 19, 1962.

24. Interview with Stewart Alsop, "Our New Strategy," *Saturday Evening Post*, December 1, 1962, p. 18.

25. See discussion of this question in Chap. V in connection with Soviet efforts to enhance the credibility of the Soviet deterrent posture.

26. See discussion of the Soviet attitude toward strategic targeting restraints in Chap. XIII.

27. *World Marxist Review*, March 1963, pp. 30–33; *Voennaia Strategiia*, 2nd ed., p. 83.

28. *World Marxist Review*, March 1963, pp. 30–35. See also article, "About 'Acceptable' War," by V. Pechorkin in *International Affairs*, No. 3, March 1963, p. 24, in which the feasibility of McNamara's concepts was challenged, though on less extended grounds than by other Soviet authors.

29. *Voennaia Strategiia*, 2nd ed., p. 84.

30. *Ibid.*

31. *Ibid.*

32. *Ibid.*

33. *Ibid.*, pp. 84–85.

34. *Ibid.*, p. 85. Elsewhere in the revised Sokolovskii edition, the authors were skeptical that the United States would in fact try to follow a set of rules in the event of war. They said, p. 365, that: ". . . the U.S. militarists do not intend to employ their nuclear weapons solely against military targets . . . they are planning to use such weapons above all against targets in the deep interior, against cities, against the peaceful population, against the economy, and also naturally against . . . the armed forces."

35. *Ibid.* See also L. Glagolev and V. Larionov, "Soviet Defence Might and Peaceful Coexistence," *International Affairs*, No. 11, November 1963, pp. 31–32; Nevsky in *World Marxist Review*, March

1963, p. 33; Pechorkin in *International Affairs,* March 1963, pp. 23–24.

36. *Voennaia Strategiia,* 2nd ed., pp. 85–86.

37. *Ibid.,* p. 86.

38. *Ibid.* See also N. Talenskii, "A NATO Nuclear Force Is a Dangerous Venture," *International Affairs,* No. 5, May 1963, p. 26; Nevsky in *World Marxist Review,* March 1963, p. 33.

39. *Voennaia Strategiia,* 2nd ed., p. 87.

40. *Ibid.* See also Nevsky in *World Marxist Review,* March 1963, p. 33; Pechorkin in *International Affairs,* March 1963, p. 24. The latter, in addition to mentioning the difficulty of target location as a problem for the United States, also implied that this would be a problem for the Soviet Union, since the location of U.S. targets would not be pinpointed for the adversary by "the U.S. Secretary of Defense." The Pechorkin argument then went on to make the point that: "Accordingly, large thermonuclear warheads would be used to blanket great expanses, which means they would inevitably hit the cities as well, especially in the densely-populated countries."

41. *Voennaia Strategiia,* 2nd ed., p. 87.

42. *Ibid.*

43. *Ibid.,* p. 88.

44. *Ibid.,* pp. 90–91. A similar view, it may be recalled, was also expressed in the article in the November 1963 issue of *International Affairs* by Glagolev and Larionov, p. 32. See discussion in Chap. V.

45. *Washington Post,* December 3, 1963.

INDEX

ABM. *See* Antimissile defense; Antimissile missiles

Adzhubei, Alexei, on reconnaissance satellites, 209

Aerial reconnaissance, importance upgraded, 181

Agriculture: 1963 "chemicalization" decisions, 265; and resource allocation, 48

Air defense: collaboration with Warsaw Pact countries, 213; evolving role of, 189; foiled by ASM-equipped bombers, 309

Air forces: evolving role of, 177–183; missions of, 181. *See also* Aerial reconnaissance; Air-to-surface missiles; Bomber aircraft; Fighter aircraft; Tactical aviation

Air reconnaissance, 181; over Cuba 209

Airborne troops, importance in future war, 174

Aircraft. *See* Air forces; Air-to-surface missiles; Bomber aircraft; Fighter aircraft; Jet aircraft; Missiles; Tactical aviation

Aircraft carriers, operations against, 185–186

Air-to-surface missiles: for attacks against carriers, 185; Soviet and US, 304; and strategic bombers, 178

Alafuzov, V. A.: on amphibious operations, 187; on ASW operations, 185; comment on Sokolovskii work, 305; on missile-launching submarines, 186

Amphibious operations: increased emphasis on, 11, 187–188; need for, 229; in Sokolovskii book, 52

Antimissile defense: claims of effectiveness, 190–193; and mass shelter program, 197–198; role of air forces, 181; in Sokolovskii book, 52; stress on, 11

Antimissile missiles, "fly in outer space," 190

Antisatellite defenses: focus of Soviet interest, 206–207; in Sokolovskii book, 52; stress on, 11

Antisubmarine warfare: in Sokolovskii book, 52; Soviet emphasis on, 11, 184–185

Armed forces: consideration of militia, 294; conventional, in local war, 122; development of, 9; economic constraints on size, 146–149; feasibility of policy changes, 21–24; Khrushchev's 1960 position on, 31; "military specialists," 100; in peacetime, 7, 52. *See also* Air forces; Airborne troops; Ground forces; Multimillion-man armies; Tank forces; Troop reduction

Arms control, 15; appeal to Soviet leadership, 237; Khrushchev reaction to NATO arms build-up, 47; lack of Soviet writing on, 238; in Soviet strategy, 23; Soviet view of, 239; understandings attained in, 257

Arms race, 16; effect on policy decisions, 20; Grechko on, 89; Malinovskii on, 84; reduction of tempo, 237; resolved by total disarmament, 236; and Soviet resource allocation, 88

ASM. *See* Air-to-surface missiles

A SELECTED LIST OF OTHER RAND BOOKS

THE FREE PRESS

Dinerstein, H. S., and Leon Gouré. *Two Studies in Soviet Controls: Communism and the Russian Peasant; Moscow in Crisis.* 1955.

Garthoff, Raymond L. *Soviet Military Doctrine.* 1953.

Goldhamer, Herbert, and Andrew W. Marshall. *Psychosis and Civilization.* 1953

Leites, Nathan. *A Study of Bolshevism.* 1953.

—— and Elsa Bernaut. *Ritual of Liquidation: The Case of the Moscow Trials.* 1954.

HARVARD UNIVERSITY PRESS

Bergson, Abram. *The Real National Income of Soviet Russia Since 1928.* 1961.

Fainsod, Merle. *Smolensk under Soviet Rule.* 1958.

Hitch, Charles J., and Roland McKean. *The Economics of Defense in the Nuclear Age.* 1960.

Moorsteen, Richard. *Prices and Production of Machinery in the Soviet Union, 1928, 1958.* 1962.

MC GRAW-HILL BOOK COMPANY, INC.

Leites, Nathan. *The Operational Code of the Politburo.* 1951.

Mead, Margaret. *Soviet Attitudes toward Authority: An Interdisciplinary Approach to Problems of Soviet Character.* 1951.

Selznick, Philip. *The Organizational Weapon: A Study of Bolshevik Strategy and Tactics.* 1952.

FREDERICK A. PRAEGER, INC.

Dinerstein, H. S. *War and the Soviet Union: Nuclear Weapons and the Revolution in Soviet Military and Political Thinking.* 1959.

Speier, Hans. *Divided Berlin: The Anatomy of Soviet Political Blackmail.* 1961.

Tanham, G. K. *Communist Revolutionary Warfare: The Viet Minh in Indochina.* 1961.

PRINCETON UNIVERSITY PRESS

Baum, Warren C. *The French Economy and the State.* 1958.

Brodie, Bernard. *Strategy in the Missile Age.* 1959.

Davison, W. Phillips. *The Berlin Blockade: A Study in Cold War Politics.* 1958.

Johnson, John J. (ed.). *The Role of the Military in Underdeveloped Countries.* 1962.

A Selected List of Other RAND Books

Smith, Bruce Lannes, and Chitra M. Smith. *International Communication and Political Opinion: A Guide to the Literature.* 1956.

Wolf, Charles, Jr. *Foreign Aid: Theory and Practice in Southern Asia.* 1960.

ROW, PETERSON AND COMPANY

George, Alexander L. *Propaganda Analysis: A Study of Inferences Made from Nazi Propaganda in World War II.* 1959.

Melnik, Constantin, and Nathan Leites. *The House Without Windows: France Selects a President.* 1958.

Speier, Hans. *German Rearmament and Atomic War: The Views of German Military and Political Leaders.* 1957.

―――― and W. Phillips Davison (eds.). *West German Leadership and Foreign Policy.* 1957.

STANFORD UNIVERSITY PRESS

Gouré, Leon. *The Siege of Leningrad, 1941–1943.* 1962.

Kecskemeti, Paul. *Strategic Surrender: The Politics of Victory and Defeat.* 1958.

―――― *The Unexpected Revolution: Social Forces in the Hungarian Uprising.* 1961.

Leites, Nathan. *On the Game of Politics in France.* 1959.

Trager, Frank N. (ed.). *Marxism in Southeast Asia: A Study of Four Countries.* 1959.

OTHER PUBLISHERS

Buchheim, Robert W., and the Staff of The RAND Corporation. *Space Handbook: Astronautics and Its Applications.* Random House. 1959.

Hsieh, Alice L. *Communist China's Strategy in the Nuclear Era.* Prentice-Hall. 1962.

Rush, Myron. *The Rise of Khrushchev.* Public Affairs Press. 1958.

Whiting, Allen S. *China Crosses the Yalu: The Decision To Enter the Korean War.* Macmillan. 1960.